BC

SEARCH AND SURVEILLANCE

*In memory of
the Gross and Sachs families of Breslau*

Search and Surveillance
The movement from evidence to information

SYBIL SHARPE
De Montfort University

Ashgate

DARTMOUTH

Aldershot • Burlington USA • Singapore • Sydney

Published by
Dartmouth Publishing Company Limited
Ashgate Publishing Ltd
Gower House
Croft Road
Aldershot
Hants GU11 3HR
England

Ashgate Publishing Company
131 Main Street
Burlington
Vermont 05401
USA

Ashgate website: http://www.ashgate.com

British Library Cataloguing in Publication Data
Sharpe, Sybil
    Search and surveillance : the movement from evidence to
    information
    1. Searches and seizures - Law and legislation - England
    2. Criminal investigation - England 3. Criminal investigation
    - England - Technological innovations 4. Criminals - Civil
    rights - England 5. Searches and seizures - Law and
    legislation - Wales 6. Criminal investigation - Wales
    7. Criminal investigation - Wales - Technological
    innovations 8. Criminals - Civil rights - Wales
    I. Title
    345.4'2'0522

Library of Congress Cataloging-in-Publication Data
Sharpe, Sybil.
    Search and surveillance : the movement from evidence to information / Sybil Sharpe.
      p.cm.
    Includes bibliographical references and index.
    ISBN 0-7546-2062-X (hbk.)
    1. Searches and seizures. 2. Electronic surveillance. 3. Evidence, Criminal. I. Title.

    K5438 .S52 2000
    345'.0522--dc21

                                          00-55870

ISBN 0 7546 2062 X

Printed in Great Britain by
Antony Rowe Ltd, Chippenham, Wiltshire

Contents

Table of Cases

England and Wales

European Court of Human Rights

United States

Preface

My intention in writing this text was not to replace standard procedural works on the Police and Criminal Evidence Act 1984 and associated legislation governing the law of search and seizure in England and Wales. I was concerned, instead, to attempt a survey of the law of search and seizure from an evolutionary perspective. The outcome of such an examination leads, inevitably, to a redefinition of orthodox notions of what constitutes a search in the context of criminal investigation. Other common law jurisdictions have already recognised that the concept now extends to the use of *any* investigatory practice that results in the finding of evidence, even when that evidence is intangible information, or even when that evidence is only discoverable through an analysis of bodily samples. Thus, new technologies, such as electronic surveillance and the power to effect DNA analysis, fall to be considered as part of the package of police methodologies that are used to effect a search and to obtain evidence against a suspect.

This redefinition has substantial implications both for law enforcers and for individual citizens. The Human Rights Act 1998 has incorporated into domestic law, for the first time, a right of privacy and the right to a fair trial. These human rights will lead to a re-evaluation of police methodology and, in the context of search in particular, an examination of whether there has been an infringement of privacy through the carrying out of an unreasonable search. The European Court of Human Rights is largely concerned with complaints arising from inquisitorial jurisdictions and the resultant case law is not, necessarily, transmutable into an adversarial system. The general nature of the precepts contained in Articles 6 and 8 of the European Convention (the right to a fair trial and to privacy) leaves considerable room for uncertainty as to the extent to which existing police powers may be held to be compatible with the Human Rights Act. However, the jurisprudence of the United States and of Canada may help us to evaluate the compliance of our current law enforcement powers with the new Convention protections. In both these jurisdictions there is a constitutionally mandated right to protection from unreasonable searches. In both jurisdictions, also, there is a due process right to trial in accordance with principles of fundamental justice. It is therefore instructive to compare the case law of these countries and to consider how our domestic law might be reformulated.

A further issue arises from the increasing use of new investigatory techniques and from the trend towards proactive policing. In many instances, police are not searching for evidence of past offending, but are keeping surveillance on targets who might offend in the near future, or are gathering information for contingent future use. These searches do not necessarily lead to the acquisition of evidence for use in a criminal trial. The primary objective of such surveillance is the acquisition of information. The creation of criminal intelligence databases, national and international, has assisted in the culture of knowledge acquisition that now pervades law enforcement agencies. This movement, from evidence to information gathering, has significant implications for the privacy rights of all citizens and raises the question of where the balance is to be drawn between the need for crime control and the need to protect each citizen from unreasonable intrusion into private affairs.

I hope that this small text may at least promote debate and that it will be of interest to legal practitioners, students of law and others concerned with the administration of justice and with civil liberties. I owe thanks to my colleagues at De Montfort University for giving me moral encouragement over the last twelve months. I, however, bear sole responsibility for any errors of typing and proof reading that may have survived my scrutiny.

Sybil Sharpe

1 Introduction

The subject matter of this text is a discussion of the powers granted to law enforcement agents to conduct searches and to gather information in support of the investigation and suppression of crime. This discussion will examine the extent and efficacy of those powers in the light of constraints imposed by human rights law, exclusionary rules of evidence and the common law concept of 'due process'. A pervasive theme is the question of whether an appropriate balance can ever be achieved between the inherently conflicting interests of the public in crime control and of the citizen in protecting personal privacy and autonomy. However, before any detailed analysis can be made, it is necessary to consider what is meant by the concept of a 'search'. The concept has developed pragmatically in common law jurisdictions. It has been moulded by many factors, including expediency, political contest, changes in the investigation and trial process and, most recently, by the introduction of electronic technologies. In order to appreciate the many faceted nature of 'search' in the context of criminal investigation, it is necessary to understand the historical evolution of the process and the widening objectives of investigators. What commenced in Anglo-Saxon times as a right to look for stolen goods, has now expanded into a general right to seek incriminatory real evidence and to seek, through electronic recording and telephone interception, evidence of self-incriminatory statements or actions made by a suspect. The distinction between evidence obtained by means of search and evidence obtained by means of interrogation has become increasingly blurred and there is no longer a firm distinction to be made between admissions and real evidence. In essence, this movement is characterised by a shift in the purpose of the search activity. That purpose is no longer confined to the discovery of tangible evidence of crime, but extends to the discovery of information about a suspect, gleaned from what a suspect says and does in his private domain. Buttressing the need for such information is the move toward targeted policing and the creation of databases of knowledge as tools of crime control.[1] The summary of the development of search powers that follows is not purely a matter of historical interest. It is a brief account of how common law jurisdictions have arrived at the concept of a search as it exists today.

The Development of Search Powers

The earliest recognised common law power of search was that of a citizen to pursue a suspected cattle thief. If the suspect had been apprehended while still driving animals, he could be taken lawfully as a 'hand-having thief' (Pollock and Maitland, 1968). This echoes the early Roman law distinction between a manifest and a non-manifest offender (Feldman, 1986). Even if the cattle had reached the marauder's land, the trail leading to the land could establish theft. The element of chase was a critical part of the process and recovery of the goods was a more usual outcome than the conviction of the thief (Pollock and Maitland, 1968). The concept of hot pursuit applied, in due course, to thieves of chattels of all kinds and was extended, by the latter part of the fifteenth century, to encompass a search of the private premises of a suspected felon. Entry by force and without consent was trespass. However, if no force was used, for instance if an outer door was open, even a non-consensual search of premises could be conducted. The concept of trespass was viewed in entirely physical terms. The issue was whether there had been a need to 'break open the door',[2] not whether there had been an intrusion into personal privacy. The only extent to which this intangible encroachment was recognised was in the distinction made between forcible entry into a dwelling house, which was trespass, and forcible entry of a non-dwelling, which was not.[3] Some acknowledgement was made, therefore, that a particular protection attached to domestic life.

In a further development, forcible entry into domestic premises, for the purpose of a search, could be made under statute or under common law by judicial authorisation. Such authorisation was called a warrant. The warrant was a contentious instrument and the arguments surrounding the legitimacy of the warrant procedure have significantly shaped the constitutional history of England and Wales and of the United States. There were two main objections to the issuance of warrants. The first related to the scope of the warrant and the second to the identity of the issuer. The development of the printing press, and therefore of mass communication, had led to the enactment of statutes empowering agents to enter and seize documents in a bid to establish censorship through a system of licensing (Polyviou, 1982). These powers were increased incrementally by the Star Chamber in order to repress both political and religious dissent. At their apotheosis, search powers existed to seek out sedition and 'unlicensed' books at any time of day or night. These wide powers did not, in fact, entirely disappear with the demise of the Star

Chamber and it was not until after the Revolution of 1688 that recognition grew of the oppressive nature of general warrants (Polyviou, 1982). The seminal case that established the need for specificity in respect of suspicion and of the items sought was *Wilkes v Wood*[4] where, reviewing a non-statutory authorisation, the Lord Chief Justice accepted that 'the law never admits of a general search warrant'. The second objection to search warrants was that they could be issued by the executive under prerogative power and thus used as a tool of political oppression. *Entick v Carrington*[5] held that such a practice, even if exercised 'since the Revolution', was illegal and that if it was to be upheld 'it would destroy all the comforts of society'.[6]

Thus, unless specifically authorised by statute, no search warrant was valid if it did not conform to the strict limits of the common law. These limits imposed a requirement of judicial control, of particularity and of reasonable belief. It will be seen that these elemental requirements remain today in respect of warrants granted in common law jurisdictions. Even so, it was a concession to crime control that, under the common law, any forcible intrusion into private property was allowed. A justice could only grant a warrant if the applicant swore on oath that a felony had been committed and that he had 'probable cause to suspect' that stolen property was in the 'house or place' to be searched. The applicant had also to show his 'reasons for such suspicion'.[7] Sir Matthew Hale viewed the warrant procedure as a coercive measure that was necessary and expedient 'in these times where felonies and robberies are so frequent'.[8] The limited power of justices to issue warrants to search for stolen goods was recognised in *Entick v Carrington*[9] and gained acceptance through long usage, even though Lord Coke denied that such a power existed.[10]

Adverse reaction to general warrants and to prerogative authority was equally evident in revolutionary America. The constitution of the newly independent United States was formed in the context of revolt against executive powers contained in 'writs of assistance'. Such writs had no real judicial origin but allowed enforcement of the Act of Frauds 1662 by conferring virtually unfettered powers of search on customs officials. The Law Reform Commission of Canada[11] went so far as to state that 'resistance to the writ, and to the customs regime that it supported, was a vital part in the sequence of events that culminated in the American Revolution'. It has also been pointed out that, even after 1688, the so-called 'judicial' magistrates sitting in America lacked the independence from the Crown that the English judiciary had achieved. 'Even when a judge issued a warrant, revolutionary America greeted the event with foreboding' (Akhil Reed Amar, 1994:773). It is not surprising then that express restrictions on the issue of warrants and upon powers of search appear in the Constitution of the United States. In its final form, the Fourth Amendment provides

> The right of people to be secure in their persons, houses, papers and effects against unreasonable searches and seizure shall not be violated and no warrants shall issue, but upon probable cause, supported by oath or affirmation, and particularly describing the place to be searched, and the persons or things to be seized.

The orthodox interpretation given to this provision[12] overturns the previously held belief that warrants were a coercive instrument of government intrusion and treats warrants as a device protective of the suspect. Criteria essential for the granting of a valid warrant are seen as safeguarding a citizen's interests. These criteria are, of course, the fundamental requirements of reasonableness, particularity, probable cause and of judicial control.[13] This interpretation has led the Supreme Court to declare in *Coolidge v New Hampshire*[14] that

> searches conducted outside the judicial process, without prior approval by a judge or magistrate are *per se* unreasonable under the Fourth Amendment – subject only to a few specifically established and well-delineated exceptions.

However, in England and Wales, the dislike of the warrant procedure, that formed an inherent part of the political struggle to establish the supremacy of the common law, resulted in a reluctance to develop any concept of a general power to grant warrants as instruments of criminal investigation. A piecemeal collection of statutes gave authority to the police to enter premises to search for prohibited items, but no coherent scheme of search and seizure powers existed prior to 1985.[15] It was not until the Police and Criminal Evidence Act 1984 (hereinafter PACE) came into force that a statutory structure existed setting out the powers of and constraints on government agents seeking tangible evidence of crime.

In order to fully understand the structure of the PACE search provisions, it is necessary to appreciate the context in which they were drafted. The Royal Commission on Criminal Procedure[16] that preceded the PACE Bills[17] was concerned to effect a 'fundamental balance' between the interests of society in bringing offenders to justice and the 'rights and liberties of persons suspected or accused of crime'.[18] There was a perceived need for clear and certain rules within which police officers should operate[19] and the openness and certainty of these rules was to be the protection of officers and suspects alike. Whilst not every proposal of the Royal Commission was adopted by the government, PACE as finally enacted, substantially replicates many of the recommendations contained therein. The major innovation effected by PACE is the creation of powers of search and seizure that are not offence specific. Instead the powers are to be exercised according to statutory criteria. These criteria attempt to maintain a 'balance' between crime control and civil liberty. A requirement of 'reasonable grounds for suspicion' predicates all search powers under PACE itself, thus, in theory, precluding an unreasonable search.[20] The specific provisions of PACE will be examined in detail in the following chapters. By way of introduction, it is worth pointing out that the powers include the right to stop and search prior to arrest,[21] to effect road checks,[22] to apply for a warrant to a justice of the peace,[23] to make a warrantless search of persons and of premises on arrest[24] and to apply to a circuit judge for a production order or a warrant to obtain sensitive and/or confidential material.[25]

The restrictions on these powers are ones both of substance and of form. Adopting the recommendations of the Royal Commission that the recording of police activity would minimise abuse of power,[26] the government incorporated detailed requirements into Codes A and B of PACE concerning the keeping of records and the notification of the basis of search to persons and occupiers. In addition, probable cause and the specificity requirement of warrant applications is enshrined in subsections 8(1)(b) and (c) which provide that a constable must satisfy a justice that there are reasonable grounds to believe that there is on the premises the material specified in the application, that such material is likely to be of substantial value to the investigation and that it is likely to be relevant evidence. The Commission was concerned that there should always be prior authority given before the 'serious intrusion' of entry onto premises took place and also that a 'compulsory power to search for evidence should be available only as a last resort'.[27] Reflecting this concern, subsections 8(1) and (3) of PACE provide that a justice may issue a warrant only when he is satisfied that there are reasonable grounds to believe that a serious arrestable offence has been committed and that the material cannot be obtained consensually. The government did not accept the Commission's historically based, but logically untenable, distinction made between searches for prohibited goods and searches for evidence.

The concerns expressed over the use of search powers affecting innocent individuals and organisations[28] have been addressed by means of the special procedure provisions contained in Schedule 1 of PACE, whilst sections 9 and 10 exempt legally privileged material from search. However, the substantial limitations on search powers contained in PACE and the Codes made thereunder have a curious loophole. Section 19 of PACE allows a constable who is lawfully on the premises to seize *any* material found thereon if he has reasonable grounds for believing that it consists of the fruits of a crime and that it is necessary to seize it to prevent its concealment or destruction. The only restriction, contained in PACE subsection 19(6), relates to items that a constable has reasonable grounds to believe are subject to legal privilege. The section allows a constable to seize material outside the scope of a warrant and does not limit the right of seizure to serious offences. It therefore legitimates general searches once an officer has entered onto the premises by means of a warrant or by consent. The section does not accord with the views of the Royal Commission that, though it was not realistic to expect a constable to ignore items found incidentally in the course of a legal search, officers should only be allowed to seize fortuitously obtained material that was evidence of a grave offence.[29] In this respect, PACE arguably grants wider powers of search and seizure than existed under the common law.[30]

Electronic Search

The discussion of the powers of search available to law enforcers has, so far, been limited to those concerning the obtaining of real evidence, that is tangible objects that in some way link the suspect to the offence being investigated. The development of audio recording and later, of video recording, has revolutionised the ability of state agents to search covertly for evidence both of prospective offending and of crimes already committed. Sometimes electronic eavesdropping does not relate to a specific offence, but is in the nature of an information gathering exercise that may prove valuable in supporting a subsequent investigation. This is particularly true of CCTV surveillance of public places where no one individual is targeted. In the United States, the Supreme Court has recognised for over 40 years that 'the protection against unreasonable searches and seizures is not limited to tangible things. It extends to intangibles such as spoken words'.[31] A considerable jurisprudence has developed concerning the reconciliation of electronic searches with the Fourth Amendment. The case law in England and Wales is embryonic by comparison and has rarely addressed the issues arising in terms of search powers,[32] judges preferring instead to consider covert recording simply as an aspect of admission evidence.[33] It may be that this different focus has been the consequence of our different constitutional heritage. In the United States, there has been an entrenched protection against unreasonable searches for two centuries. In England and Wales, due process protections arise from common law and statute law. The absence of a clearly recognised tort of privacy or of any express right to be free from unjustified intrusions into private life, has left English lawyers with little room to manoeuvre when seeking to exclude electronically recorded evidence. Instead they have fallen back upon PACE, which controls the obtaining of confessions.[34] However, incorporation into domestic law of the European Convention for the Protection of Human Rights and Fundamental Freedoms has been effected by the Human Rights Act 1998. Article 8(1) of the Convention is of more general application than the Fourth Amendment and confers a presumptive right to respect for private life, family life, home and correspondence.[35] Incorporation will permit of arguments that have previously only been brought before North American courts.[36] These arguments will be addressed more particularly in the chapters dealing with electronic eavesdropping. At this juncture, it is sufficient to examine the potential conflict that arises between the need for the effective suppression of crime and the need to maintain the privacy of the presumptively innocent citizen.

This conflict was addressed many years ago by the report of the Committee of Privy Councillors appointed to Inquire into the Interception of Communications.[37] The Councillors pointed out that the 'freedom of the individual is quite valueless if he can be made the victim of the law breaker. Every civilised society must have the power to protect itself from wrongdoers'. Concerns that innocent citizens would suffer an interference with liberty, should their messages necessarily be intercepted along with those of targeted individuals, were rejected. It was said that there were 'no harmful results' from such an outcome and that the citizen must endure this inevitable consequence in order that the main purpose of detecting and preventing crime should be achieved'. The justification for powers of interception was regarded as one of expediency, for even prior to concerns over drug importation and international fraud, it was accepted that criminals used the telephone as a means of communication and that interception might provide the evidence necessary to prefer charges. However, in England and Wales, the debate did not encompass any discussion of unreasonable searches.[38]

The concept of search for 'information', as opposed to search for physical objects, was not recognised and, until 1985,[39] no clear statutory procedures were put in place to govern telephone tapping. Of course, electronic monitoring covers a wide range of activity from the interception of satellite based communication to the basic 'wiring' of an individual or the 'bugging' of premises. However, no theoretical connection was made between these forms of search and no coherent principles were adopted in respect of surveillance activity. The result has been an *ad hoc* collection of administrative directions, case law and statutes, many of which provide no scope for judicial authorisation.[40] In the United States, on the other hand, the crucial issue is not so much the means used to effect the surveillance as the *impact* of that surveillance on the Fourth Amendment.[41] The most significant single decision is the case of *Katz v US*.[42] *Katz* firmly overturned earlier authority by viewing the protection from unreasonable search as an aspect of privacy rights rather than as a safeguard from trespassory interference. Whilst earlier cases[43] had focused upon whether there had been a physical intrusion into the individual's 'constitutionally protected area',[44] *Katz* affirmed that 'the Fourth Amendment protects people, not places'.[45] The reasonableness of a search did not depend upon whether there had been an interference with property rights, but upon whether the object of the surveillance had a justifiable expectation of privacy and whether this right had been overridden.

This seismic shift in the jurisprudence of the United States has led to the development of principled criteria for all forms of surveillance activity. However, because it is necessary, in the interests of controlling crime, that government investigators have the power to monitor conversations and actions of suspects and of targets, even a reasonable expectation of privacy is not absolute. Instead, it may be overridden under prescribed safeguards, similar to those governing applications for search warrants to look for tangible property.[46] Legitimate, non-consensual[47] monitoring of private conversations may only take place under a judicial warrant based upon adequate showing of probable cause. The offences being investigated, the individuals, the premises[48] and the types of conversation to be intercepted must be specified. There must be a time limitation on surveillance. Such constraints transport the elemental concepts of judicial control, of reasonable grounds and of particularity to electronic search. A major question to be determined, following the enactment of the Human Rights Act 1998, is whether existing surveillance procedures in England and Wales uphold those concepts and, if they do not, whether they are none the less in accordance with Article 8.

The point has already been made that, at present, in England and Wales, the interception or recording of conversations for the purposes of criminal investigation takes place under legislation dealing separately with telephone interception[49] and with the bugging of property.[50] Whether a police officer, judge or government minister is responsible for granting the statutory authorisation will depend upon the specific provisions of the legislation relied upon. There is no underlying rationale for why, under the Police Act 1997 section 92, the police should be the organisation primarily responsible for the bugging of premises, whilst under the Interception of Communications Act 1985 section 2(1), a Secretary of State grants warrants to intercept post or the public telecommunications system. However, to make matters even more complicated, there are many categories of electronic search that are not covered by any statutory authority simply because they fall outside a literal reading of existing enactments.[51] At present, there is also one general exception to the need for authorisation in accordance with law and that is the exception of consensual eavesdropping. Where an individual is persuaded to wear a hidden recorder, or consents to have his telephone calls intercepted or his premises bugged, the need for adherence to statutory procedures and for authorisation thereunder disappears.[52] The purpose of such consensual activity is usually to obtain evidence against a suspect when conventional police methods of investigation are likely to fail. There are serious and difficult evidential questions raised when participating informants lead others into taking action that would not otherwise have been taken, or into making admissions that would not have been made in response to questioning under caution by a police officer.

The first difficulty is that this form of electronic search may overlap with the use of undercover operatives as *agents provocateurs*. Arguments concerning the admissibility of the recording in a criminal trial may turn on whether, under section 78 of PACE, entrapment by the undercover agent has so tainted the evidence that reliance upon it 'would have such an adverse effect on the fairness of the proceedings that the court ought not to admit it'. The section provides an express judicial discretion to exclude prosecution evidence for potential unfairness. The impropriety of investigators, rather than the breach of any statutory provision in respect of recording or transmitting words or actions, may lead to the exclusion of the evidence.[53] Courts will also have to bear in mind that Article 6 of the European Convention provides a right to a fair trial and that this includes the right of one with no criminal predisposition not to face trial solely on the basis of evidence obtained by entrapment.[54] A second difficulty is that there may be issues of trickery and implied deception in recording statements or actions when the subject is unaware that he is incriminating himself. The courts in England and Wales have, so far, followed the approach adopted in North America[55] and have not excluded electronically recorded evidence obtained prior to custodial interrogation through the use of 'mere strategic deception'.[56] In the United States, a greater protection exists for a suspect under the Sixth Amendment,[57] but even after charge, passive listening will not result in the suppression of evidence so long as there is no deliberate attempt to elicit information.[58] A similar approach prevails in Canada where, after charge, the question is whether the deception 'unfairly deprived the suspect of the right to choose whether to speak to the authorities or not'.[59] It remains to be seen whether, following the implementation of the Human Rights Act, English judges will exercise their exclusionary discretion in cases where admissions have been made on the basis of some deception, but do not result from the interrogation. A third and equally contentious issue was that of certain 'consensual' telephone taps. Calls made via a public telecommunications system fall within the Interception of Communications Act 1985. Normally intercepts of such calls cannot be adduced against an accused,[60] but those that were believed to be intercepted with consent could, until recently, be used in evidence. The reception of such communications called into question whether an accused had had a fair trial, since the Act precludes any challenge on the issue of reasonable belief in consent.[61]

Bodily Samples

A distinction has been made between searches for tangible items and searches for information. A further distinction can be made between searches for tangible evidence that incriminates a suspect by virtue of its existence and searches for tangible evidence that incriminates only by virtue of forensic analysis. Blood stains, semen, fingerprints and hairs may link a suspect to the victim or to the scene of the crime. Such bodily samples will become probative when matched to the DNA profile of the suspect. The power to take bodily samples in order to support a criminal prosecution originated in road traffic legislation. The Road Traffic Act 1988 contains the current powers of police to obtain such samples. That Act requires any person who is reasonably suspected of having committed driving offences premised upon the consumption of alcohol or drugs[62] to provide a sample of breath, blood or urine.[63] Prior to PACE, a requirement to provide a specimen of breath for analysis was viewed as conflicting with the privilege against self-incrimination and as amounting to compelling evidence of a quasi-confessional nature.[64] PACE, as amended by the Criminal Justice and Public Order Act 1994, now provides that non-intimate bodily samples and fingerprints are obtainable by compulsion and may be used for the purpose of a speculative search into criminal offending.[65] Such samples are not invalidated by reason of their self-incriminatory quality.[66] Traditionally, the taking of a sample from a suspect has not been treated as an aspect of search and seizure, although the sample frequently becomes probative only as a consequence of linking the suspect to the forensic evidence obtained in searches made in the aftermath of crime. Instead, bodily samples have been treated as a subcategory of identification evidence (Blackstone's, 1999:2219). However, in the United States and in Canada, such evidence *is* regarded as obtained through a process of search; a search of the person of the suspect.[67] Although other factors such as the privilege against self-incrimination and the right to counsel[68] have also entered into a consideration of the admissibility of bodily samples, the reasonableness of police action in making the 'search' is a crucial factor.[69] In contrast, those procedures under PACE that allow for speculative searches need not be based on reasonable suspicion in respect of the crime under investigation.[70]

Due Process Rights Relevant to Search

In this introduction, I have attempted to give a brief overview of the different kinds of search that may take place in the course of criminal investigation. It is appropriate to conclude this chapter with an analysis of those due process constraints that may affect the validity of searches. It is axiomatic that the outcome of any challenge to the legality of a search depends upon judicial interpretation and application of domestic evidence law and of constitutional and human rights law. It is instructive, therefore, to compare protections afforded by the European Convention with those granted by the American Constitution and the Canadian Charter of Rights and Freedoms. Whilst there may be differences of emphasis and of detail, there are similarities of principle and it is possible to draw analogies with the more developed jurisprudence of those jurisdictions. One important distinction is that Article 8 of the European Convention makes no specific reference to powers of search. As stated earlier, Article 8(1) creates a general right to privacy by stating:

> Everyone has the right to respect for his private and family life, his home and his correspondence.

This wider right must necessarily include the right 'to be let alone'.[71] It also includes the right of the individual to be protected against spying, interference with correspondence and misuse of private communications.[72] However, the right of privacy under Article 8 is not absolute. Article 8(2) permits derogation by a 'public authority'. Such derogation must be '*in accordance with the law*' and be necessary in a democratic society in the interests of one of the following;

national security, public safety, the economic well-being of the country, *the prevention of disorder or crime*, the protection of health and morals or the protection of rights and freedoms of others.[73]

There is no express prohibition on unreasonable searches, but there is, none the less, good reason why a search of any kind, other than on reasonable grounds, may violate the Article. The general principle of proportionality applies to all decisions of the European Court and the European Court of Human Rights. This principle demands that action taken is strictly limited to that necessary to obtain lawful objectives. If a search is made without reasonable suspicion or 'probable cause',[74] it cannot be justified as a necessary activity in the prevention of crime and thus would arguably be unlawful, despite any adherence to statutory procedures. One real difficulty with this analysis is that any individual seeking to disprove the existence of probable cause has an uphill struggle because the information on which warrants and authorisations are granted is likely to be subject to public interest immunity. This immunity relieves the Crown from the normative obligation to disclose unused material in criminal proceedings where this material might 'undermine the case' for the prosecution[75] or 'might reasonably be expected to assist the accused's defence as disclosed by the defence statement'.[76] The immunity attaches to 'sensitive material'[77] which is stated to include the identity of informants, covert surveillance locations and material supporting applications for search warrants.[78]

It is ultimately for a judge to decide whether the sensitive material should be disclosed to the defence, claims of immunity notwithstanding. The criteria for this decision making and the practical difficulties for a defendant seeking to obtain this disclosure are discussed in chapter 6. Further, whilst some hope for criminal suspects is contained in dicta of the Court of Human Rights to the effect that any incursion into the right of privacy must be 'interpreted narrowly' and must be 'convincingly stated',[79] that Court has not condemned the absence of judicial review or the secrecy surrounding our domestic law in respect of telephone interception. The circumstances surrounding that form of electronic search may not be examined or challenged under the Interception of Communications Act 1985, yet the procedure has been sanctioned by the Court as being 'in accordance with the law'.[80] Questions therefore arise as to whether Article 8 is in reality focused on legal formalism and whether it will prove as potent an instrument as the Fourth Amendment or the Canadian Charter in striking down unreasonable searches.

In the United States, the Fourth Amendment is specifically concerned with prohibiting unreasonable searches. The Fourteenth Amendment, containing the requirement that no person shall be deprived of life, liberty or property without 'due process of law', has the effect of subjecting all states to the Fourth Amendment.[81] In a shorter, but equally specific provision, section 8 of the Canadian Charter of Fundamental Rights and Freedoms states that 'everyone has the right to be secure against unreasonable search and seizure'. This right is buttressed by the Canadian equivalent of the Fourteenth Amendment. Section 7 of the Charter grants the right not to be deprived of life, liberty and security of person other than in accordance with 'principles of fundamental justice'. From the viewpoint of an accused, the linguistic difference between these provisions and Article 8 is, perhaps, of less significance than the rules of evidence governing any criminal trial in which they may fall to be considered. The adversarial common law culture that applies to proceedings in the United States and Canada permits argument that evidence should be excluded, despite its inherent reliability, if it is obtained in violation of powers granted to law enforcement officers.

The view that state officials must not act in arbitrary disregard of the law has a long constitutional history. One method of curbing such actions is to deprive the state from benefiting from the fruits of an illegal search by suppressing the evidence in any resultant criminal proceedings. The suppression of evidence of a search resulting from criminal investigation provides a direct and effective remedy for any person charged as a consequence of an illegal search. It does not, of course, protect citizens who are not made the subject of criminal proceedings.[82] In the United States, suppression is achieved by an 'automatic' exclusionary rule. However, this rule is subject to judicial determination as to its applicability to the facts of any particular case[83] and, in respect of search, to common law and statutory exceptions in respect of the warrant requirement.[84] In Canada, the trial judge must exclude evidence under section 24(2) of the Charter if the evidence was obtained in a manner that denied or infringed Charter rights and if it is established that, having regard to all the circumstances, 'the admission of it in the proceedings would bring the administration of justice into disrepute'. The judge therefore has to balance the suppression of reliable evidence of criminal offending against the gravity of the Charter violation. If the violation is sufficiently serious, the administration of justice is brought into greater disrepute by the admission of evidence than by its exclusion.[85]

In England and Wales, there was, prior to PACE, a rhetorically acknowledged, but rarely applied judicial discretion to exclude improperly and illegally obtained evidence.[86] This discretion has now been supplanted by the judicial discretion to exclude prosecution evidence under section 78(1) of PACE which provides

> In any proceedings the court may refuse to allow evidence on which the prosecution proposes to rely to be given if it appears to the court that, having regard to all the circumstances, including the circumstances in which the evidence was obtained, the admission of the evidence would have such an adverse effect on the fairness of the proceedings that the court ought not to admit it.

Whilst there have been examples of exclusion of evidence under this section when there have been flagrant breaches of PACE,[87] it is unusual for evidence obtained as the result of a search to be excluded in order to deter the police from impropriety.[88] The inherent reliability of this kind of evidence means that a trial judge is likely to conclude that the fairness of the proceedings is not adversely affected despite of the way in which it was obtained. The Court of Appeal in *R v Chalkley and Jeffries*[89] has endorsed this approach stating that, other than in the case of confessions and evidence obtained from the accused after the crime, 'there is no discretion to exclude evidence unless its quality was or might have been affected by the way in which it was obtained'. In England and Wales, therefore, maintaining the reputation and integrity of the criminal justice system is not the crucial concern when judicial discretion to exclude evidence is being exercised.[90]

Whenever the subject of a search seeks legal redress, whether in the form of a civil action, or a prerogative order quashing the search and seizure, or even by seeking suppression of the evidence resulting from the search, the enactment of the Human Rights Act 1998 requires judges to determine if the search has been conducted 'according to the law' in the light of the right to privacy and personal autonomy contained in Article 8. Section 3(1) of the Act states that a court, so far as it is possible to do so, must read primary and subordinate legislation 'in a way which is compatible with the Convention rights'. Section 2 requires courts to take account of the jurisprudence of the European Court of Human Rights and of the Commission. As stated above, uncertainties arise as to the extent to which certain searches may be validated under Article 8(2). Further, in respect of accused persons, Article 8 may well prove to be a less effective due process weapon in trial proceedings than the Fourth Amendment or the Canadian Charter.[91] How generously Article 8 is applied in relation to defendants, or to others subjected to criminal searches, is ultimately a matter for judges in England and Wales to decide. The Human Rights Act provides new scope for judicial interpretation. Rights to privacy, to a fair trial and to freedom of speech are now to be precepts against which the propriety of all criminal investigation is to be judged. In the following chapters of this text, I examine the various kinds of search powers outlined above and evaluate the extent to which they might survive challenge under the Human Rights Act. In the final chapter, an assessment is made of the impact on the right to privacy of increasing European co-operation in the storage and exchange of police intelligence.

Notes

1. The Police Act 1997 created the National Criminal Intelligence Service and the National Crime Squad. The Criminal Justice and Public Order Act 1994 established a DNA database. The Europol Convention came into effect on 1st October 1998. The Convention provides for a European-wide 'information system'.
2. *Lee v Gansel* (1774) 1 Cowp 1, 98 ER 935; *Semayne's Case* (1604) 5 Co Rep 91a, 77 ER 194; *Maleverer v Spinke* (1537) 1 Dyer 35b, 73 ER 79.
3. *Penton v Browne* (1657) 1 Sid 186, 82 ER 1047; see also Feldman (1986). Compare the Police Act 1997 Part Three, below and chapter 4.
4. (1763) 19 How St Tr1153, 98 ER 489; *Crozier v Cundy* (1827) 6 B&C 232, 108 ER 429.
5. (1765) 19 How St Tri 1030, 95 ER 807.
6. *Ibid.*
7. See Sir Matthew Hale's *The History Of The Pleas Of The Crown* (vol.2) republished in London Professional Books 1971.
8. *Ibid.*
9. Above.
10. 4 Co Inst 176–177.
11. Report On Writs Of Assistance And Telewarrants (1983) no. 19; see also *Stanford v Texas* (1965) 379 US 476.
12. There is some debate as to whether a correct interpretation of the Fourth Amendment does require a search to be by warrant, or merely requires it to be reasonable; see Amar (1994).
13. See *Trupiano v US* (1948) 334 US 699. Exceptions to the warrant requirement exist in exigent and other circumstances; see chapter 2.
14. (1971) 403 US 443.
15. For instance, stolen goods, drugs, firearms and explosives. There was also power to seek evidence of offences contained in specific statutes, e.g. illegal gaming under the Gaming Act 1968.
16. The Phillips Report Cmnd. 8092 (1981).
17. There were two PACE Bills, in 1982 and 1983. A general election disrupted the passage of the first Bill.
18. Para. 1.11.
19. Paras. 2.18–2.24.
20. Searches may be made other than on reasonable grounds in respect of individuals and vehicles under the Prevention of Terrorism (Temporary Provisions) Act 1989 sections 13A (inserted by The Criminal Justice and Public Order Act 1994 s.81) and 13B (inserted by the Prevention of Terrorism (Additional Powers) Act 1996 s.1) and also under CRIMPO 1994 s.60 (prevention of incidents of serious violence); see chapter 2.

21. Sects. 1–3 of PACE and Code A.
22. Sects. 4–5.
23. Sects. 8, 15, 16 and Code B.
24. Sects. 18, 32 and Code B.
25. Sects. 9, 11–14 and Schedule 1.
26. Cmnd. 8092 paras. 3.24–3.28 and 3.46.
27. Paras. 3.38–3.47.
28. *Ibid* paras. 3.40–3.41.
29. At paras. 3.48–3.49.
30. See *Chic Fashions West Wales v Jones* [1968] 1 ALL ER 229 and *Ghani v Jones* [1969] 3 ALL ER 1700. Despite some incursion into the specificity limitation (*Wilkes v Wood* (1763) 19 How St Tri 1153 and above) the right of seizure was limited to related or serious offences. Compare *Arizona v Hicks* (1987) 480 US 321 for a more restrictive approach; but note that the doctrine of 'plain view' may legitimate seizure of items not specified in the warrant where an officer is lawfully on the premises, *Washington v Chisman* (1982) 455 US 1.
31. *US v On Lee* (1952) 343 US 747 per Barton J. (dissenting) – a covert recorder and transmitter were used.
32. *R v Khan* [1996] 3 ALL ER 289 is an exception. Issues of trespass and the significance of the (then unincorporated) Article 8 of the European Convention were addressed.
33. *E.g. Christou v Wright* [1992] 4 ALL ER 559 and *R v Bailey and Smith* [1993] 3 ALL ER 513. For the theoretical link between search and self-incrimination see the now somewhat discredited case of *Boyd v US* (1886)116 US 616.
34. There is no longer a meaningful distinction between an admission and a confession. PACE sect. 82(1) defines a confession as including 'any statement made wholly or partly adverse the person who made it, whether made to a person in authority or not and whether made in words or otherwise'.
35. Derogations from this right are permissible in the interests of (*inter alia*) national security, public safety and the prevention of disorder or crime; see below.
36. Canada also has constitutional protection against unreasonable searches under sect. 8 of the Charter of Rights and Freedoms; see below.
37. (1957) Cmnd. 283 (Birkett Report).
38. Though the Report of the Committee on Privacy (1972) Cmnd. 5162 (Younger Report) did recommend the creation of a criminal offence of surreptitious surveillance by a technical device. The police would, probably, have been exempted.
39. The Interception of Communications Act 1985 was passed in response to the case of *Malone v UK* (1984) 7 EHRR 14.
40. *E.g.* The Interception of Communications Act 1985; the Security Service Act 1989; the Intelligence Services Act 1994. Even the Police Act 1997 provides only for retrospective judicial review other than in a limited number of cases; For pending reform and generally; see chapter 5.
41. See The Electronic Communications Privacy Act 1986 amending the Omnibus Crime Control Act 1968.
42. *Katz v US* (1967) 389 US 347.
43. *Olmstead v US* (1928) 277 US 438 and *Silverman v US* (1961) 365 US 505.
44. *E.g.* private homes, but also offices (*Gouled v US* (1921) 255 US 298) and hotel rooms (*Lustig v US* (1949) 338 US 74); cp. Police Act 1997 Part Three.

45. Above, per Mr. Justice Stewart.
46. See USCA 18 paras. 2510–2520.
47. Title 111 of the Omnibus Crime Control Act 1968 does not extend to the recording of a conversation with the consent of one of the conversants or to participant bugging or interception where there is an 'assumed risk' of disclosure of the conversation; *US v White* (1971) 401 US 745; *US v Caceres* (1979) 440 US 741 and cp. *R v Rasool and Choudhary* [1997] 2 Cr App. R 190 *R v Hallsworth* C.A. 03/04/98 and *Barker v R* (1994) 127 ALR 280.
48. But note the possibility of 'roving surveillance' under Title 111 of the Omnibus Crime Control and Safe Streets Act 1968.
49. The Interception of Communications Act 1985 and the Security Service Act 1996.
50. The Police Act 1997.
51. *E.g.* the bugging of persons rather than premises, bugging where no physical trespass takes place and the interception of cordless telephones and pagers; see chapters 5 and 6.
52. Interestingly, the Police Act makes no specific mention of consensual bugging, presumably because it validates certain police action, rather than outlawing activity that does not conform to statutory criteria. See chapter 5 for reform proposals under the Regulation of Investigatory Powers Bill.
53. *R v Smurthwaite and Gill* [1994] 1 ALL ER 898; *R v Shazad and Latif* [1996] 1 ALL ER 335.
54. *Teixera De Castro v Portugal* (1998) 44/1997/828/1034 [1998] Crim LR 751. Since there was a violation of Article 6, the Court did not go on to determine whether Article 8 had been violated; see chapter 6.
55. See *US v White* (1971) 401 US 745; *Hoffa v US* (1966) 385 US 293; *Illinios v Perkins* (1990) 496 US 292.
56. *Illinois v Perkins* (above) per Mr. Justice Kennedy. See *R v Christou and Wright* [1992] 4 ALL ER 559.
57. The Sixth Amendment applies after charge and contains, *inter alia*, the right to counsel. Undercover questioning after charge violates this right.
58. *Kuhlman v Wilson* (1986) 477 US 436; cp. The Australian case *R v Swaffield, Pavic v R* (1998) 151 ALR 98.
59. *R v Herbert* (1990) 57 CCC (3d) at 39 and see *Broyles v The Queen* (1991) 68 CCC (3d) 308 at 319; cp. dicta of Lord Justice Taylor in *Christou and Wright* (above) at 566 and chapter 6.
60. *R v Preston* [1994] 2 AC 130; *Preston v UK* (1997) EHRLR 695; *Morgans v Southwark Crown Court* [1999] 2 Cr. App. R.99 (DC) and chapter 5.
61. ICA 1985 sects. 1(2)(b) and sect. 9(1) as interpreted in *R v Owen and Stephen* [1999] 2 Cr. App. R.59.
62. Road Traffic Act 1988 sects. 3A, 4 and 5.
63. RTA 1988 sects. 6 and 7. It is an offence to fail, without reasonable excuse, to provide a specimen, RTA subsects. 6(4) and 7(6).
64. *R v Payne* [1962] 1 ALL ER 848; *R v Court* (1960) 44 Cr App. R 242; *R v Sang* [1980] AC 402.
65. PACE 1984 sects. 61, 63, 63A, as amended by CRIMPO 1994 sects. 54–59.
66. *Saunders v UK* [1996] 23 EHRR 313 and Sharpe (1998).
67. *R v Dyment* (1988) 55 DLR (4th) 503; *Stillman v The Queen* (1997) 144 DLR (4th) 193; *US v Weir* (1981) 657 F2d (8th Cir) 1005; *Schmerber v State of California* (1966) 384 US 757.

68. *R v Milne* (1996) 107 CCC (3d) 118; *R v Stillman* (above); *Winston v Lee* (1985) 470 US 753; but cp. *Schmerber v California* (above).
69. *Stillman* (above); *R v F(S)* (1997) 153 DLR (4th) 315.
70. PACE sect. 63A and H.O. Circular no. 16/95 – The National DNA Database; cp. the Canadian Criminal Code sect. 487.09 (1) and (2).
71. Cooley on Torts 2nd ed. (1888) at 29 and Warren and Brandies (1890).
72. See the conclusion of the Nordic Conference of Jurists on the Right to Respect for Privacy (May 1967).
73. Compare the wording of Article 12 of the UN Declaration of Human Rights 1948 which gives protection against 'arbitrary' interference with privacy, family, home and correspondence and the almost identically worded Article 17 of the International Covenant on Civil and Political Rights 1966. There is no express derogation to these rights.
74. In this text the terms 'probable cause' and 'reasonable grounds for belief' are used interchangeably.
75. Criminal Procedure and Investigations Act 1996 sect. 3(1)(a).
76. CPIA 1996 sect. 7(2)(a); for a fuller discussion of the link between pii and probable cause; see chapter 6.
77. See the Code made under CPIA at para. 6.12.
78. *Ibid.* see also Sharpe (1999).
79. *Cremieux v France* (1993) 16 EHRR 357; *Funke v France* (1993) 16 EHRR 297.
80. Sects. 1(2) and 9, *Christie v UK* App. No. 21452/93DR78; *Preston v UK* App. No. 24193/94 (1997) EHLR 695. See chapter 5.
81. *Mapp v Ohio* (1961) 367 US 643.
82. Such a person may sue in tort for trespass (*Ghani v Jones* [1969] 3 ALL ER 1700) or for the malicious procuring of a search warrant (*Gibbs and ors. v Rea* The Times 4th Feb. 1998). Judicial review of the search/seizure may also be sought (*R v Chief Constable of Warwickshire and ors. v Fitzpatrick and ors.* [1998] 1 ALL ER 65).
83. *E.g.* that the Fifth Amendment does not apply to bodily samples, *Schmerber v California* (1966) 384 US 157 or that the Fourth and Fifth Amendments do not apply where there is an 'assumed risk' of disclosure of conversation, *US v White* (1971) 401 US 745; see also Kamisar Y (1987).
84. *Coolidge v New Hampshire* (1971) 403 US 443 stating that searches conducted outside the judicial process are *per se* unreasonable, subject to established exceptions such as exigent circumstances, plain view searches and searches incidental to arrest. However, the search must still be reasonable; see chapter 2.
85. *Collins v The Queen* (1987) 38 DLR 508 and *R v Richard* (1996) 99 CCC (3d) 441.
86. *Kuruma v The Queen* (1955) AC 197; *Callis v Gunn* [1964] 1 QB 495; *R v Sang* [1980] AC 402.
87. See *R v Quinn* [1995] 1 Cr App. R 488; *R v Canale* [1990] 2 ALL ER 187; *R v Raphaie* [1996] Crim. L.R. 641.
88. *Matto v DPP* [1987] Crim. L.R. 641 was a rare early example. See also Sharpe (1998a).
89. [1998] 2 ALL ER 155 at 178–9.
90. See *R v Khan* [1996] 3 ALL ER 289 (HL). See chapter 6.
91. Sharpe (1997).

2 Warrantless Searches for Real Evidence

Searches by Consent of People and Premises

If a search is by consent, the statutory powers of search are not needed to legitimate the activities of law enforcement officers. There is no need for the search to be based upon reasonable grounds. In the context of a physical search of individuals, the safeguards incorporated into the revised Code A of PACE[1] will not apply. This Code governs pre-arrest police powers to stop and search persons in public places. However, Code A1.3 states that it governs 'the exercise by police officers of statutory powers'. Nothing in Code A affects

(a) the routine searching of persons entering sports grounds or other premises with consent as a condition of entry; or

(b) the ability of an officer to search a person in the street with his consent where no search power exists. In these circumstances, an officer should always make it clear that he is seeking the consent of the person concerned to the search being carried out by telling the person that he need not consent and that without his consent he will not be searched.[2]

Since the Code does not apply in these situations, there is no formal requirement as to what information is to be given to a volunteer, nor as to recording the search. However, there is some attempt in the Notes for Guidance paragraph 1D, quoted above, to ensure that consent is freely given. Further, where there is some doubt about the capacity of an individual to give informed consent, whether through mental handicap, disorder, or otherwise, that person should not be subjected to a 'voluntary search'.[3] If an officer acts in an 'improper manner', this will vitiate consent.[4] However, 'improper manner' is not defined in the Code and it is unlikely to extend to the subtle and internalised intimidation that inevitably exists whenever a police officer requests a citizen, however, properly, to permit a search in public of his outer clothing and personal property.

Consent is, in reality, likely to be no more than co-operation. There is little distinction between the compliance of the subject of a consensual search and the compliance of one searched under statutory authority. Research shows that the majority of officers carry out 'consensual' stops and that only a minority exercise their statutory powers (Bottomley, 1991; McConville, 1991). The use of unregulated authority allows a police officer to search without having to establish reasonable suspicion that he will find stolen or prohibited articles. It also relieves an officer from the detailed recording requirements that exist under PACE.[5] It is hardly surprising therefore that officers prefer not to have to justify their actions in an official record. The degree of intrusion into personal autonomy is at a fairly low level in a stop and search. Only outer coat, jacket and gloves are removed in public[6] and no strip or intimate search can be made.[7] None the less, there is an invasion of privacy and the possible risk of incrimination. Article 8 of the Convention could be relied upon where it is alleged that informed consent was not truly given and that there is no reasonable basis for the search.[8] The difficulty is that ultimately the legality of the search turns on the credibility of the police officer concerned compared with that of the aggrieved subject. Further, unless the search results in a seizure of incriminating items, there is unlikely to be any challenge to police action. It is hardly surprising, therefore, that there is a marked absence of authority on the issue and that consent, as distinguished from co-operation, has not been the subject of judicial analysis in England and Wales.

Searching premises by consent differs from stop searches in that Code B of PACE *does* apply to searches 'undertaken for the purpose of investigation into an alleged offence, with the occupier's consent'.[9] This endorses the view of the Royal Commission on Criminal Procedure that it is 'only rarely that the police do not receive consent to enter'.[10] Code B5.4 requires an officer to make an initial attempt to take to gain entry by co-operation even where a warrant has been obtained or when he is relying upon a statutory power to search without warrant.[11] To ensure that there is no evasion of the reasonable grounds requirement that would normally attach to a non-consensual search of premises, Code B4.2 provides

> Before seeking consent the officer in charge of the search shall state the purpose of the proposed search and inform the person concerned that he is not obliged to consent and that anything seized may be produced in evidence.

A person is entitled to be told if he is not a suspect at that time and certain specified information must be given.[12] This information must be provided to an occupier regardless of whether the search is by consent, by warrant, or under PACE powers to make a search on arrest.[13] The 'Notice of Powers and

Rights' must be in a standard format and must explain the extent of powers of search and seizure under PACE, the availability of compensation for any damage caused and that there is a right to consult the Code at any police station.[14]

The only exception to the requirement to provide a copy of this document is where an officer considers that it is 'impracticable' to provide the notice. This exception cannot apply in a consensual search and, indeed, Code B4.1 states that the consent must, if practicable, be given in writing on the Notice of Powers and Rights before search takes place. The Code also provides that consent is to be given by 'a person entitled to grant entry to the premises' and stipulates that an officer must make enquiries to satisfy himself that 'the person is in a position to give such consent'.[15] There may be more than one occupant of the premises and, in this situation, the consent of one occupier may 'bind' another. Thus a wife may consent to the search of a house occupied jointly with her husband,[16] but a spouse out of occupation may not consent to police entry against the wishes of the occupying spouse.[17] A parent may consent to the search of a house in which an adult child still resides. However, the converse is probably not true to the extent that a parent could countermand consent given by such a child having no proprietary interest in the premises.[18] Proprietorship, or, at least, control of the premises, seems to be a necessary requirement for being in a position to give consent. This view is endorsed by the case of *R v Edwards*,[19] where the Canadian Supreme Court rejected an argument that the accused had a reasonable expectation of privacy in respect of an apartment belonging to his girlfriend. He had a key, but was essentially 'just a visitor', albeit one who was 'an especially privileged guest'. He did not contribute to the rent, kept few personal possessions in the apartment and, crucially, had no control over access to the premises.

The 'enquiries' made by the police must therefore encompass the possible co-existence of registered title, equitable interests, leases and licences. Where occupants are resident in separate units such as a 'lodging house', the consent of the landlord is insufficient unless the lodger or tenant is unavailable and the matter is urgent.[20] Consent is not irrevocable and can be withdrawn at any time before the search is completed.[21] Code B therefore attempts to ensure that, within certain restraints of practicability, consent is informed, voluntary and is given by the individual whose privacy is being invaded. Once permission to enter has been given, however, subsections 19(2) and (3) of PACE authorise a police officer to seize anything that he has reasonable grounds to believe is evidence of or the proceeds of *any* offence. It need not concern the offence being investigated, provided that he also has reasonable grounds to believe that seizure is necessary to prevent the concealment, loss, alteration or destruction of the item. The only restriction is that of legally privileged material.[22]

This uncontrolled power of seizure, rather than the consensual entry that precedes it, may be subject to criticism. Not only does it go further than previous common law powers by enabling the police to seize items that are not related to the offence under investigation nor, necessarily, evidence of grave offences,[23] but it entitles officers to seize confidential material that would otherwise only be obtainable through the order of a circuit judge. This is because there is no restriction, under section 19, on the seizure of 'excluded' or 'special procedure' material that falls within Schedule 1 of PACE.[24] Whilst section 19 applies equally to searches that are initially effected by warrant or other statutory authority, it has a particular impact in respect of consensual searches taking place in the premises of unsuspected third parties. There may be a substantial invasion into the privacy of an individual as a consequence of a third party permitting a police officer to enter an office, or consulting room, in order to search through personal records or other material held in confidence. The protection of privacy interests is therefore frequently dependent on the ethics governing the professions likely to be affected. Whilst doctors, nurses, spiritual advisers, counsellors or journalists may place a high premium on retaining the confidentiality of their patients or clients, there is always the risk that administrative staff may unwittingly give access to such documentation.

Stop Searches under PACE

PACE section 1(2)(a) gives a constable[25] a power to search any person or vehicle, or anything which is in or on a vehicle, for stolen or prohibited articles or for a bladed or pointed object to which the Criminal Justice Act 1988 section 139 applies. Section 1(1) provides that this power arises in respect of any place to which the public or a section of the public has access. The basis of this power is that a constable has *reasonable grounds to suspect* that articles of the specified categories will be found.[26] The definition of 'prohibited article' is contained in subsection 1(7). Offensive weapons are the first class of prohibited articles. The term 'offensive weapon' is further defined in subsection 1(9) as any article

(a)   made or adapted for use for causing injury to persons; or
(b)   intended by the person having it with him for such use by him or by some other person.

This definition is identical to that in the Prevention of Crime Act 1953.[27] Thus the case law surrounding that statute can be applied equally to section 1 of PACE. Weapons made to cause injury, sometimes referred to as offensive *per se*, are weapons that are considered to have no innocent purpose. Such items would include flick knives,[28] rice flails,[29] and coshes. Whether an article is adapted to cause injury is a matter for the court to determine. A bottle that had been smashed in order to create jagged glass[30] and a razorblade inserted into a potato[31] have been held to fall within this category. The third category depends upon establishing an intention on the part of the possessor that someone should be injured.[32] It is therefore not justifiable for police to search on the basis that an article is intended for use only to scare persons away. Inevitably, this third category creates difficulties for police officers effecting stop searches in that perfectly legitimate tools of trade, such as a workman's hammer,[33] may be offensive weapons under the statute, but reasonable suspicion must exist prior to the search, at which point intent may be difficult to establish.

An interesting combination of rights issues arises when a person asserts that an offensive weapon is being carried as a measure of private defence. In these circumstances there may be possession of a legitimate item such as kitchen knife, but a conditional intent to injure only if attacked. Alternatively, the possessor may be carrying an article that is made for inflicting injury, such as a CS gas canister or a mace spray, but again have no intention to use it other than *in extremis*. The right to bodily autonomy under Article 8 then coincides with the right to life under Article 2 of the European Convention. At present, there appears to be no standing right to carry articles for self-protection. Unless there is an immediately perceived threat, neither the common law right of self-defence nor the Criminal Law Act 1967 section 3 will apply to legitimate possession of the weapon.[34] Thus a woman who is known to advocate the carrying of anti-rape sprays and who regularly walks along a dark and secluded road late at night could be stopped and searched and, if a large pair of scissors or a mace spray is found in her handbag, she could be charged as a consequence. It is arguable that the search in those circumstances could violate Article 8. The search would be in 'accordance with the law', but might not be necessary in the interests of public safety or necessary for the prevention of disorder or crime, since the objective of the possessor would be the *avoidance* of crime through the use of necessary force. The right of self-defence against unlawful violence is recognised in Article 2(2)(a) of the European Convention as extending even to the taking of life, so long as the level of force used is not more than is 'absolutely necessary' and is proportional to the violence offered.[35] It is possible, therefore, that the search could be outside the permitted derogation contained in Article 8(2).

The other class of prohibited article is defined in section 1(7)(b) as one made, or adapted, or intended for use in the course of or in connection with specified offences. The relevant offences are listed in section 1(8). They are burglary, theft and offences under the Theft Act 1968 sections 12 and 15. It is clear that the section is aimed at facilitating convictions under the Theft Act 1968 section 25 for 'going equipped' for the commission of these offences. Section 1 does not include in the definition of prohibited articles many items that are subject to independent stop and search powers. Searches in public for drugs,[36] intoxicating liquor[37] and hunting or poaching equipment[38] are all governed by PACE Code A, but do not fall within section 1. Searches for Firearms are authorised by the Firearms Act 1968 section 47, but a firearm would almost inevitably also be an offensive weapon within subsection 1(7). The procedural safeguards contained in sections 2 and 3 of PACE are stated to apply to *all* statutory powers to search persons and vehicles prior to arrest.

Section 2 requires a constable to take reasonable steps to bring to the attention of the subject of the search documentary evidence that he is a constable (if not in uniform) and the officer's name and station. Section 2(3) also requires the subject to be told the object of and grounds for the proposed search and that he is entitled to a copy of the record of the search.[39] In the case of a search of an unattended vehicle, a notice containing the above information, apart from the object and grounds for the search, must be left inside the vehicle.[40] When assessing the legality of police action, the cause of suspicion forming the *basis* for the search is the crucial issue. This should be preserved in the record of search that must be made under section 3 of PACE. The record, which should be made contemporaneously unless this is not practicable,[41] must state both the object of the search and the 'grounds for making it'.[42] Section 3 is therefore instrumental in verifying whether reasonable grounds to suspect exist prior to the search taking place. However, PACE itself does not provide clarification as to what might or might not amount to reasonable grounds in the context of a stop and search, nor what level of intrusion is justified in carrying out such search. Such guidance, as there is, appears in Code A.

The degree of intrusion into personal privacy is limited. As in the case of consensual searches, only searches of outer clothing of a person can be made in public. Detention is only possible for 'such time as is reasonably required to permit a search to be carried out either at the place where the person or vehicle was first detained or nearby'.[43] However, the permitted extent of a vehicle search is not set out in Code A. In Canada, stop searches for traffic violations or breaches of the highway code do not justify searches of the contents of containers such as trunks or bags,[44] or of a load being carried on a vehicle.[45] In England and Wales, the general power to stop a vehicle derives from the Road Traffic Act 1988 section 163(1). This provides that a person driving a motor vehicle on a road 'must stop' on being requested to do so by a constable in uniform, but there is no attendant search power. The section is primarily aimed at facilitating requests to produce documents and details of identity following accidents and traffic violations. Additionally, under section 23(2) of the Misuse of Drugs Act 1971, a constable may stop a vehicle if he has reasonable grounds to suspect that drugs may be found therein. All searches effected under PACE must be predicated on reasonable grounds to suspect that prohibited or stolen articles will be in the vehicle. Should a vehicle have been stopped under section 163, it may be difficult for a constable to argue that it is reasonable to search the baggage in a car simply because the driver turns out to be disqualified from driving or to be driving without insurance.[46] Even if it could be argued, on the particular facts, that driving without required permits gives reasonable grounds to suspect that weapons of offence, stolen items, or drugs may be present in the car, an extreme measure such as ripping open upholstery or dismantling body work would probably be excessive and parallel an intrusive or strip search of the person.[47]

The level of suspicion justifying a stop and search is not as high as that justifying an arrest, but a stop and search carried out purely on a 'hunch' is unreasonable. There are sound reasons why this should be so. From the perspective of the civil libertarian, any search, however superficial, that is carried out on this basis is an unjustified interference with personal autonomy. From the perspective of the law enforcer, there is a substantial risk that searches based on grounds that cannot be objectively verified will lead to public resentment and to a worsening of relations between civilians and police. It was disquiet with the implementation of stop and search powers prior to PACE, that led the Royal Commission on Criminal Procedure[48] to recommend that there should be a 'stricter application of the criterion of reasonable suspicion'. The Scarman enquiry that took place in the wake of the Brixton Disorders[49] and subsequent research into the use of stop and search by the Metropolitan Police (Smith and Gray, 1983) revealed that, in a substantial minority of cases, there was an exercise of power without justifiable suspicion, that few arrests actually resulted from the exercise of these powers and that there was an apparent racial bias in the selection of subjects.

Code A of PACE attempts to address these issues by setting out exemplars of what might and what might not be reasonable suspicion. The Code states that, whilst the circumstances of each case must vary, there must always be 'some objective basis' for suspicion.[50] This may be supported by a person 'acting covertly or warily or attempting to hide something', or by a person carrying an article 'at an unusual time or in a place where a number of burglaries or thefts are known to have taken place recently'.[51] Reasonable suspicion may be based on 'reliable information or intelligence' which indicates that members of a particular group or gang habitually carry offensive weapons or controlled drugs.[52] However, with the exception of indicia of membership of groups or gangs in these categories, 'reasonable suspicion can never be supported on the basis of personal factors alone without supporting information or intelligence'.[53] Code A1.7 explicitly rejects colour, age, hairstyle, manner of dress and even knowledge that the subject has a previous conviction for possession of an unlawful article as a sufficient basis for search. Nor may search be founded on 'stereotyped images of certain persons or groups'. Code A therefore contains a specific injunction against racial bias in the exercise of police powers.

In the United States, there has been argument about the extent to which a profile of 'probabilistic' evidence may justify stop searches. In *US v Sokolow*,[54] the Supreme Court held that there may be reasonable suspicion that criminal activity is afoot even where such suspicion is based on factors that *individually* could be consistent with lawful conduct. In that case, the stereotype of a paradigmatic drug courier was held to have probative significance. This approach obviously reduces any requirement of fact based suspicion in respect of the subject of a search when that subject happens to exhibit several features attributable to offender profiling. Whether Code A gives greater protection and ensures that, in England and Wales, all stop searches are indeed based on particularised reasonable grounds, is a question that is perhaps better answered by considering both judicial decisions and Home Office statistics, rather than case law on its own. The reason for this is that the legality of a stop and search is rarely raised in the context of criminal proceedings,[55] and is unlikely to form the substance of a civil action for trespass unless some aggravating feature, such as the use of unreasonable force occurs.[56]

The case law that does exist suggests that police officers do not always act on particular and reasonable grounds. In *Tomlinson v DPP*,[57] the appellant contested his conviction for assaulting a police officer. In the context of this appeal, the High Court had to decide whether a stop and search effected under the Misuse of Drugs Act 1971 was based on reasonable suspicion. Two police officers had observed Mr. Tomlinson walking 'aimlessly' around the Soho district of London. On several occasions he stopped and looked at people, but he did not approach anyone. The officers were aware of the prevalence of drug usage in that part of London. After some 15 minutes, they approached the appellant and asked him what he was doing. They alleged that they had received a verbally abusive answer and that, when they attempted a search for controlled drugs, a struggle ensued in the course of which one officer was bruised and scratched. The appellant denied the police version of events. He claimed that he was on his way to a cab office, had noticed the officers, and that he was watching them when he was searched without any explanation. The Crown Court was of the opinion that the police had a 'genuine and reasonable suspicion' that the appellant might be in possession of controlled drugs. However, Lord Justice Nolan was in no doubt that while the officers 'genuinely believed' their suspicion, the crucial question was whether there were *grounds* for this belief. He concluded that there were not. Walking around aimlessly in Soho was behaviour that could also be consistent with being lost, being mentally ill, looking for a taxi, or seeking some other illegal activity such as prostitution. His Lordship stated:

> We have not reached the stage where the prevalence of a particular type of activity in an area can justify the detention and search under section 23(2) of a man who is doing no more than walking aimlessly and looking at other people during the dark hours of the night, even if that takes place in Soho.

In subsequent cases concerning stop and search, the High Court has continued to take a strong line on the necessity for reasonable grounds. In *Black v DPP*,[58] it was held that the visiting of premises, at the time that they were being lawfully searched for drugs under a warrant, was not sufficient conduct to give reasonable grounds to search the visitor. This person might be there in some lawful capacity such as a salesman or gasman.[59] Further, the behaviour of the subject on being searched was to be disregarded. The court stated that reasonable suspicion must exist 'immediately prior to the moment of detention'. It could not be retrospectively supported by the reaction of the subject of the search. In *French v DPP*, [60] the court declined to accept that non-specific third party information could constitute a valid basis for search. In that case a constable had received a message over his radio that a man had been seen dealing in drugs in a particular road. He went there and found the appellant being spoken to by two female officers. It was 'plainly reasonable' for the constable to conclude that the appellant was the person to whom the message related, but it was not reasonable to act on the message alone. It was unverified and might have been 'false, inaccurate and possibly even relating to another person'. The constable had no evidence from a 'prime source' to show that there were reasonable grounds to suspect the appellant, whose conviction for obstruction was quashed.[61]

The decision may have been different if the officer had been acting on the basis of targeted surveillance. In the Canadian case of *R v Debot*,[62] the trial judge held that a stop and search of a vehicle and its occupants based on instruction received from another member of a surveillance team was unreasonable because the officers 'did not exercise any direct independent mind of their own to determine whether or not what they were doing was arbitrary'. The search was based on 'suspicion and hope'. However, the prosecution appeal was allowed on the basis that reasonable grounds for belief existed in the mind of the searching officers. It was said to be

> unrealistic and incompatible with effective law enforcement and crime prevention when a police officer is requested by a superior or fellow officer to arrest or search a person suspected of the commission of crime and to be fleeing from the scene, to require that police officer to obtain from his or her superior or fellow officer sufficient information about the underlying facts to enable him or her to form an independent judgement upon which to arrest or search the suspect.

In the United States, third party information, in the form of the tip off from an anonymous informer, may support reasonable belief, particularly if the information is sufficiently corroborated by subsequent surveillance.[63] Clearly, behaviour by the suspect, that does take place in the *presence* of the constable effecting the search and which precedes the search, may substantiate suspicion. Thus in *Slade v DPP*,[64] the appellant was observed at Brixham Quay close to premises known to have been used for the supply of drugs. The appellant appeared to notice the officer. He put a hand in his trouser pocket and seemed to give 'a smug smile.' When later asked to turn out his pockets pursuant to a stop and search, he dropped some folded silver paper and instructed others to 'kick it'. The paper landed in the Quay. The High Court was satisfied that there had been reasonable grounds to effect the search even though only those actions that had taken place *prior* to the search could be relied on and thus the deliberate destruction of the paper wrap could not be taken into account.

The focus on the need for objective grounds for suspicion should not lead to disregard of the additional requirement that an officer must subjectively believe that grounds to effect a search exist. This principle is extrapolated from *Chapman v DPP*[65] which, though a case concerning reasonable belief justifying arrest, is applicable on this point to stop and search powers. The above discussion shows that there is some authority on what might constitute reasonable suspicion in certain circumstances. However, there is a dearth of discussion, in England and Wales, as to whether there is any difference in the degree of suspicion required for this relatively superficial intrusion as compared to that required to support an arrest or to support a full search of premises.

In the United States, the matter has been specifically addressed. In *Terry v Ohio*,[66] the Supreme Court considered the level of suspicion needed to justify a 'frisk' of persons who had been observed loitering outside a store, causing an officer to suspect that they were 'casing a job, a stick up'. Firearms were found in the overcoat pockets of two of the three suspects. A major issue that had to be decided was 'whether in all the circumstances of this on-the-street encounter', the petitioner's 'right to personal autonomy was violated by an unreasonable search and seizure'. The Court acknowledged that there was a balancing of interests involved in this situation. In dealing with

> rapidly unfolding and often dangerous situations on city streets the police are in need of an escalating set of flexible responses graduated in relation to the amount of information they possess.

On the other hand, the constitutional requirement of probable cause prevented police activity where there was no voluntary co-operation and insufficient grounds to make an arrest. The argument that a stop and frisk was not a search or seizure within the Fourth Amendment was rejected. It was said that whenever a police officer accosts an individual, restrains his freedom to walk away and explores the outer surfaces of clothing all over his body, there is 'a serious intrusion upon the sanctity of the person which may inflict great indignity and arouse strong resentment'.[67] The Supreme Court effected a solution by strictly limiting the extent of pre-arrest powers of search. There was 'a narrowly drawn authority' to permit a reasonable search for weapons for the protection of officers. This applied when there was reason to believe that an officer was dealing with armed and dangerous individuals and applied regardless of whether there was probable cause to arrest. The *Terry* principle has created some subsequent problems for courts in determining just how far this 'narrowly' limited authority extends. Ultimately each case must depend on its facts and upon a balancing of the 'strong government interest in solving crimes and bringing offenders to justice' against 'the individual's interest to be free of a stop and search detention that is no more extensive than permissible in the investigation of imminent or ongoing crimes'.[68] In *US v Hensley*,[69] even a search in relation to a completed crime was justified where the police had reasonable suspicion grounded in specific and articulable facts.

In England and Wales, PACE powers are not limited to the protection of the police, or even to the protection of citizens, although this must be implicit in any search for offensive weapons. The purpose of the powers is clearly the detection of crime.[70] A literal interpretation of subsection 1(3) of PACE, and of the other statutory provisions falling under Code A, would lead to the conclusion that, in many cases, the grounds to support stop and search should also be grounds to support an arrest.[71] This is because the *possession* of many prohibited items, as opposed to any use to be made of them, frequently creates an offence. There is, surely, only a semantic difference between having reasonable grounds to suspect that a search will reveal the presence of controlled drugs on the person of an individual and having reasonable grounds to suspect that a person is guilty of possessing controlled drugs.[72] The same argument applies to offences under the Theft Act 1968 section 25.[73] Whilst, in respect of non-arrestable 'possession' offences,[74] the use of stop and search may assist the police in establishing an 'arrest condition' under section 25 of PACE,[75] it is less easy to see the detective function of the power in relation to arrestable possession crimes. It is, of course, possible for a person to be in innocent possession of a stolen or prohibited article[76] and, in this situation, the distinction between reasonable grounds for suspicion justifying a power to stop and search and reasonable grounds for suspicion justifying arrest is a real one.

One way of determining whether the power to stop and search under PACE is being used reasonably and only so far as is necessary 'for the prevention and disorder of crime'[77] might be to consider the outcome of searches effected under section 1 of PACE. Whilst there can be no *ex post facto* justification by reason of a suspect's conduct occurring after a decision to search has been made, statistics showing that that a high proportion of such searches result in an arrest may indicate that objective grounds for suspicion existed prior to most stop searches. Conversely, statistics on the use of the powers that indicate that certain ethnic groups are stopped and searched more frequently than others, might suggest a purely subjective use of the power based on stereotyping and prejudice. Home Office statistics for 1997/1998[78] show that 20% more people were stopped and searched in that year than in the preceding year. In excess of one million searches took place and out of this number the two most frequent reasons were to search for stolen goods (38%) and drugs (33%). The number of arrests following the use of this power rose at almost the same rate as the increase in the number of searches,[79] but the overall number of stop searches that led to arrest was (at 10%) at its lowest proportion since the commencement of PACE. Thus the vast majority of stop searches remain unproductive in the detection of crime. This fact must raise questions as to the reasonableness of the grounds that form the basis of the search. A further concerning feature of the use of these powers is that, overall, black people are five times more likely to be stopped than whites.[80] Whilst there is considerable variation in statistics between police forces, stop searches appear to be affected by ethnic considerations and substantial doubt is cast on whether power is objectively exercised and can be justified as 'necessary' under Article 8(2). The issue of ethnic or racial bias has attained a higher profile due to accusations of 'institutional racism' that have recently been levelled at police forces in the United Kingdom.

Stop Searches Based on Expediency

The power of the police to stop and search has been extended by statute to situations where there need be no reasonable grounds in respect of the individual or vehicle searched. The common link in these various powers is the perceived need to protect the public from serious crime and from acts of terrorism. The privacy intrusion that takes place is the price to be paid for greater bodily security. Any reasonableness justification is transposed from the subject of the search to the wider goal of the prevention of disorder or crime. Certain of these 'public protection' searches are predicated on reasonable grounds for belief in respect of the factual situation that triggers the exercise of the power. This applies to the conduct of road checks under section 4 of PACE. Subsection 4(4) requires that the authorising officer[81] has reasonable grounds to believe that a serious arrestable offence has been, or is about to be, committed and that the person sought in connection with that offence is, or is about to be, in the locality in which vehicles would be stopped if the road check were authorised. Alternatively, there must be reasonable grounds to suspect that a person unlawfully at large is, or is about to be, in the locality. A road check permits officers to stop *all* vehicles in the locality during the period of the power, or to stop vehicles 'selected by any criterion'.[82] Section 4(1) provides that the purpose of the search is to ascertain whether a vehicle is carrying a person as described above, or a witness to a serious arrestable offence. The initial authorisation may be for a continuous period of up to seven days and this may be extended for a further seven days.[83] Despite detailed recording requirements contained in section 4, the objection remains that this random power is exercisable in respect of less than 'grave' offences.[84] This is not the only statutory power of search that hinges on the basic concept of serious offending.[85] On closer analysis, it will be seen that the definitions applicable to these powers also embrace medium range offending. Section 116 of PACE defines 'serious arrestable offence' as including an offence causing 'serious financial loss' to a person, but this loss is to be evaluated subjectively by reference to the impact that it has on the victim.[86] The reference in that section to an offence causing 'serious injury' must be read in the light of the reality that many such crimes are dealt with under section 20 of the Offences Against the Person Act 1861, an either way offence.[87] The consequence is that there is, in theory, a very wide power to cordon off areas and to stop and search inside vehicles on an indiscriminate basis. In practice, this power seems to be used more sparingly in the wake of legislation permitting the random search of persons and vehicles under the Prevention of Terrorism (Temporary Provisions) Act 1989.[88]

The other power that requires an objective suspicion as to background circumstances is that existing under section 60 of the Criminal Justice and Public Order Act 1994,[89] to stop and search in anticipation of violence. A police officer of the rank of inspector or above,[90] must reasonably believe that incidents involving serious violence may take place in any locality in his area and that authorisation under the section is 'expedient' to prevent their occurrence.[91] Alternatively, he must reasonably believe that persons are carrying 'dangerous instruments or offensive weapons' in any locality in his police area without good reason.[92] The authorisation entitles a constable in uniform to stop 'any person or vehicle and make any search he thinks fit whether or not he has reasonable grounds for suspecting that the person or vehicle is carrying weapons or articles of any kind'.[93] Clearly, therefore, individualised suspicion is irrelevant. The power may last for up to 24 hours and be renewed for that period.[94] In the most recent extension to this power, section 4A authorises the removal and seizure of any item 'which the constable reasonably believes that person is wearing wholly or mainly to conceal identity'.[95] Although the section does not specify that the 'item' must cover the face, the marginal note refers to 'masks etc.' and the revised Code A refers to 'face coverings'.[96] There is no knowing whether a wig and/or dark glasses would be within the section. It is equally unclear whether a false beard that only obscures the lower jaw would be a 'covering'.

The power was intended to be a major support to the police in the prevention of public order offences, yet subsequent extensions of the power reduce the prevention of disorder element to an alternative *raison d'etre*. It would not be difficult to justify an almost constant belief, in certain force areas, that more than one person in a locality is carrying a 'dangerous instrument' or an 'offensive weapon'. Code A attempts to curtail the use of the provision by emphasising that the power should be used for the minimum period necessary to deal with the risk of violence.[97] The Code also restates that an officer must believe that the purpose of the removed face covering is to conceal identity. However, in a rather bizarre and apparently conflicting paragraph, there is reference to the removal of face coverings worn by Muslim women for 'religious reasons'.[98] If this is a genuine reason, it is difficult to imagine such a practice giving rise to a lawful search power and it is likely that Article 9, granting the right to freedom of religion and to manifest this religion in practice and observance, might be violated alongside Article 8.

The final statutory powers of stop and search require neither individualised suspicion, nor even reasonable belief that a particular set of circumstances is imminently about to happen. The powers exist under the Prevention of Terrorism (Temporary Provisions) Act 1989. Section 13A was inserted by section 81 of the Criminal Justice and Public Order Act 1994. The section permits stop searches of vehicles on the basis that it is 'expedient to do so to prevent acts of terrorism'. Authorisation must be by an officer of the rank of commander or assistant chief constable or above.[99] Whilst the occupants of vehicles can be searched under this provision, pedestrians are subject to search under the similarly worded section 13B. This was inserted by section 1 of the Prevention of Terrorism (Additional Powers) Act 1996. The reworded section authorises search both of the pedestrian and also of 'anything carried by him'.[100] Under both sections, the power is exercisable by a constable in uniform and may take place at 'any place' within the force area or in a 'specified locality' in the area for a period of up to 28 days.[101] The authorisation must be in writing and must identify the area to which it applies. The purpose of the search is to find 'articles of a kind which could be used for a purpose connected with the commission, preparation, or instigation of acts of terrorism'.[102] The sections expressly state that there is no necessity that a constable has 'any grounds' for suspicion.[103] Thus random search is legitimated. The justification rests not only on the prevention of disorder and crime, but also on the need to preserve 'national safety' and 'public security'.[104] Because the derogation from privacy rights is based on graver considerations, the margin of appreciation may well apply to validate the legislation. The provisions of Code A1.16 emphasise that the selection of persons stopped 'should reflect an objective assessment of the threat posed by various terrorist groups active in Great Britain'. The Code also states that, whilst there should be no unwarranted discrimination against members of ethnic minorities, international terrorist threats posed by particular groups might entitle an officer to take account of ethnic origins. The fact that there was a substantial drop in the use of these powers in 1997/1998 is explained by a 'general drop in activity by the various terrorist organisations'.[105] Since information concerning these activities will inevitably be covered by public interest immunity, there is always an element of trust in accepting justifications for the exercise of these powers, but there does seem to be an attempt to comply with the proportionality principle, as evidenced by a dramatic reduction in their use.

Search on Arrest

In England and Wales, search on arrest is now entirely governed by statutory powers under PACE. The origin of these powers is the historic concept of hot pursuit[106] and its development under the common law allowed officers to search an arrested person and his surroundings. It was available only when there were reasonable grounds for believing the person arrested had a weapon which he could use to effect an escape or to cause injury, or had evidence material to the offence for which he was arrested.[107] These common law powers have resonance in other jurisdictions, but the jurisprudence of the United States and of Canada has redefined the extent of these powers in the context of whether they are compatible with a 'reasonable expectation of privacy'.[108] Prior to PACE, the legitimacy of a more intrusive police search of an arrested individual at a police station or a search of premises occupied and controlled by that person, was uncertain. PACE attempts to clarify police authority in these situations and to provide certain safeguards for the subject of the search in terms of recording procedures and in respect of the persons who may authorise and carry out 'intimate' searches. The provisions are set out in specific, but textually unrelated sections and it is a matter of some surprise that there has been little case law upon them. This may be a reflection of the view that challenge is pointless because the evidence discovered will be admitted, the illegality of the search notwithstanding.[109] A fatalist self-fulfilling dynamic may occur to stifle challenge on the legality of police action. It may also be a reflection of the previous non-existence of a right to privacy under English law. The enactment of the Human Rights Act 1998 may require judges to look more carefully at the exercise of power under these sections.

Section 18 of PACE contains the power to search the premises 'occupied or controlled by' a person who has been arrested for an arrestable offence.

The concept of control is not defined, but it is likely that it would extend to the manager of premises and might even include security personnel such as a night watchman (Lidstone and Palmer, 1996). A constable may search if he has reasonable grounds for suspecting that there is on the premises evidence that relates to that offence or to some other arrestable offence which is connected with or similar to that offence.[110] The search may not include items 'subject to legal privilege'. The proportionality principle is applicable to these searches by virtue of subsection 18(3) which states that there is only a power 'to search to the extent that is reasonably required for the purpose of discovering such evidence'. Authorisation must normally be provided in writing by an officer of the rank of inspector or above, although there may be retrospective verbal notification to such person where a search is conducted prior to arrival at a police station and the presence of the suspect is 'necessary for the effective investigation of the offence'.[111] There is a recording requirement as to the nature and grounds of the search, but this requirement is considered to be weaker than the requirement concerning the initial authorisation. Whilst *R v Badham*[112] established that the authorisation 'meant more than a mere record of verbal authority' and must consist of an independent document, the record of the search has been held to be a 'directory' rather than a 'mandatory' requirement and, thus, a failure to make such record need not affect the legality of the search.[113] There is clearly an issue as to the correctness of treating the recording requirement as anything other than mandatory, since it provides a means to challenge probable cause and the reasonableness of the search.

Although section 18 permits a search on arrest, there is no element of exigency and it may be conducted at any time after arrest. This is a considerable extension of a warrantless search power that is usually linked to urgency or exigent circumstances.[114] The power may be challenged under Article 8, since there is no requirement of judicial scrutiny even in those circumstances where it would be feasible to obtain a warrant. To this extent the pre-PACE case of *McLorie v Oxford*,[115] holding that there was no common law power to enter and search a dwelling house several hours after the arrest of an occupier, may be reinstated and section 18 confined in scope. Section 32 of PACE, by contrast, provides a power of search that is clearly based upon immediacy. It permits search upon arrest at a place other than a police station. A constable may search the arrested person if he has reasonable grounds for believing that that person may present a danger to himself or others. He may also search for anything that might be used to assist the arrestee to escape from lawful custody or which might be evidence relating to an offence.[116] Subsection 32(2)(b) allows a constable to enter and search any premises in which he was when arrested or immediately before he was arrested for evidence relating to the offence for which he has been arrested.

By virtue of section 23 of PACE, 'premises' includes vehicles, vessels, aircraft and any movable structure.

This power is apparently more circumscribed than section 18 in that the search is restricted by requirements of urgency and particularity. Only evidence relating to the relevant offence may be searched for. There is also a limitation on the extent of a body search, restricting it to outer clothing, although mouth orifices are now within the section.[117] The degree of intrusion into personal autonomy is therefore limited and, traditionally, this has been a significant factor in upholding the reasonableness of warrantless searches.[118] However, it should be remembered that, under section 19, a constable may seize *anything* that he has reasonable grounds to believe is evidence of or the fruits of an offence in order to prevent its destruction or alteration.[119] Thus, once lawfully on premises under section 32, an officer may seize evidence of unrelated offending, so long as the search is limited to that reasonably required to discover items falling within the section.[120] Further, the section applies in respect of any offence, not simply an arrestable one. It could therefore apply in respect of very minor offending. Finally, there is some uncertainty about the meaning of 'immediately' since the Act specifies no time limits. In *Badham*[121] the Crown Court considered that a delay of 3-4 hours prevented the police from searching under section 32 and that a proper authorisation under section 18 should have been obtained. However, in *R v Heap*[122] the Court of Appeal refused to interpret the immediacy requirement as making a section 32 search only 'available at or very soon after a person has been arrested'. Relying on editorial criticism of *Badham*, the Court rejected the notion that the powers under these two sections had to be used sequentially. Uncertainty as to the actual scope and application of section 32 renders it as liable to challenge on the basis of lack of judicial authorisation as section 18 of PACE.

The development of warrantless search powers in the United States has been constrained by the reasonableness requirement of the Fourth Amendment. Viewed essentially as 'exceptions' to the normative warrant procedure,[123] such searches are validated by three distinct lines of argument. The first is that the urgency of the situation necessitates an immediate search, despite the absence of judicial authorisation. The second is that there is a minimal level of intrusion caused by the search and therefore no violation of privacy. This argument may be linked to the third justification, which is that there is no reasonable expectation of privacy in the circumstances existing at that time. In *Agnello v US* [124] the Supreme Court, whilst recognising a right to search both a person 'lawfully arrested' and 'the place where the arrest is made', stressed that this right is 'an incident of the arrest'. Thus, the search of an accused's premises 'several blocks' from the scene of the arrest and after all the accused were in custody elsewhere, violated the Fourth Amendment. This approach contrasts noticeably with judicial interpretation of the PACE provisions discussed above. It has been affirmed in more recent jurisprudence that draws a distinction between those circumstances where there is opportunity to obtain a warrant [125] and those of urgency and hot pursuit. [126]

The problem that has faced American courts has been to define the *limits* of an exigent search. The case of *US v Robinson* [127] established that a full body search can be made on arrest, even though the search is unlikely to reveal a weapon or destructible evidence relevant to the offence for which the person has been arrested. It was a 'reasonable intrusion' once probable cause to arrest existed. The extent of the power to search premises on arrest is less certain. To what extent may it allow a search of rooms other than those in which an arrest is actually made? Can items not in open view, such as the contents of drawers, be searched for? In the seminal case of *Chimel v State of California*, [128] the exigency justification for searches on arrest was reiterated. The Supreme Court, drawing analogies with stop search cases such as *Terry v Ohio*, [129] affirmed that a search of the person and of the area 'within his immediate control' was reasonable to protect officers and ensure that the arrest could take place. There was 'ample justification' to look for weapons and for destructible evidence that was under the immediate control of the arrestee. There was *no* justification, however, for a routine search of 'any room other than that in which an arrest occurs' or for a search 'through all the desk drawers or other concealed or closed areas in that room itself'. However, in *Maryland v Buie*, [130] some attempt was made to loosen the restraints placed on police officers by *Chimel*. It was said that it was reasonable for officers to undertake a 'protective sweep' of premises in order to search for anyone who might 'pose a danger' to those effecting the arrest. This 'sweep' need not be confined to the room in which the arrest had taken place, but it should not be a 'full-blown' search 'top-to-bottom' of the premises. It needed to be based on 'reasonable, articulable suspicion' that the premises harboured a wanted or dangerous person. This extension of powers does not, in itself, permit substantially wider powers of search. What it does do is to open the door to the other justifications for warrantless search, in other words, that there is minimal intrusiveness in the activity, or that there is the lack of any reasonable expectation of privacy.

In *Maryland v Buie*, the item seized was in 'plain view' of the officer who was checking the basement from which the arrestee just had emerged to see if there was anyone else 'down there'. The effect of the decision is that items that are not stored in cupboards or wardrobes and are observable on a superficial inspection of the premises may, under the exigent circumstances principle, be admitted in evidence even if seized without a warrant. This, arguably, extends the plain view doctrine by applying it, even absent probable cause in respect of the items seized, to private premises and not simply to public or to open land.[131] The application of the plain view doctrine is less contentious when it is supported by the argument that there can be no reasonable expectation of privacy. The doctrine has justified searches of 'open fields',[132] even where the land concerned has been fenced and aerial observation has taken place. It has also justified a search of the contents of garbage bags left outside the curtilage of a home.[133] In these cases *Katz v US*[134] has been 'interpreted' to allow warrantless searches on the basis that the *venue* of the search precludes any reasonable claim to privacy rights. It has links with the other *Katz* 'limitation principle', which is that the search itself is so superficial that no intrusion into privacy takes place. In *Cardwell v Lewis*[135] the exigent circumstances rationale was less important than the fact that the car searched had been towed by police from a public parking lot and the search was limited to external observation in the form of taking paint samples and inspecting tyre tread. The later case of *New York v Belton*[136] appears to have validated more intrusive automobile searches by equating vehicles with searches of the person, rather than with searches of premises. In the United States, property is granted a greater protection from warrantless search than is the person of the arrestee. This is not a distinction recognised in PACE sections 18 and 32 and it appears to have evolved as a matter of pragmatism rather than of principle.[137]

In Canada, the reasonableness of warrantless searches depends upon reconciliation with section 8 of the Charter of Rights.[138] Certain statutes, that were passed before the Charter was enacted, have had to be re-evaluated in the light of the Charter. The seminal case of *Hunter v Southam*[139] laid down criteria for this reconciliation. Dickson J. stated

> Section 8 is an entrenched constitutional provision. It is not therefore vulnerable to encroachment by legislative enactments in the same way as common law protections. There is, further, nothing in the language of the section to restrict it to the protection of property or to associate it with the law of trespass. It guarantees a broad general right to be secure from unreasonable search and seizure.

Thus privacy rights are protected regardless of whether the statute under consideration deals with searches of persons or of premises. A statute may be struck down to the extent that it is considered to be incompatible with such rights.[140] This highlights one major structural difference between the application of the Canadian Charter, the Fourth Amendment and the Human Rights Act 1998. In England and Wales there is no 'entrenched' constitutional right to privacy. The legislation conferring this right may be repealed like any other enactment. Further, any pre-existing legislation will not automatically be repealed to the extent that it is inconsistent with that Act (Butler, 1997). The English courts must strive to interpret statutes in accordance with the Act and with European Convention jurisprudence. Where this is impossible a 'declaration of incompatibility' may be made under section 4. 'Striking down' is not within the hands of the judiciary, but in those of a government minister who may, by order, make amendments to the incompatible legislation if he considers that there are 'compelling reasons' to do so.[141] The extent to which sections 18, 19 and 32 of PACE may be circumscribed by reasonableness criteria such as those discussed above is affected by the structural difference in constitutional protections existing between England and other common law jurisdictions.

Searches at Police Stations

Under PACE, certain searches may only take place at a police station. Section 54, states that the custody officer[142] must search a detained person and make a record of all items in his possession. The officer may seize clothes and personal effects, where he believes that the items may be used to harm persons or property, to interfere with evidence, or to assist the arrestee to escape. He may also seize items where he 'has reasonable grounds for believing that they may be evidence relating to an offence'.[143] A body search may therefore be made on arrival at a police station and evidence of *any* offending may be retained. The section is not, in fact, limited to those brought to the police station under criminal detention and applies to those brought in compulsorily for their own safety under mental heath legislation. In certain circumstances the detained person may be strip searched. This involves the removal 'of more than outer clothing'. However, PACE Code C Annex A makes it clear that such action should not be routinely carried out and is only justified where the custody officer reasonably considers that items capable of seizure are being concealed. The search must, under Code C, be carried out in a private area and by a person of the same sex as the person searched. Where the search involves the exposure of intimate parts of the body, there must be a second person present, but the sex of that individual is not specified. The search 'shall be conducted with proper regard to the sensitivity and vulnerability of the person' and every effort must be made to obtain co-operation and to minimise embarrassment. Whilst this rhetoric would seem to accord with the proportionality principle and thus with the derogation in Article 8, there is undeniable humiliation caused to a person who may be required to allow a visual examination of 'genital and anal areas' and, so long as no 'physical contact is made with any body orifice', there is no requirement that a doctor or nurse be in attendance.

The custody officer is not empowered to make 'intimate searches'. An intimate search is a physical examination of body orifices other than the mouth.[144] These searches must be made on the authorisation of an officer of the rank of superintendent or above. The officer must have reasonable grounds for believing, under PACE section 55(1)(a), that the person to be searched has concealed on him any thing which could be used to physically injure himself or others whilst in custody. Alternatively, under section 55(1)(b), the officer must have reasonable grounds to believe that the detainee has concealed on him a class A drug intended for supply or export. Further, there must be reasonable grounds to believe that the intimate search is necessary to reveal the item sought. Except in cases of urgency in relation to items that may cause injury, the 'suitably qualified' person to carry out this search is a registered medical practitioner or nurse. Section 55 and Annex A of Code C stipulate that searches may only take place at a hospital, a surgery or, in the case of items likely to cause harm, at a police station. In May 1999, the British Medical Association advised doctors not to carry out non-consensual intimate searches and stated that the informed consent of the detainee should be sought whenever possible.[145] The only exception is where the search may be justified in order to save the patient's life. Where consent is not obtained, searches under section 55(1)(a) will, of necessity, be carried out by a police officer of the same sex as the subject of the search. It remains to be seen how far this guidance operates to protect medical practitioners from allegations of assault, rather then to protect the bodily privacy of the detainee, who may be at risk of being searched in any event. The only question may be by whom. Some officers are already taking the view that drugs can constitute an item that could 'cause physical injury' and validating police searches for class A drugs on that basis.[146]

It might be thought that there would be some connection with the taking of intimate samples in respect of the loss of bodily autonomy involved.

However, developments in technology have enabled forensic scientists to extract DNA samples from hair and from saliva. Thus, whilst there may be substantial issues of self-incrimination involved in the non-consensual taking of samples, the question of whether there is an assault upon bodily integrity is arguably less substantial than in the case of intimate searches. The taking of intimate samples is dealt with in chapter 4.

Notes

1. Laid under PACE sect. 66. The Code applies to PACE itself and to the retained pre-PACE powers such as the Misuse of Drugs Act 1971; see Annex A. The most recently revised edition is effective from 1st March 1999.
2. Code A Notes for Guidance 1D(a) and (b).
3. Notes for Guidance 1E.
4. *Ibid.*
5. Sect. 3 and below.
6. But under Code A3.5 a 'more through search' can be done 'out of public view' where there are reasonable grounds to consider this is necessary. Also, a person may voluntarily remove more than outer clothing. Notes for Guidance 3A.
7. Code A 3.5. No search involving exposure of intimate parts of the body may take place in a police van.
8. In the United States, the Supreme Court has stated in *Florida v Royer* (1983) 460 US 491 that consent to a search must be proved by the State to have been 'freely and voluntarily' given and 'mere submission to a claim of lawful authority' will not suffice.
9. Code B1.3(a).
10. Cmnd. 8092 (1981) paras. 3.41–3.42.
11. *I.e.* PACE sects. 17, 18, 19 and 32. There is an exception in B5.4(iii) when there are reasonable grounds to believe that alerting the occupier would frustrate the object of the search or endanger officers or others.
12. Code B4.1 and 4.2.
13. PACE sects. 17,18 and 32.
14. Code B5.7.
15. Code B4.1.
16. *R v Thornley* (1980) 72 Cr. App. R 302.
17. *McCleod v UK* [1999] Crim. L.R. 155, a breach of Article 8 occurred since no breach of the peace was threatened and thus PACE sect. 17(6) did not apply.
18. See *R v Jones and Smith* [1976] 3 ALL ER 54. It would seem illogical to confine the parent's ability to limit permission given by an adult child to entry for an illegal purpose.
19. (1996) 132 DLR (4th) 31; see also *R v Belnavis* (1996) 107 CCC (3d) 195.
20. Notes for Guidance 4A. Cp. *Chapman v US* (1961) 365 US 610; *Stone v California* (1964) 376 US 483. Search is also permitted without the occupiers' consent where it is reasonable to assume that an innocent occupier would agree *e.g.* where a check of gardens is being made in pursuit of a fleeing suspect.
21. Code B4.3.

22. PACE sect. 19(6) and Code B6.2.
23. *Ghani v Jones* [1969] 3 ALL ER 1700.
24. See chapter 4 for a discussion of powers to search for confidential material under Schedule 1 of PACE.
25. 'Constable' is used throughout PACE in the common law sense of the office of constable and therefore includes all police officers of whatever rank.
26. Sect. 1(3).
27. As amended by the Public Order Act 1986.
28. *R v Lawrence* (1971) 57 Cr. App. R 64; *R v Allanby* [1974] 1 WLR 1494; *R v Simpson* [1983] 3 ALL ER 784.
29. *Copus v DPP* [1989] Crim. L.R. 577.
30. *R v Simpson* (above).
31. *R v Williamson* (1977) 66 Cr. App. R 35 at 38.
32. It is unclear whether this extends to injury to one's self. Compare *Bryant v Mott* (1975) 62 Cr. App. R 71 and *R v Fleming* [1989] Crim. L.R. 71.
33. *Ohlson v Hylton* [1975] 1 WLR 724.
34. *Evans v Hughes* [1972] 3 ALL ER 412; *R v Densu* [1998] 1 Cr. App. R. 400; but cp. *R v Fegan* (1972) NI 80 and *Attorney-General's Ref. (No. 2 of 1983)* [1984] 1 QB 456. In these latter cases, convictions for possession of material in breach of the Explosive Substances Act 1883 were overturned on appeal because of feared future threats of violence from unidentified individuals.
35. *McCann and Others v UK* (1996) 21 EHRR 97; though it is generally assumed that Article 2 is more restrictive than the common law right to self-defence.
36. Misuse of Drugs Act 1971 sect. 23.
37. Sporting Events (Control of Alcohol etc.) Act 1985 sect. 17.
38. *E.g.* Poaching Prevention Act 1862 sect. 22; Badgers Act 1992 sect. 11.
39. Other than in the case of a search of an unattended car, or a search under the Aviation Security Act 1982 sect. 27(2).
40. Subsect. 2(6). This notice must also state that an application for compensation for any damage caused can be made to the police station named in the document.
41. Subsect. 3(1) and (2). If a non-contemporaneous note is made, this should be done 'as soon as practicable' after completion of the search.
42. Sect. 3(6)(a).
43. PACE sect. 2(8).
44. *R v Belnavis and Lawrence* (1996) 107 CCC (3d) 195; 151 DLR (4th) 443, a search of a trunk when a vehicle was stopped for speeding was unreasonable and *R v Mellenthin* (1992) 76 CCC (3d) 481, a routine stop did not justify the search of a bag on a car seat. Cp. the 'plain view' doctrine in the United States, see *Texas v Brown* (1983) 460 US 730.
45. *R v Higgins* (1996) 141 DLR (4th) 737, a search of the load carried by a vehicle was unreasonable as it went beyond a search to ensure compliance with the Highway Code.
46. It does not follow that such evidence will be excluded. See *R v McCarthy* [1996] Crim. L.R. 818; *R v Belnavis* (above); *R v Higgins* (above) and see chapter 6.
47. But see *Ornelas v US* US Court of Appeals 7th Circuit May 28th 1996, the removal of a loose panel under the back seat of a car was justified by probable cause based on an offender profile and the fact that the occupants of the car were on a Federal database of known or suspected drug traffickers (NADDIS).
48. Cmnd. 8092 at para. 3.25. This criterion was to be protected by the procedures now incorporated into PACE sects. 2 and 3.

49. Sir L. Scarman 'The Brixton Disorders: 10–12th April 1981' Cmnd. 8427 (1981) HMSO.
50. Code A1.6.
51. *Ibid.*
52. Code A1.6A and below for a further discussion of 'reliable information'.
53. Code A1.7.
54. (1989) 490 US 1.
55. It sometimes arises as an aspect of a defence to a charge of assaulting an officer in the execution of his duty; see *King v Gardener* (1979) 71 Cr. App. R. 13; *Black v DPP* CO/877/95 (11th May 1995) DC; *French v DPP* CO/2507/96 (27th Nov. 1996) DC.
56. PACE sect. 117 authorises a constable to use 'reasonable force' whenever this is necessary to exercise a power under the Act.
57. CO/2491/90 (7th February 1992) QBD.
58. CO/877/95 (11th May 1995) QBD.
59. The appellant was visiting premises occupied by his brother.
60. CO/2507/96 (27th Nov. 1996) QBD. See also *Castorini v Chief Constable of Surrey* (1988) 138 NLJ 380. Cp. *R v Debot* (1986) 30 CCC (3d) 207.
61. The appellant was alleged to have swallowed a wrap of drugs. He claimed that he had inadvertently swallowed chewing gum when an officer applied pressure to his throat.
62. (1986) 30 CCC (3d) 207; (1989) 52 CCC (3d) 193. See also *R v McComber* (1988) 48 CCC (3d) 185.
63. See *Alabama v White* (1990) 496 US 325, details were given of the suspect's departure time, the vehicle to be driven and probable destination.
64. CO/1678/96 (22nd Oct. 1996) QBD.
65. (1989) 1 Cr. App. R. 190.
66. (1968) 392 US 1. See also *Sibron v New York, Peters v New York* (1968) 392 US 40.
67. See also *US v Marshall* (1980) 446 US 554. Cp. *Antoniades v The CPS* CO/1973/91 (5th Dec. 1991) DC, there was no search when a torch shone through a car window revealed a pick axe handle inside the vehicle.
68. *US v Hensley* (1985) 469 US 221; suspicion was based on a 'wanted flyer' issued in connection with an armed robbery and on the carrying of a weapon by the passenger in the car.
69. (Above). See also *US v Sokolow* (1989) 490 US 1, discussed above.
70. See RCCP Cmnd. 8092 at para. 3.17.
71. Under PACE sect. 24, a constable must have reasonable grounds to suspect that an arrestable offence has been committed, is being committed, or is about to be committed by the individual arrested. Where an arrest is by a police officer, there is no requirement that an offence actually be committed. Cp. *R v Self* (1992) 95 Cr. App. R. 42.
72. Misuse of Drugs Act 1971 sect. 5(2). See *Slade v DPP* (above) on the relationship between sect. 23(2) and this section.
73. See above.
74. Such as possession of an offensive weapon under the Prevention of Crime Act 1953, or bladed articles under the Criminal Justice Act 1988 as amended by the Offensive Weapons Act 1996.
75. *E.g.* that the constable has reasonable grounds for believing that an arrest is necessary to prevent the relevant person causing harm to himself or another person, or to prevent damage to property under sect. 25(3)(d).
76. Code A1.7A. In these circumstances every effort should be made to secure the consensual production of the article.

77. European Convention Article 8(2).
78. Home Office Statistical Bulletin 2/99 Operation Of Certain Police Powers Under PACE.
79. *Ibid.* Arrests rose by 19%.
80. Statistics on Race and the Criminal Justice System (1998) Home Office. Under Notes for Guidance 4DA, supervising officers should consider whether there is any evidence that officers are exercising their discretion on the basis of stereotyped images of certain persons or groups.
81. The officer must be of the rank of superintendent or above, unless the matter is one of urgency, in which case it must be reported to a superintendent as soon as possible; see subsects. 4(3)(5)(6) and (7).
82. PACE sect. 4(2).
83. Subsects. 4(11) and (12).
84. Cp. RCCP Cmnd. 8092 (1981) para. 3.32.
85. *E.g.* sect. 8 and Schedule 1 of PACE (serious arrestable offence) and the Interception of Communications Act 1985 and the Police Act 1997 (serious crimes).
86. PACE subsects. 116(6) and (7).
87. The accused can be dealt with summarily in the magistrates' court, or tried on indictment in the Crown Court.
88. See Home Office statistical Bulletin 2/99. A large increase in the number of road checks occurred in 1993–1994 in the City of London. This was prior to amendments to the Prevention of Terrorism Act; see below.
89. The section has now been amended twice; by the Knives Act 1997 sect. 8 and also by the Crime and Disorder Act 1998 sect. 25.
90. The power was originally only entrusted to an officer of the rank of superintendent or above. Where an inspector grants the authorisation, a superintendent must be notified as soon as practicable, sect. 3A (as inserted by the Knives Act 1997).
91. Sect. 60(1)(a).
92. Sect. 60(1)(b). This ground was added by the Knives Act 1997.
93. Sect. 60(5). However, the police must supply details of their names and station or the search is unlawful; *Osman v DPP The Times* 28th September 1999.
94. Sect. 60(1) and 60(3) as amended by the Knives Act 1997. Renewal must be by a superintendent.
95. Sect. 4A inserted by the Crime and Disorder Act 1998 sect. 25.
96. Notes for Guidance 1A.
97. Note A1.8 and Notes for Guidance 1F.
98. Notes for Guidance 1AA. There is no power to search *for* facial covering though it may be seized if it is found incidentally pursuant to a search for something else.
99. Sect. 13A (a)–(c).
100. Sect. 13B(2). There is no power to compel the removal of clothing other than outer clothing that may be removed in a stop search under PACE, see 13B(4).
101. Sect. 13A(1); sect. 13B(2) and (9). In the case of a search under sect. 13B, the Secretary of State must be notified of the use of the power and he may cancel authorisation at any time. Any further use of the power under sect.13A requires a new authorisation, sect. 13A(8) and Code A1.11.
102. Sect. 13A(3) and 13 B(2).
103. Sect. 13A(4) and 13B(3).
104. Article 8(2) of the European Convention. At present, the sections do not cover acts of

terrorism 'connected solely' with the U.K., apart from Northern Ireland, but see the Terrorism Bill 2000.

105. Home Office Statistical Bulletin 2/99. There were 43,700 stop searches under the PT(TP) Act 1989 in 1996/1997 and only 15,400 in 1997/1998.

106. See chapter 1.

107. See RCCP Cmnd. 8092 (1981) paras. 3.114–3.122.

108. See below.

109. See *R v Hughes* (1994) 99 Cr. App. R.160; *R v Heap* CA 13th October 1994.

110. Sect.18(1).

111. Sect. 18(5). Problems have arisen under this provision in connection with unrecorded and unauthorised pre-police station interviews taking place during the search; see Code C11.1 and *R v Joseph* [1993] Crim. L.R. 206.

112. [1987] Crim. L.R. 202.

113. *Krohn v DPP* CO/3920/96 (18th March 1997) QBD.

114. Cp. *Warden v Hayden* (1967) 387 US 294; *Chimel v California* (1969) 395 US 752; *Feeney v The Queen* (1997) 146 DLR (4th) 609.

115. [1982] 1 QB 1290. Note that the RCCP (Cmnd. 8092) rejected the proposal that all such searches should be by warrant, stating at para. 3.121 'that it is preferable to put the responsibility on the police'.

116. Sect. 32 (1) and 32(2)(a).

117. Sect. 32(4), as amended by CRIMPO 1994 sect. 59(2). More intrusive searches can be conducted in private. Mouth swabs are no longer intimate samples; see chapter 4.

118. *Cardwell v Lewis* (1974) 417 US 583; *California v Greenwood* (1988) 486 US 35.

119. Except legally privileged material.

120. Sect. 32(3). This argument applies equally to the wider search power under sect. 18.

121. Above.

122. CA 13th Oct.1994; see also *R v Junior Beckford* (1992) 94 Cr. App. R. 43.

123. *Coolidge v New Hampshire* (1971) 403 US 443 and see chapter 3.

124. (1925) US 20. This case also demonstrates a now largely discredited link between the Fourth and Fifth Amendments.

125. See *Trupiano v US* (1967) US 699.

126. *Warden v Hayden* (1967) 387 US 294.

127. (1973) 414 US 218. In this case, a search following arrest for a driving offence revealed a cigarette packet containing heroin.

128. (1969) 395 US 752 and see *Mincey v US* (1978) 437 US 385; *Adams v Williams* (1972) 407 US 143.

129. Above.

130. (1990) 494 US 325.

131. Cp. *Payton v New York* (1980) 445 US 573, citing *Semaynes's Case* 5 Co Rep 91a, 77 ER194.

132. *California v Ciraolo* (1986) 467 US 207, where a backyard surrounded by a high fence was observed from the air and *Dow Chemical Company v US* (1986) 476 US 90.

133. *Greenwood v Van Houten* (1988) 486 US 35.Cp. *R v Lauda* [1998] 2 SCR 683.

134. (1967) 389 US 347 and see chapter 1.

135. (1974) 417 US 583 and see *US v Chadwick* (1977) 433 US1.

136. (1981) 453 US 454. It was held that after arrest of the occupants of a motor vehicle, a search of the passenger compartment and of containers therein was reasonable. See also *R v Caslake* [1998] 1 SCR 51.

137. An example of this pragmatism is a recent decision holding that, though a vehicle is defined as 'premises' under PACE and there is no power to seize 'premises', sect. 18 gave power to seize 'anything' searched for and that this included the moveable premises themselves; *Cowan v Commissioner of Police of the Metropolis* The Times August 31st 1999.
138. See chapter 1.
139. (1984) 11 DLR (4th) 641. This case is also discussed in chapter 3.
140. As in *R v LePlante* (1987) 48 DLR (4th) 615, holding that the Food and Drugs Act RSC 1970, purporting to authorise warrantless searches of non-dwellings, gave rise to a 'basic inconsistency' with section 8. Cp. *Simmons v The Queen* (1988) 55 DLR (4th) 673.
141. Human Rights Act 1998 sect. 10.
142. The officer designated under PACE to safeguard the due process rights of suspects on arrest by informing the suspect of his rights and by recording details of custodial detention.
143. Sect. 54(4)(b).
144. PACE sect. 65 as amended by CRIMPO 1994 sect. 59(1). Cp. *R v Hughes* (1994) 99 Cr. App. R. 160.
145. The detainee should be permitted to speak privately to the doctor prior to giving consent and the doctor should explain the grounds on which the search is based, the options available to the detainee and the procedure for undertaking the search. Where refusal is likely to imply guilt, this should also be explained.
146. There is reference to this practice in the BMA circular. It is stated to be 'totally unacceptable'.

3 Searches of Premises by Warrant

The Nature and Purpose of Warrants

The warrant is a document by which searches of premises are judicially authorised and legitimated. As has been outlined in the introductory chapter, the oppressive historical reputation of these authorisations led to constitutional conflict during the seventeenth and eighteenth centuries both in the United Kingdom and in the United States. The eventual outcome of these conflicts was that the common law judges succeeded in imposing strict constraints upon the circumstances when a warrant might issue and required that the issuance itself to be a judicial act.[1] Because of the fetters placed upon the granting of warrants, certain common law jurisdictions came to view the warrant procedure as a due process safeguard rather than as a coercive means of obtaining incriminating evidence through an exceptional intrusion into a person's privacy. The inexorable product of this hypothesis is that all searches by warrant are considered to be 'good' and all searches without warrant are 'bad'. This theory is most evident in the rhetoric of the United States' Supreme Court in cases such as *Coolidge v New Hampshire*,[2] where it was stated that, as a general proposition, warrantless searches were unreasonable.[3] A similar doctrine is evident in Canada where the seminal case of *Hunter v Southam Inc.*[4] stated that the absence of a warrant makes a search *prima facie* unreasonable. It is then for the Crown to establish that it is none the less reasonable and, as stated in chapter 2, pre-existing common law or statutory powers of search will not necessarily survive scrutiny under section 8 of the Canadian Charter.

The other theory, and the one to which English judges traditionally subscribed, is that warrants are indeed coercive instruments and they must therefore be limited to those situations that have been expressly set out in statute, as a result of democratic process. This somewhat more cautious view of the nature and purpose of warrants resulted in the absence of any statutory power to search by warrant that was not 'offence-specific' and it was not until the enactment of PACE that a comprehensive power to issue search warrants was granted to magistrates.[5] However, with the exception of section 26(2) of the Theft Act 1968,[6] the piecemeal legislation that pre-dated PACE has not been repealed. Section 8(5) of PACE states that the 'power to issue a warrant conferred by this section is in addition to any such power otherwise conferred'. That said, these various powers are now subject to the same due process limitations that apply to PACE warrants by virtue of section 15 and Code B 1(3)(c) of the Codes of Practice.[7] PACE applies only to 'constables' and, by extension, to other law enforcers investigating offences, such as officers of Customs and Excise.[8] It does not apply to administrative officers carrying out purely routine inquiries.

There is a debate about the point at which statutory rights of entry granted to persons such as trading standards officers, or to gas or electricity officials give rise to a 'search' within PACE. If these individuals are merely inspecting 'goods, equipment or procedures' and the power that they are exercising is 'not dependent on the existence of grounds for suspecting that an offence has been committed', nor are there 'reasonable grounds for such suspicion',[9] then PACE is irrelevant. However, officials may enter with the intention of effecting a routine inspection and then, incidentally, discover evidence of offending. In this situation the courts may decide the substance of Code B applies even though, on a literal interpretation of section 15 of PACE, it should not do so.[10] Such an approach extends the protections given to suspects beyond the situation of the formal warrant application and demonstrates the need to recognise that it is the reasonableness of the search, not, necessarily, the formal authority that preceded it, that is the crucial issue in deciding whether there has been a violation of privacy rights (Sharpe, 1999a).

In order to assess the extent to which warrants serve to safeguard legitimate expectations of privacy, certain aspects of the warrant process must be considered in more detail. The first question is whether the required judicial scrutiny provides a real control upon the exercise of search powers. Linked to this, but a distinct issue in itself, is the sufficiency of information provided by the applicant to the issuer of the warrant. Proof of reasonable grounds to believe not only that a serious offence has been committed, but also that there will be evidence of it on the premises to be searched, may be necessary to comply with the derogation from the right to privacy contained in Article 8(2) of the European Convention. Finally, the scope of the power of search and seizure provided by a warrant is of enormous importance, bearing in mind the attacks on 'general warrants' in the eighteenth century.[11] A warrant legitimises entry to search for certain items, but does it also legitimise the seizure of *any* evidence of crime found as a consequence?

Judicial Scrutiny

Prior to PACE, there was criticism to the effect that 'magistrates may exercise insufficient care in ensuring that a warrant is necessary; and that too often they merely rubber stamp police requests'.[12] The recommendation of the Royal Commission[13] was that a first stage application should be made to a court for a summons to allow inspection of the evidence sought. Failure to comply with this order would result in the issuance of a warrant.[14] It was suggested that the 'seriousness of the intrusion' effected by the order or warrant might be 'marked by making the issuing authority a circuit judge'.[15] Magistrates would only have retained their then existing powers to authorise search for 'prohibited goods'.[16] The Royal Commission seems to have assumed that seeking 'evidence of crime' frequently involved searching innocent third parties and obtaining evidence of a confidential nature.[17] The non consensual search for and seizure of confidential material is now subject to a procedure similar to that suggested by the Commission,[18] but the non consensual search for and seizure of other evidence has, under section 8 of PACE, been placed in the hands of justices of the peace who are, usually, not legally qualified.[19] Thus, in England and Wales, there is a two tier procedure for warrants. Applications to search for evidence comprising material such as personal records, journalistic material or confidential business records may only be heard by a circuit judge under Schedule 1 of PACE. The statutory scheme provides an acceptance of the fact that the most sensitive and intrusive searches require the scrutiny of a professional lawyer. Applications to search for other evidence may be heard by the magistracy.

Section 8(1) of PACE requires a justice of the peace to be satisfied, before issuing a warrant, that there are reasonable grounds for believing

a) that a serious arrestable offence has been committed; and
b) that there is material on premises specified in the application which is likely to be of substantial value (whether by itself or together with other material) to the investigation of the offence; and
c) that the material is likely to be relevant evidence; and
d) that it does not consist of or include items subject to legal privilege, excluded material or special procedure material; and
e) that any of the conditions specified in subsection (3) below applies.

A 'serious arrestable offence', as defined in section 116 and Schedule 5 of PACE, embraces the most serious crimes that are indictable only, such as murder, rape and hi-jacking. Also included are certain either way offences of pornography and obscenity.[20] Section 116(3) extends the concept of a serious arrestable offence to one that has led to certain specified consequences, or is intended or likely to lead to those consequences. These consequences include 'serious financial loss to any person' and 'substantial financial gain to any person'.[21] The subjective nature of these concepts widens the potential application of section 8 to medium range offending.[22]

The conditions referred to in section 8(1)(e) above are those limiting the use of warrants to the 'last resort' principle. They permit a warrant to be granted only in three situations. These are, firstly, that it is 'not practicable' to communicate with a person entitled to grant entry (or to grant access to the evidence). The second situation is where entry will only be granted on production of a warrant. The third is that the purpose of the search may be 'frustrated or seriously prejudiced' unless immediate entry is gained by a constable. These are fairly stringent threshold requirements and it seems that their very stringency deters the police from seeking a warrant when a search can be effected consensually or under sections 18 or 32 of PACE (Bevan and Lidstone, 1996:98). However, where they do so, there is some concern that the magistracy (and even judges in Schedule 1 situations) may not be examining applications as rigorously as they should. One difficulty in determining the level of scrutiny accorded to warrant applications under section 8 is that they are heard *ex parte* and the keeping of notes by the justices' clerk, although frequently endorsed as being 'good practice' is not mandatory.[23] A few reported cases indicate that the 'rubber–stamping' of applications does occur. In *R v Reading Justices, Chief Constable of Avon and Somerset and Intervention Board for Agricultural Produce ex parte South West Meat Ltd.*,[24] the Divisional Court considered that the facial errors in and generality of the warrant 'raised questions as to how closely the justices had enquired into it'. Here the previous (co-operative) relationship between the Intervention Board and the subject of the application and the lack of specificity on the face of the warrant produced external evidence of rubber-stamping. It was not necessary to know details of the *ex parte* application itself to come to this conclusion. Similarly in *R v Southwark Crown Court and HM Customs and Excise ex parte Sorsky Defries*,[25] a circuit judge considered an application on behalf of Customs and Excise for a search warrant directed at a firm of accountants and concerning money laundering activities that had taken place in the United States.[26] The lawyer acting for Customs took no part in the application. The judge was advised that that it was an 'unusual one', but was not told of the particular jurisdictional and other issues involved in the case. The judge had never dealt with such an application before, yet he did not 'take his time', nor had he 'asked to be referred to the relevant statutory provisions and authorities'. Instead, he granted the application within 'a couple of minutes'. The Divisional Court stated that for all 'these reasons, it was clear that the judge could not in fact have been satisfied out of those matters of which he was obliged to be satisfied before issuing a warrant'.

However, in *R v Marylebone Magistrates' Court and anor. ex parte Amdrell Ltd. and ors.*,[27] the Divisional Court held that the magistrate had applied his mind to the 'relevant considerations'. This conclusion was based on the affidavits of the police applicant and of the magistrate. There were no notes of the hearing. The absence of extraneous grounds to quash the warrants worked against those seeking to challenge what had occurred during the hearing of the *ex parte* application. Thus, although it has been said that the appropriate judicial authority should himself be satisfied that the criteria for granting a warrant are satisfied and that 'it does not suffice for the person laying the information to say that he is',[28] it is often impossible to obtain an impartial account of the hearing and thus to challenge the issuance of a warrant effectively.

The same concerns about potential inadequacy of scrutiny exist in North America. Empirical research carried out by the National Center for State Courts showed that magistrates frequently failed to ask a single question during the warrant application and, in some cases, colluded with the police in granting illegal warrants (Van Duizand, Sutton and Carter, 1984). Indeed, it has been said that this study reveals 'a litany of perversions of the Fourth Amendment' (Dripps, 1986:1408). The research does not simply raise the question of the reality versus the rhetoric of judicial scrutiny. It raises a further and more substantial issue which is the role that justices see themselves as performing within the judicial process. The historical justification for the warrant procedure was to provide an impartial and independent control over the powers of the State to intrude into private dwellings. Yet justices may often not view themselves as impartial, but as an arm of the law enforcement agency seeking to effect the search. Where *prima facie* evidence of this partiality is established, the warrant will be invalidated. Thus in *Coolidge v New Hampshire*,[29] warrants relating to a murder investigation were issued by the State Attorney General, acting as a justice of the peace. Prior to issuing the warrants, the Attorney General had personally taken charge of all police activities relating to the investigation. He later served as a chief prosecutor at the trial. The Supreme Court held that the search resulting from these warrants breached the Fourth Amendment. The Court relied upon some seminal dicta in the case of *Johnson v US*.[30]

> The point of the Fourth Amendment, which often is not grasped by zealous officers, is not that it denies law enforcement the support of the usual inferences which reasonable men draw from evidence. Its protection consists in requiring that those inferences be drawn by a neutral and detached magistrate instead of being judged by the officer engaged in the often competitive enterprise of ferreting out crime. Any assumption that evidence sufficient to support a magistrate's disinterested determination to issue a search warrant will justify an officer in making a search without a warrant would reduce the Amendment to a nullity and leave the people's homes and offices secure only in the discretion of officers.

Where there is evidence of ostensible bias, as in *Coolidge*, the Supreme Court is likely to invalidate the warrant even in the absence of proof of actual partiality. Thus in *Connally v Georgia*,[31] a justice issued a search warrant under a statutory scheme whereby he received no salary, but was paid a prescribed fee for the issuance of every warrant. No fee was payable where a warrant was denied. The justice had testified in pre-trial hearings that he was a justice primarily because he was 'interested in a livelihood'. The issuance of the warrant was a breach of the Fourth and Fourteenth Amendments.

In *Conally v Georgia*, the justice had a 'direct, personal, substantial, pecuniary interest' in making a determination. However, partiality can arise for more indirect and non-financial reasons. In *Commonwealth v Davis*,[32] the issuing justice was a former employee of the district attorney's office and, on the particular facts of the case, was shown to have 'a strong tendency to accept whatever the police told him as true'. This unquestioning trust in police veracity might, arguably, be said to exist amongst some of the magistracy in England and Wales. It can arise not through previous employment connections, but simply through the day to day contact that arises between magistrates and police officers and the creation of a collaborative culture. Research studies have shown that there is a higher chance of acquittal before a judge and jury than in a summary court (Vennard, 1985). Whilst one reason for this may be the high percentage of judge directed acquittals in Crown Court trials,[33] the perception of accused persons is that they receive a fairer trial before a jury because magistrates are imbued with 'police' court culture (Bottoms and McClean, 1976; Hedderman and Moxon, 1992). If magistrates are not regarded, by those at risk, as sufficiently impartial to deliver a fair trial, it must be questioned whether they are always sufficiently impartial to act neutrally in a search warrant procedure that does not allow for defence representation.

Partiality may also arise as an aspect of abdication of responsibility of a justice. In *Lo-Ji Sales Inc. v New York*,[34] the magistrate signed what was, in effect, an 'open' search warrant in respect of an adult bookstore. The warrant had been issued after the magistrate had viewed two sample films purchased from the store by the police investigator. The magistrate accompanied the police to the bookstore for the purpose of ascertaining whether any material found on the premises might be obscene. This action was not only an improper delegation of judicial power to the police, it demonstrated a clear lack of neutrality. The justice had allowed himself to become a member of 'the search party which was essentially a police operation' and had acted as 'an adjunct law enforcement officer'.

The requirement that the issuer of the warrant be 'neutral and detached' does not necessarily mean that he has to be legally qualified. In *Shadwick v City of Tampa*,[35] the Supreme Court held that a court clerk could issue a warrant (an arrest warrant) for breaches of municipal ordinances. It is most unlikely that a valid search warrant could be issued by a court clerk (Goldstein, 1987:1184). However, it is clear from the dicta in *Shadwick* that non lawyers may grant warrant applications. It was stated that the terms 'magistrate' and 'judicial officer' had been used interchangeably in case law and there was nothing in the Fourth Amendment to require that 'all warrant authority must reside exclusively in a lawyer or judge'. The Supreme Court's approval of lay justices was reiterated in *North v Russell*.[36] The Canadian Supreme Court has taken a similar approach to the United States in regarding neutrality and detachment as more important than legal qualification. In *Hunter v Southam Inc.*[37] it was stated that for an authorisation procedure 'to be meaningful' it is necessary for the person authorising the search to be able to assess the evidence 'in an entirely impartial and neutral manner'. However, this assessment need not be made by a judge. It must be made by someone who would 'at a minimum be capable of acting judicially'.[38] The question of detachment is not one that has, to date, much vexed the English courts, but the absence of jurisprudence on this matter may be short-lived. The decisions that come from the European Court of Human Rights demonstrate that Article 8 requires not only legal certainty in the application of search procedures, but also, at least where evidence from that search is later relied on by the prosecution,[39] the scrutiny of an independent judge.[40]

Sufficiency of Information

Closely related to the adequacy of scrutiny accorded to a warrant application is the question of whether enough information has been presented to a magistrate to enable a proper decision to be made. In England and Wales, PACE section 15 and Code B2.6 of the Codes of Practice stipulate that certain material *must* be put before a justice. This minimum detail must include the premises to be searched and (so far as possible) the articles or persons to be sought. There must also be a statement of the *grounds* on which the application is made. This includes, where the purpose of the search is to find evidence of an alleged offence, an indication of how the evidence relates to the investigation.[41] Code B2.8 provides that where an application is refused, there may not be a fresh application in respect of the named premises unless supported by additional grounds. Further safeguards appear in Code B paragraphs 2.1 to 2.3. The investigating officer must take 'reasonable steps' to check that any information he has received 'is accurate, recent and has not been provided maliciously or irresponsibly'. In addition, an application 'may not be made on the basis of information from an anonymous source where corroboration has not been sought'. Notes for Guidance 2A states that the identity of the informant need not be disclosed, but that the applicant should be prepared to deal with questions concerning the accuracy of previous information provided by that source or any other related matters.

Whilst the rhetoric of Code B mandates that careful evaluation should be given to all information received by police officers,[42] the reality is that effective monitoring of compliance with this rhetoric is frustrated by claims of public interest immunity. Public interest immunity includes the American concept of informer privilege, but goes well beyond the protection of informers. It creates difficulties for those seeking to challenge the basis of a search, whether that search is a physical search for tangible evidence, or whether it is an electronic search for incriminating statements. The problem is that law enforcers frequently work on the basis of a tip off or on the basis of undercover observation and are loathe to reveal preliminary sources of information. English law enforcers have a considerable immunity from the production of these sources. The Code laid under the Criminal Procedure and Investigations Act 1996 (hereinafter CPIA) specifies, in paragraph 6.12, a long list of 'sensitive material' that need not be disclosed unless the court so orders. The list includes general categories such as 'material given in confidence', but also specifies, more particularly, 'material upon the strength of which search warrants were obtained'. Added to this is any material that might reveal the identity of informants, undercover officers, the location of surveillance operations and the techniques or methods used in police investigation. The content of this list makes it likely that *any* challenge to the sufficiency of information provided and, thus, to the validity of a warrant will be met by a claim of public interest immunity.

A judge will only order the disclosure of sensitive material when 'the disputed material may prove the defendant's innocence or avoid a miscarriage of justice'.[43] In the case of *R v Turner*,[44] Lord Taylor C.J. deprecated the increased tendency of defendants to allege that they had been set up or had acted under duress. He stated that such claims should be scrutinised with great care. A 'robust approach' should be taken by the judiciary. Only in those cases where a defendant can show a 'reasonable possibility that information about the informant will bear upon the issues'[45] may actual compliance with Code B of PACE be tested in court. In the United States and Canada, a similar approach exists in that a distinction is made between disclosing information that is seen to bear directly on the innocence of the accused and that which is seen simply to affect the legitimacy of police action. In *McCray v State of Illinois*,[46] it was stated that when 'the issue is not guilt or innocence' but is 'the question of probable cause for an arrest or search', the identity of an informant need not, ordinarily, be revealed. Despite a dissenting opinion,[47] that such an approach would leave the police free to act as their own arbiters of 'probable cause', the principle continues to be applied.[48]

There is a clear public policy interest in protecting sources of information and details of police methodology. Although the privilege is now frequently linked to the increasing use of covert investigations and offender targeting, its origin and justification pre-dates the use of new technologies. As the Canadian Supreme Court stated in *Leipert v The Queen*,[49]

> Informer privilege is an ancient and hallowed protection which plays a vital role in law enforcement. It is premised on the duty of all citizens to aid in enforcing the law.

The privilege is not considered to be inconsistent with the Canadian Charter of Rights and Freedoms, so long as the 'innocence at stake' exception is maintained.[50] Since it has been stated that the privilege does not offend against the right, contained in section 7 of the Charter, to a trial in accordance with 'principles of fundamental justice',[51] it can probably be assumed that, in England and Wales, the maintenance of such an immunity at common law will not be found to violate the Human Rights Act 1998. Article 6 of the European Convention grants the right to a fair trial. However, the European Court of Human Rights has recognised that the right of the defendant to receive a fair trial must be balanced against the 'interests of society'.[52] Fairness is therefore a relative, rather than an absolute, concept and that Court has failed to uphold claims by English defendants who have submitted that there was an unfair trial because of non-disclosure of information relating to informants.[53] This issue will be discussed more fully in the chapters dealing with electronic search. In such situations, the participation of the informer in the crime charged, or the fact that the informer is a material witness[54] may bring the 'innocence at stake' exception in issue.

As far as challenging warrants is concerned, however, the exception is only likely to apply where a defendant alleges that he was framed by another suspect, or by the police.[55] Despite the difficulties caused by the immunity attaching to police investigations, it may be possible to argue that, as a matter of law, the information presented to a justice cannot establish probable cause[56] upon which to issue a warrant. In England and Wales, the express wording of PACE subsection 8(1) preserves this requirement by stating that a warrant may only be issued where there are '*reasonable grounds*' to believe that there is material on the premises specified that is likely to be of substantial value to the investigation and that it is likely to be relevant evidence. Despite this express incorporation of the reasonableness principle, there is comparatively little case law on the issue in the context of section 8 applications.[57]

Jurisprudence in the United States has evolved over the years through challenges raised under the Fourth and Fourteenth Amendments. Supreme Court review has shifted in its perspective. Rather than focusing narrowly upon the evidence supporting the application, the Court has given consideration, more recently, to the extent to which such applications afford protection to justices and law enforcers. The dual character of warrants allows for their use as a shield against legal liability on the part of those involved in their issuance and execution. Where such immunity exists, it also protects the fruits of the search from evidential exclusion in subsequent criminal proceedings. However, this protection, in the form of qualified immunity from suit, depends on the objective reasonableness of the officer's good faith reliance on the information presented to the justice. It was held in *Malley v Briggs*[58] that an officer could not simply rely upon judicial approval of an application. He must himself exercise 'reasonable professional judgement'. The same standard of conduct applies when the suppression of evidence, obtained as a consequence of executing a warrant, is being considered.[59] There are therefore certain basic and immutable requirements that exist before a warrant will legitimate a search and the seizure of any items resulting therefrom. The first requirement is that the applicant must not knowingly mislead the magistrate with information that he knows is false. In *US v Leon*,[60] it was stated that where an officer displays a 'reckless disregard of the truth', suppression remains an 'appropriate remedy'. A second requirement is that a magistrate must not 'wholly abandon his judicial role'[61] and, where this occurs, the applicant cannot rely on the magistrate's probable cause determination because he patently has not made one. The third requirement enunciated in *Leon* is that the warrant is facially valid. It may be facially deficient in failing to specify the place to be searched or the things to be seized and, in such a situation, 'the executing officers cannot reasonably presume it to be valid'.

The requirement of facial validity does not mean that every officer authorised to execute the warrant must be individually named,[62] nor that every single detail concerning the object of the search must be particularised. The knowledge of the police officer carrying out the search may, on occasion, supplement the description of items contained in the warrant.[63] However, where a warrant is issued to search for a large amount of published material, a higher standard of particularity is required because the right to free speech and freedom of the press conjoins with the right to privacy.[64] In such situations, where the warrant is frequently issued to search for subversive or obscene material, the borderline between criminality and a lawful titillation is not necessarily clear cut and the courts are more likely to strike down imprecise wording.[65] Where the warrant relates to premises different from those specified, no good faith exception can save the search. Thus in *Schroeder v US*,[66] the police searched the wrong mobile home as a consequence of entering from a direction not specified in the warrant. It was said that the crux of the error that led the trial court to admit the evidence lay not in the finding that the search warrant was written with sufficient particularity, but in finding that the search warrant identified the appellant's residence at all. In the English case of *R v South Western Magistrates' Court ex parte Cofie*,[67] the Divisional Court granted judicial review of the issuance of a search warrant where the warrant gave the correct address of premises in multi-occupancy but did not specify the actual flat to be searched.

Leon stated that the fourth requirement of a legally protected search was that the warrant is not 'so lacking in indicia of probable cause as to render official belief in its existence entirely unreasonable'. This last requirement is at the crux of reasonableness determinations. If there is apparent insufficiency of probable cause, then the search is an unreasonable one. It has been said that the Fourth Amendment acts as an 'imperfect divining rod' to separate the legitimate detection of crime from illegitimate government prying (Loewry, 1983:1244). If an individual has given reasonable grounds to the police to search for evidence of crime, then he cannot complain of a privacy violation since there is no right to secrete evidence of offending. This principle is implicit in the American Constitution and in section 8 of the Canadian Charter. It is explicit in Article 8(2) of the European Convention on Human Rights. Article 8(2) allows derogation from the right to privacy where a public authority is acting 'in accordance with the law' and the derogation is 'necessary in a democratic society for the prevention of disorder or crime'. An unreasonable search is not a 'necessary' one and whilst probable cause does not separate out the guilty and innocent with precision, it goes a long way toward doing do (Sharpe, 1999a).

The major question is what information establishes probable cause and what information fails to do so? In the seminal case of *Illinois v Gates*,[68] the Supreme Court had to determine the vexed question of whether information originally derived from an anonymous tip off amounted to probable cause. A police department had received an anonymous hand-written letter stating that Mr. and Mrs. Gates 'strictly made their living selling drugs'. Details were given of their drug trafficking *modus operandi* and the letter stated the date on which the next consignment would be brought in from Florida. The letter ended with the words 'I guarantee if you watch them carefully you will make a big catch'. A confidential police informant verified that Mr. Gates had booked a flight to Florida and Drugs Agency surveillance was arranged. A search warrant for the Gates' house was issued on the basis that the *modus operandi* (a rendezvous in Florida) had been confirmed by subsequent observation. Police were waiting on the Gates' return and, on searching their car and home, found drugs, weapons and other contraband. The majority of the Court concluded that the information provided a 'substantial basis' for determining that probable cause existed and held that the search warrant was therefore properly issued. In reaching this conclusion, Justice Rehnquist reviewed previous Supreme Court authority[69] and rejected any inflexible 'two-pronged test' that required a warrant affidavit to reveal not only the *basis* of knowledge of the informant (for instance the means by which he came by the information), but also evidence of veracity or reliability of the informant.

An informant's veracity, reliability and basis of knowledge were said to be 'highly relevant in determining the value of his report', but they should not be understood to be 'entirely separate and independent requirements to be rigidly exacted in every case'.[70] Instead, the totality-of the circumstances' approach should be employed. It was said that

> Probable cause is a fluid concept – turning on the assessment of probabilities in particular factual contexts – not readily, or even usefully, reduced to a neat set of legal rules. Informant's tips doubtless come in many shapes and sizes from many different persons.

The issuance of warrants was to depend on 'non-technical, common sense judgements of laymen'.

The effect of *Illinois v Gates* is that police officers may supplement *any* information received by further investigation. The fact that the initial tip off does not, of itself, give rise to probable cause is no longer determinative. There is an issue about the loss of privacy for those, potentially innocent, citizens who are targeted as a result of such tips. However, arguably, the greater problem is judicial acceptance of what amounts to corroborative information obtained by the police. There is no requirement for the facts or circumstances relied on by the police to be independent of the informer. In *US v Harris*,[71] a warrant was issued on the basis of a report from an informant whose identity was not revealed to the magistrate. The corroborative facts were that the informant had himself purchased illicit whiskey from the suspect for more than two years and had done so within two weeks of notifying the police. It was stated that admitted participation in offending made it more likely that the statement was reliable. It is true that the informant was technically incriminating himself. Nevertheless, the tendency for criminals to 'grass up' one another does not necessarily mean that the resultant information is more credible just because it emanates from past or present associates, particularly when a police deal may be the objective of the informant. Even more worrying is the statement in *Jones v US*[72] that predisposition was a factor corroborating information received. Whilst a previous drugs supplier is more likely to be engaged in further similar activity, it is equally likely that such a person is at risk of being set up by associates.

In Canada, a similar approach has been taken. The information presented must indicate reasonable grounds to believe that the search will afford evidence with respect to the commission of an offence,[73] but the 'totality-of-circumstances' standard is applied in determining whether reasonable grounds exist.[74] The starting point is that the affidavit in support of the application must 'contain sufficient detail to enable a justice of the peace to properly exercise his or her discretion'.[75] Where police are seeking to search the premises of innocent third parties, there is a 'much higher' requirement as to the sufficiency and accuracy of the information put before a justice of the peace.[76] The Canadian courts have grappled with the informant problem in the context of probable cause and have established some judicial criteria that make full acknowledgement of the need to reconcile societal interest in the suppression of crime with the rights of citizens not to be subjected to unreasonable searches. In *R v Garofoli*,[77] Sopinka J. set out some fundamental 'propositions' concerning probable cause, stating that these were applicable to searches by warrants and also to warrantless searches.

The first proposition is that 'a tip from an informer, by itself, is insufficient to establish reasonable and probable grounds'. Secondly, in assessing the reliability of the 'tip' the court must look at a variety of factors including

(a)   the degree of detail of the 'tip',
(b)   the informer's source of knowledge;
(c)   the indicia of the informer's reliability such as past performance or confirmation from other investigative sources.

Finally, it was stated that the results of a search could not retrospectively validate the issuance of a warrant. In *R v Solomon*,[78] it was conceded that, whilst anonymous complaints are not, in principle, inadmissible, they must be treated 'with prudence' because of the impossibility of verifying the credibility of the complainant. Such lack of verification could, however, be compensated for by 'the quality of the information, the detail and corroborating evidence'. Thus tips (even those anonymously received) may found the preliminary basis of a warrant application, but the police will need to demonstrate further why the tip is a credible and reliable one. They may do this by reference to the content of the information itself and/or by reference to an existing police/informant relationship. Their own investigative efforts may add corroboration. A 'first time tipster' may be relied upon when he provides detailed information and the police are able to confirm the information before search, but information that merely describes 'innocent and commonplace conduct' and emanates from an untested, anonymous informant cannot on its own establish reasonable grounds.[79]

Factual support for the issuance of a warrant may come from a previous warrantless search, but the warrantless search must itself be reasonable within section 8 of the Charter or it cannot be relied upon to support an application.[80] For example, police officers may obtain evidential support from a pre-warrant search that does not violate any reasonable expectation of privacy. Thus in *R v Plant*,[81] a 'Crime Stoppers' tip that cannabis was being cultivated by the accused was confirmed by a computer search of the electricity consumption at the premises in question. The search revealed that consumption was four times the average. The Supreme Court considered that the check of computerised electrical records did not 'reveal intimate details of the appellant's life'. The appellant therefore had no reasonable expectation of privacy in this minimally intrusive activity. The decision in *Plant* is of some consequence as it considers the wider issue of the need for a reconciliation between societal interests in protecting 'individual dignity, integrity and autonomy' and the need for effective law enforcement. Information received may be firmed up by subsequent police investigation, but only where this subsequent investigation constitutes a reasonable search.[82] The gloss that this puts upon *Illinois v Gates* and, by implication, upon Code B of PACE, is that whilst apparent probable cause is an essential component of a warrant application, it may only be established by an initial investigation that *itself* complies with the Fourth Amendment,[83] or with Article 8 of the European Convention.

The Permitted Scope of Search and Seizure

If warrants are regarded as safeguards against unreasonable searches and if there is a requirement, under section 15 of PACE, for the warrant application to specify both the premises to be searched and the material that is to be sought, it might be assumed that law enforcers can only search for and seize that specified material. PACE provides otherwise. Despite the common law revulsion against general searches,[84] the extent of a search is limited but the *fruits* of that search are not constrained by the terms of the warrant. Section 16 of PACE contains requirements to ensure that the execution of a warrant is effected in a reasonable manner and therefore provides statutory recognition of the proportionality principle. The search must be conducted at a reasonable hour, unless it appears to the constable executing the warrant that this would frustrate the purpose of the search.[85] The search must take place within one month from the date of issue.[86] Entry is authorised on one occasion only.[87] Most importantly, subsection 16(8) provides that 'A search under a warrant may only be a search to the extent required for the purpose for which the warrant was issued'. Code B paragraph 5.9 enlarges on this by stating that regard must be had to 'the size and nature' of whatever is sought. It further stipulates that a search under warrant cannot continue once all the items specified in the warrant have been found, or the officer in charge is satisfied that they are not on the premises. Searches should be conducted with 'due consideration for the property and the privacy of the occupier'[88] and another person such as a friend or neighbour should be allowed to witness the search, unless there are reasonable grounds to believe that this would hinder the investigation or endanger officers.[89]

These safeguards do not, however, preclude the police from seizing material other then that specified in the warrant. Even pre-PACE, the law had evolved to allow for seizure of such material. In *Chic Fashions West Wales*

Ltd. v Jones,[90] the common law power of arrest for theft and of search for the stolen items was extended to a police officer who was executing a search warrant in respect of the premises in which stolen goods, not specified in the warrant, were found. Dubious though this extension might be, it had some tenuous historical precedent (Feldman, 1986:14). The slightly later case of *Ghani v Jones*[91] created a further extension of seizure powers in respect of any material that was believed to implicate the subject of the search in other offending. This judicial endorsement of serendipity was motivated by the need to help the police 'in their efforts to track down criminals'[92] and Lord Denning was not troubled by the absence of pre-existing legal authority to support the decision.[93] *Ghani v Jones* was an exemplar of judicial creativity. There is some uncertainty, however, whether *Ghani v Jones* had the effect of authorising the seizure of *any* items found regardless of the level of suspected offending. Whilst Lord Denning does speak of goods that show the suspect 'to be implicated in some other crime', he later appears to qualify this statement by setting out four requisites for lawful seizure. The first of these is that the police officers must have reasonable grounds for believing that 'a serious offence has been committed – so serious that it is of the first importance that offenders be caught and brought to justice'. The second requisite is that the officers have reasonable grounds for believing that the article in question is either the fruit of the crime, an instrument of the crime or evidence of the crime. The first two requisites would indicate that unless serious crime (however that is defined) is reasonably believed to have taken place, the property cannot be removed.

The Royal Commission on Criminal Procedure did not rule out the seizure of items not specified in the warrant, but thought that such seizure should be limited to 'prohibited goods or evidence of a grave offence'.[94] To this extent, it was considered that evidence found 'incidentally in the course of a lawful search' should be admissible. The manner of the search was to be determinative. If police officers did not search appropriately under the warrant and fulfil their recording obligations, they could not rely upon the fruits thereof. Section 19 of PACE goes further than the recommendations of the Commission. Although, as has been mentioned above, the *manner* in which the search is conducted may be crucial in considering the issue of whether material has been lawfully seized, the fact that the property has no relationship either to the crime being investigated, or to the subject of the search, is irrelevant. Nor is it relevant that there are no reasonable grounds to believe that the property is evidence of serious crime. Section 19(1) provides that a constable 'who is lawfully on the premises' has certain powers of seizure. There is no requirement that the constable be on the premises in order to execute a search warrant. It may be (as in *Ghani v Jones*) that he has been 'invited' onto the premises and is there by consent. Whatever the basis of the lawful entry, a constable has a virtually unlimited power to seize any item where he has reasonable grounds for believing that the item has been obtained in consequence of the commission of *an* offence, or that it is evidence in relation to an offence which he is investigating or *any other offence*.[95]

There are two caveats to what is, in effect a general licence to take away *any* suspect evidence. The first is that the constable must have reasonable grounds to believe that it is necessary to seize it in order to prevent the evidence 'being concealed, lost, damaged, altered or destroyed'.[96] Lidstone and Palmer (1996:142) consider that this requirement precludes the seizure of items that can be photographed or copied by an officer under subsection 20(5) of PACE. However, a constable may consider, in the light of the 'best evidence rule' that it is preferable to retain the original, which could be destroyed or defaced if not removed immediately. In England and Wales, the surviving scope of this rule, in respect of documentary evidence, is subject to academic debate.[97] A police officer might well not consider himself qualified to judge whether the rule has been effectively eradicated by section 27 of the Criminal Justice Act 1988 (which provides for the reception in evidence of certified copies of documents) or merely confined in its application. Sections 19(4) and 20 also allow a constable to require information contained in a computer and accessible from the premises to be produced in a form in which it can be taken away. Although there is no longer any special requirement concerning the admissibility of computer generated evidence, the provisions of the Criminal Justice Act 1988, concerning the reception of hearsay evidence in documentary form, would still apply to much of this material before it could be relied upon in court.[98] A constable is therefore not always in a position to judge whether seized material will be usable evidence, even if he reasonably believes that it will be concealed or destroyed if not immediately removed, and the taking of copies is no guarantee that the evidence will subsequently be admitted at trial.

The second caveat is that, under section 19(6), the constable may not seize an item that he has reasonable grounds for believing is 'subject to legal privilege'. Legal privilege is not a straightforward concept and the English case law thereon will be discussed in the following chapter. Essentially, it protects from production those communications that have come into existence as a consequence of advice sought by a client and given by a lawyer in the context of legal transactions.[99] Whilst difficulties over the seizure of legally privileged material usually arise in the context of applications made under

Schedule 1 of PACE, the seizure of documents under a section 8 warrant has been the subject of challenge on the basis that legal privilege may have applied.[100] Even where there is only a '*prima facie*' claim of privilege, the police should not seize documents, but should proceed under Schedule 1. If it is inappropriate for a justice to consider the scope of legal privilege,[101] it is surely even more inappropriate for a police officer at the scene of the seizure to do so. Another curious feature of subsection 19(6) is that it does *not* exclude from seizure special procedure, or excluded material. Again, these concepts are explored in the next chapter, but the commonality between them is the confidential nature of the information contained in the material sought. Such material is precluded from seizure under magisterial warrant[102] but not from seizure by a police officer.

As stated above, the search itself must be proportional to the purpose for which the warrant was issued.[103] Thus where a large number of documents are being sought, the temporary seizure and removal of all documents on the premises, in order to permit the police to sort them elsewhere would be objectionable. The removal of files (rather than specific pieces of paper within the files) might be justified, if the police reasonably believe that each file contains the material sought. It should be hard to justify the legitimacy of such conduct where a search is conducted under section 8 of PACE, since it is almost inevitable that, where material of such volume and complexity is involved, there is likely to be special procedure, excluded, or even legally privileged material contained therein. In the recent case of *R v Chesterfield Justices and ors ex parte Bramley*,[104] Lord Justice Kennedy stated that those searching under section 8 were not empowered to remove items to 'sift through' them to see whether they fell within the scope of the warrant. However, where a large quantity of material was involved, it was conceded that it might be impracticable to make a complete and final check of the materials seized whilst on the premises. Any item that was later discovered to be subject to legal privilege, must be returned, but it was thought that the search itself would not, thereby, be invalidated.

In the United States, the 'plain view' doctrine permits the seizure of articles not comprised in a warrant and this is not considered to be a violation of the Fourth Amendment.[105] In particular, it was stated in *Horton v California*[106] that inadvertence is not a necessary condition of legitimate plain view searches and, thus, that an officer may 'be interested in finding other evidence' connecting the suspect to the offence whilst searching for the items specified in the warrant.[107] Whilst the discovery of plain view items need not be entirely fortuitous, the Supreme Court in *Horton* made clear that 'plain view alone is never enough to justify the warrantless seizure of evidence'. The incriminating character of the item must be 'immediately apparent'. A similar distinction was made, as exists under PACE, between search powers (which are constrained by the Fourth Amendment) and a power of seizure. Seizure was said not to involve any privacy rights in circumstances where an officer has lawful access to an item in plain view. It was pointed out in the dissenting judgment that seizure might not affect privacy interests, but that it did affect possessory interests.[108] The point remains equally unanswered in England and Wales and demands equal attention since Article 8 gives a right to respect for 'home and correspondence'. Possessory interests are therefore implicitly protected, in addition to privacy rights. Section 19(6) grants the equivalent of 'general warrant' powers to officers operating at street level and it is surely inevitable that challenge will be made under the Human Rights Act 1998.

Remedies in Respect of Improperly Issued Warrants

The first difficulty in establishing any claim that a search of premises, by warrant or otherwise, is improper is that public interest immunity will almost certainly be raised by the police to defeat any challenge to the sufficiency of information upon which the warrant was granted.[109] Public interest immunity applies equally to civil proceedings and it will only be overridden where a weightier public interest requires disclosure of the privileged documents.[110] Thus, regardless of whether the remedy sought is a civil one or whether the objective is to exclude the evidence obtained in a criminal trial, it may be impossible to establish that a warrant should not have been issued. Where this evidential immunity does not prevent challenge to the warrant procedure, there are three possible routes by which the subject of a search may seek redress. The first avenue is to take independent proceedings against the police. However, unless no criminal proceedings were in fact instituted, or those proceedings were unsuccessful, it is unlikely that the claimant can sue for damages as an 'innocent' citizen whose rights have been violated. Probable cause is almost certainly bound to have existed in respect of the search should a conviction result.[111] For this reason, writers have suggested that a civil action should be the primary remedy available in respect of the wrongful application for and issuance of a warrant, since it distinguishes between innocent and guilty targets.[112]

However, it has also been pointed out that not only are citizens reluctant to sue the police in tort, where physical damage to property may be minimal, but also that juries may be reluctant to award damages in such actions (Spiotto, 1973:272). Unless it can be established that there has been oppressive, arbitrary or unconstitutional conduct by government servants, no punitive or exemplary damages may be awarded.[113] Added to the 'not worth the cost' attitude of those who have endured a search under an invalid warrant, there is the difficulty that only certain civil actions may be open to them. In England and Wales, the doctrine of 'immunity from suit' protects those who investigate crime from certain liability. It is not possible to sue the police for misfeasance in public office. It was stated in *Docker and ors v Chief Constable of West Midlands Police*[114] that, save in actions for abuse of process of the court, there was absolute civil immunity from action in respect of things said or done in the course of the judicial process 'even if falsely and maliciously and without reasonable cause'. The 'judicial process' extended to 'conduct which could fairly be said to be part of the investigatory and preparatory process of investigating crime or possible crime' prior to prosecution. For the same reason, a civil action in defamation does not lie against the police.[115]

However, in *Gibbs v Rea*,[116] it was held that an action for maliciously procuring a search warrant could be brought since its true foundation is the 'intentional abuse of the process of the court'. It was stated that, in asserting that the defendant did not have reasonable and probable cause to make the warrant application, the plaintiff must show that the defendant lacked any *bona fide* belief that he or she was placing before the issuing judge material sufficient to meet the conditions for the issue of the warrant sought. The plaintiff must also establish malice on the part of the defendant. This required more than the absence of 'reasonable cause' although that itself could be evidence of malice. The burden placed on the potential plaintiff is therefore a heavy one in view of the fact that, under section 8 of PACE, the application will have been made *ex parte*.[117] The other civil action that may be brought is that of trespass on the basis that there has been a physical entry onto and interference with property.[118] No action exists at present for any invasion of personal autonomy that occurs as a consequence of the execution of an improperly obtained warrant. It can be seen that a civil action does not look a hugely attractive option so far as a potential plaintiff is concerned. Further, it does nothing to assist an individual, charged with an offence, who is claiming that patent lack of moral integrity on the part of the police should be sanctioned by the exclusion of the resultant evidence.

The debate about whether the exclusionary rule should be employed in order to discipline the police and deter future misconduct has been continuing unabated in the United States for nearly forty years, ever since the Supreme

Court held in *Mapp v Ohio*[119] that the Fourth and Fourteenth Amendment required evidence obtained from an illegal search to be suppressed in both Federal and State courts. There are two main objections to the judicial exclusion of illegally obtained real evidence.[120] The first is that there is no empirical research to support the hypothesis that exclusion does in fact deter improper police activity (Oaks, 1970). This assertion has been challenged subsequently (Orfield, 1987) and it would appear that, as with reliance upon any statistical data, support can be found for either view depending on the criminal justice values held by those seeking to justify them.[121] The second major objection is one of policy. It is said that the exclusionary rule benefits those very people who least deserve protection. Thus the 'cost' of the rule to society as a whole is too high and its benefit is too small. However, Stewart (1983:1383) points out that there is another dimension to excluding the evidence of an illegal search. This is the fact that suppression is a constitutionally mandated remedy for violation of the Fourth Amendment.

In England and Wales no such constitutional perspective has yet been taken toward excluding real evidence. The reliability principle has been paramount and, illegality notwithstanding, such evidence has been admitted.[122] It will be interesting to see whether judicial attitudes may change following the incorporation of Article 8 into domestic law. An interesting comparison may be made with the impact in Canada of the Charter of Rights and Freedoms. Evidence may be excluded under section 24 of the Charter either on the basis that its reception would render the trial unfair, or on the basis that its admission would bring the administration of justice into disrepute. There is therefore more opportunity for judges to utilise exclusion as a means of maintaining the integrity of the criminal justice system. In *Collins v The Queen*,[123] it was accepted that although the cost of excluding reliable evidence was high and although the trial was not necessarily rendered unfair by the admission of the item(s) found, there could be circumstances where 'the administration of justice would be brought into greater disrepute' by admitting evidence and condoning police conduct that amounted to a 'serious and flagrant violation of the rights of an individual'. This approach was followed in *R v Croucher*,[124] where evidence discovered as a result of a the execution of a search warrant was excluded even though the deficiency in the warrant arose purely through the Crown's reluctance to identify their informer and thus to manifest probable cause. In *R v Silveira*[125] the Canadian Supreme Court took a different view and held that 'exigent circumstances' validated police action in placing both the appellants and their property under house arrest prior to applying for a search warrant. The entry had been at gun-point and the judicial officer issuing the warrant had not been informed of the occupation of the house by the police. Nonetheless, the serious nature of the offence (drug trafficking) and the perceived need to preserve potential evidence were seen as overriding factors in determining whether to exclude evidence under section 24(2). It is clear that, where real evidence is concerned, the public interest in crime control frequently trumps respect for integrity on the part of investigators and that judges are willing to find reasons to uphold searches that bend the rules.

Perhaps for that reason, in England and Wales, the most successful challenges to searches conducted by warrant have been through the medium of judicial review. Judicial review is specifically concerned with the decision-making process itself. The reviewing court looks at whether the decision-making authority exceeded its powers, committed an error of law, or breached the rules of natural justice. In the context of a warrant application, judicial review will lie where a justice accedes to a request on the basis of information that no reasonable magistrate could consider sufficient, or issues a warrant that is so obviously invalid on its face that no reasonable magistrate would issue it.[126] The remedy of *certiorari* has the effect of retrospectively quashing the issuance of a warrant. A declaration as to the unlawfulness of any activity carried out under the warrant may also be obtained. The consequence of granting such remedies is that property seized will be returned and the parties will be put back, so far as is possible, into the position that they would have been had the warrant not been issued.[127] Since judicial review is aimed at controlling an excess or abuse of power by public authorities, it provides a more direct form of control in respect of the warrant process than does the suppression of any resultant evidence. It is hardly surprising therefore that those challenges to section 8 warrants brought in the form of judicial review proceedings have been more successful than those brought under section 78 of PACE.

The case of *R v South Western Magistrates' Court and anor. ex parte Cofie*[128] is a clear example of the striking down by the Divisional Court of a facially defective warrant. In *R v Reading Justices, Chief Constable of Avon and Somerset and Intervention Board for Agricultural Products ex parte South West Meat Ltd.*[129] inadequate magisterial scrutiny combined with a facial lack of particularity vitiated the warrant. These rare instances of section 8 warrants being struck down by a reviewing court show the potential for this remedy. Yet it is, in fact, in respect of warrants granted under Schedule 1 of PACE that judicial review is generally sought. The reasons for this are linked to the special nature of applications under that Schedule. Whilst the remedy applies equally to those who are not themselves criminal suspects and to those who are considered to be potentially guilty, the citizens most likely to be disquieted by the wrongful issuance and execution of a warrant are those who are innocent custodians of material that the police consider is 'likely to be of substantial value' to their investigation. Further, even if the subjects of the Schedule 1 application are themselves suspected of criminality, they are more likely to be professional men or involved in commercial activity and to have the capability and resources to instruct lawyers on their behalf.[130] This situation creates its own dynamic of judicial favouritism. Judges are more likely to be critical of the issuance of warrants when they affect the privacy of people who have a certain status in society.

In the *Crown Court at Southwark, The Commissioner of the Police for the Metropolis, The Secretary of State for the Home Dept. ex parte Gross*,[131] an application was made under Schedule 1 and under the Criminal Justice (International Co-operation) Act 1990. The United States' authorities were seeking documents in connection with alleged deception and false accounting in respect of claims for medical services rendered. Despite the fact that the police had acted in good faith, there had been a catalogue of errors occurring throughout the process. Apart from mistakes in the execution of the warrant, there had been a failure to make reasonable initial inquiries and inadequate information had been presented to the judge about the innocent subject of the search. This subject was 73 years old, was a retired Professor Emeritus with distinguished academic qualifications and he had an exemplary war record. It followed that, even though the material sought related to the son of the subject, the reviewing judges were reluctant to assume that someone who 'had led a blameless life for 73 years would assist his son to defend a serious criminal charge beyond that which was permissible'. There was no reason, therefore, why an order to give access to the relevant material would not have sufficed.[132] This case is a fairly extreme example of a warrant being used when it was not necessary to do so. Under Article 8 it would not be considered to be a proportionate derogation from the right to privacy. Whilst judicial review applies to suspect and to non suspect alike, in considering whether a warrant is necessary as a tool of last resort to secure evidence,[133] the court may well take account of the character and reputation of the holder of the material sought in determining whether a judicial officer acted in error in issuing a warrant. Although this would seem to introduce some subjectivity into the scrutiny of warrant procedures, it is, arguably, justified since warrants are coercive and intrusive instruments and should not be issued where other means of obtaining the material would be effective. In the following chapter, further consideration will be given to the use of search powers in respect of third parties who may have no connection with the crime being investigated.

Notes

1.   See chapter 1.
2.   403 US 443 (1971) and see chapter 1.
3.   Subject to 'a few specifically established and well delineated exceptions'. Some of these exceptions have been considered in chapter 2.
4.   (1984) 11 DLR 4th 641. See also *R v Klimchuk* (1991) 67 CCC (3d) 385; *R v Collins* (1987) 33 CCC (3d) 1; *R v Rao* (1984) 9 DLR (4th) 542.
5.   See chapter 1.
6.   Repealed by Schedule 7 of PACE. The section authorised a police superintendent to issue authority to search.
7.   *E.g.* Misuse of Drugs Act 1971; Firearms Act 1968.
8.   PACE sect. 114. See also *R v Twaites* (1990) 92 Cr. App. R. 106 and PACE sect. 67 (9). The Codes apply to 'persons other than police officers who are charged with the duty of investigating offences or charging offenders'.
9.   Code B1.3B.
10. See *Dudley Metropolitan Borough Council v Debenhams* (1994) 159 JP 18 (DC). Cp. *Camara v Municipal Court* 383 US 808 and *See v City of Seattle* (1967) 387 US 541.
11. See *Wilkes v Wood* (1763) 19 How St Tri 153, 98 ER 489 and chapter 1.
12. RCCP Cmnd. 8092 at para. 3.37.
13. Above.
14. Para. 3.42. This two-stage procedure is now reserved for special procedure and excluded material; see chapter 4.
15. *Ibid.*
16. Para. 3.45.
17. Para. 3.41.
18. See chapter 4.
19. In England and Wales stipendiary magistrates are professional lawyers, but the vast majority of justices are 'lay' justices with no legal qualifications.
20. Protection of Children Act 1978 sect. 1 and Obscene Publications Act 1959 sect. 2.
21. Sect. 116(6).
22. *E.g.* the theft of a pensioner's weekly payment and see chapter 2 pp. 32–33.
23.   See *R v Marylebone Court and anor. ex parte Amdrell Ltd. and ors.* DC 31st July 1998, 148 NLJ 1230 and cp. *R v Chief Constable of Warwickshire Constabulary ex parte Fitzpatrick and ors.* [1998] 1 ALL ER 65.
24. [1992] Crim. L.R. 672.
25. [1996] Crim. L.R. 195, CO/283/95.
26. The search was pursuant to a request from authorities in the United States under the Criminal Justice (International Co-operation) Act 1990 and PACE sect. 9 and Schedule 1. This is an *ex parte* procedure.
27. (1998) 148 NLJ 1230.
28. *IRC v Rossminster Ltd.* [1980] 1 ALL ER 80 at 87 per Viscount Dilhorne. See also *R v Crown Court at Lewes ex p Hill* (1991) 93 Cr. App. R. 60.
29. (1971) 403 US 443.
30. (1948) 333 US 10.
31. (1977) 429 US 245.
32. (1973) 310A 2d 334.

33. See RCCP Cm. 2263 pp. 76–77.
34. (1979) 442 US 319.
35. (1971) 407 US 443.
36. (1976) 427 US 328.
37. (1984) 11 DLR (4th) 641.
38. *Ibid.*
39. See *Preston v UK* (1997) 6 EHRLR 695, information obtained through telephone tapping is not admissible against an accused when obtained under a warrant issued by the Secretary of State. See chapters 5 and 6.
40. *Klass v Federal Republic of Germany* (1978) 2EHRR 214 at para. 55; *Cremieux v France* (1993) 16 EHRR 357.
41. Where an application for a search warrant is made under Schedule 1 of PACE, the application shall also indicate why it is believed that service of the notice of application for a production order may seriously prejudice the investigation. See Code B2.7 and chapter 4.
42. Code B2.4 provides that, other than in cases of urgency, an officer of the rank of inspector or above must authorise all such applications.
43. *R v Keane* [1994] 2 ALL ER 478.
44. [1995] 2 Cr. App. R. 94.
45. *Turner* (above) at 98.
46. (1967) 386 US 300; see also *Rugendorf v US* (1964) 376 US 528.
47. Justices Douglas, Brennan and Fortas.
48. See the more recent cases of *Schmid v State of Alkaska* (1980) 615 P2d 565; *US v Frazier* (1988) 856 F2d 196.
49. (1997) 143 DLR (4th) 38 at 43 and see *Roviaro v US* (1957) 353 US 53.
50. There is an evidential burden on the defendant to show that sych an exception exists (*ibid* p.48) and see *R v Turner* (above) and CPIA 1996 sect. 8.
51. See *R v Stinchcombe* (1991) 3 SCR 326 and *R v O'Connor* (1993) 105 DLR (4th) 110.
52. *Kostovski v The Netherlands* (1989) 12 EHRR 434 at para. 44.
53. *Jasper v UK* App. No. 27052/95; *Fitt v UK* App. No. 29777/96 ; cp. *Rowe and Davis v UK* Application No. 28901/95
54. See *R v Scott* (1990) 61 CCC (3d) 300.
55. *R v Baker* [1996] Crim. L.R. 55. The defendant alleged that there had been no real informant, as alleged by police, and that after the improper obtaining of a warrant drugs were planted on him.
56. See PACE sect. 8 criteria set out above; 'reasonable grounds' and 'probable cause' will be used interchangeably. In Canada, the terms are treated as being synonymous.
57. But see *R v Reading Justices, Chief Constable of Avon and Somerset and Intervention Board for Agricultural Produce ex parte South West Meat Ltd.* [1992] Crim. L.R. 672 where lack of magisterial scrutiny precluded an assessment of probable cause.
58. (1986) 475 US 335.
59. *US v Leon* (1984) 468 US 897.
60. Above. See also *Franks v Delaware* (1978) 438 US 154.
61. As in *Lo-ji Sales v New York* (1979) 442 US 319 discussed above and *Marcus v Search Warrant* (1961) 367 US 717.
62. *R v Hunt* [1994] Crim. L.R. 747.
63. *Massachusetts v Sheppard* (1984) 468 US 981.

64. *Stanford v Texas* (1965) 379 US 476; *Marcus v Search Warrant* (above); but *Zurcher v Stanford Daily* (1978) 436 US 547.
65. *Darbo v DPP* [1992] Crim. L.R. 56. 'sexually explicit' did not necessarily mean 'obscene'.
66. (1997) 129 F 3d 439.
67. [1997] 1 WLR 885 and see *R v Atkinson* [1976] Crim. L.R. 307. A warrant granted under the MDA 1971 gave the wrong number of the flat to be searched.
68. (1983) 462 US 213.
69. *Spinelli v US* (1969) 393 US 410 and *Aguiler v Texas* (1964) 378 US 108.
70. *Illinois v Gates* (above) per Rehnquist J.
71. (1971) 403 US 573. See also *Jones v US* (1960) 302 US 257.
72. Above. The predisposition test also causes difficulty in the context of the entrapment defence, see Choo (1990) and Sharpe (1996).
73. Canadian Criminal Code RSC 1985 sect. 487(1).
74. *R v Garofoli* (1990) 60 CCC(3d) 161.
75. *Canadian Broadcasting Corp. v Attorney-General for New Brunswick* (1991) 85 DLR (4th) 57.
76. *Canadian Broadcasting Corp. v Lessard* (1991) 3 SCR 421. Cp. Schedule 1 of PACE discussed in chapter 4.
77. Above. *Garofoli* was a case on telephone interception.
78. (1996) 139 DLR (4th) 625.
79. *R v Lewis* (1998) 122 CCC (3d) 481; *R v Zammit* (1993) 84 CCC (3d) 112 and *R v Bennett* (1996) 108 CCC (3d) 175.
80. *R v Plant* (1993) 84 CCC (3d) 203; *R v Wiley* (1993) 84 CCC (3d) 161 and *R v Grant* (1993) 3 SCR 223.
81. Above.
82. See also *R v Sandhu* (1993) 82 CCC (3d) 236; *R v Dersch* (1993) 85 CCC (3d) 1.
83. Clancy (1995) points out that the United States Supreme Court has yet to address this issue and that lower court decisions are in direct conflict.
84. See chapter 1.
85. Subsection 16(4); see also Code B paras. 5.1–5.3.
86. Subsection 16(3).
87. Subsection 15(5).
88. Code B5.10.
89. Code B5.11.
90. [1968] 1 ALL ER 229. It is perhaps significant that this was an action in trespass against a Chief Constable and not a criminal case. The judgment therefore extended the warrant immunity of the police.
91. [1969] 3 ALL ER 1700.
92. *Chic Fashions West Wales v Jones* (above) at 236 and *Ghani v Jones* (above) at 1703.
93. But he did state that the earlier decision of *Elias v Pasmore* [1934] 2 ALL ER 380 went too far in endorsing otherwise unlawful seizure by the State of documents, if they are evidence of crime committed by *anyone*.
94. Cmd. 8092 para. 3.49.
95. Subsections 19(2) and 19(3).
96. *Ibid.* Note that the word damaged does not appear in subsect. 19(3), but his is probably an error in drafting.
97. It is stated in Blackstones' *Criminal Practice* (1999) that sect. 27 CJA 1988 may be confined to the various types of hearsay contained within the Act itself and may not

affect the proof of the content of a document in its own right. Cp. Cross and Tapper (1999:641).

98. PACE sect. 69 has now been repealed by the Youth Justice and Criminal Evidence Act 1999 sect. 60 which removes the additional admissibility conditions previously attaching to computer evidence. However, unless the evidence resulted from the purely automated function of a computer and involved no human input, it would still need to fall within one of the documentary exceptions to the hearsay rule; see *R v Shephard* [1993] AC 380.

99. See *R v Crown Court ex parte Baines and Baines* [1987] 3 ALL ER 1025 at 1030. The advice does not have to be connected to litigation, but legal documents not connected with advice (such as conveyancing transaction documents) are not privileged. See chapter 4.

100. *R v Guildhall Magistrates' Court ex parte Primlacks Holdings Co. (Panama) Inc.* [1990] 1 QB 261. Judicial review of the warrant was granted on the basis that even where there was doubt about the existence of the privilege, the matter should have been considered by a circuit judge.

101. See *Primlacks Holdings* (above).

102. Subsection 8(1)(d).

103. Sect. 16(8) and above.

104. *The Times*, November 10th 1999 and see *Reynolds and anor. v Commissioner of Police of the Metropolis* [1984] 3 ALL ER 649.

105. See chapter 2.

106. (1990) 496 US 128.

107. *Coolidge v New Hampshire* (1971) 403 US 443 was declared not to be binding precedent on this particular point.

108. Justices Brennan and Marshall dissented. The Fourth Amendment, of course, specifically protects against both unreasonable search *and* seizure.

109. The elements of public interest immunity are mentioned above.

110. *R v Horseferry Road Magistrates' Court ex parte Bennett (no. 2)* (1994) 99 Cr. App. R. 123 at 126 D.C. Even if there is not the secrecy required by a pending prosecution, information received in relation to one investigation may form part of a continuum of police activity.

111. Although victims who are convicted and incarcerated on the basis of illegally obtained evidence would suffer the largest *actual* damage.

112. See Oaks (1970:757) and Akhil Reed Amar (1997:40). Cp. Stewart (1983:1388).

113. *Rookes v Barnard* [1964] AC 1129.

114. (1998) The Times 29th April C.A.

115. *Taylor v Serious Fraud Office* [1997] 4 ALL ER 887 C.A.; affirmed [1998] 4 ALL ER 801 H.L.

116. [1998] 3 WLR 72 P.C. In this case, the issuance of the warrant itself caused damage because the plaintiff lost his job as a consequence.

117. In *R v Aylesbury Justices Ex parte Wisbey* [1965] 1 ALL ER 602 it was held that an accused is not entitled to see the sworn information that forms the basis of the warrant application.

118. *Ghani v Jones* [1969] 3 ALL ER 1700.

119. (1961) 367 US 643.

120. Stewart (1983:1393) raises four criticisms, but their essence can be reduced to these two.

121. The Supreme Court has seized upon research casting doubt on the efficacy of the rule to curtail the effect of *Mapp v Ohio*; see *US v Calandra* (1974) 414US 338.

122. *R v Hunt* [1994] Crim. L.R. 747; *R v Wright* [1994] Crim. L.R. 55; *R v Stewart* [1995] Crim. L.R. 500 and see dicta in cases on electronic search to be discussed in chapter 6 *viz. R v Khan* [1996] 3 ALLER 289; *R v Chalkley* [1998] 2 ALL ER 155.
123. (1987) 38 DLR (4th) 508.
124. (1996) 112 CCC (3d) 428.
125. (1995) 2 SCR 297 (LaForest J. dissenting).
126. *Associated Picture Houses Ltd. v Wednesbury Corporation* [1947] 2 ALLER 680 and Cp. *R v Lord Saville of Newdigate ex parte A* The Times June 22nd 1999. Note that this remedy is only available in the context of criminal proceedings prior to the matter becoming one 'on indictment'; see Supreme Court Act 1981 sect. 29(3).
127. There may still be an issue over the return and usage in evidence of copies of documents and an order of the reviewing court may be sought in that respect.
128. [1997] 1 WLR 885 and see the discussion on facially defective warrants, above.
129. [1992] Crim. L.R. 672.
130. As in *R v Southwark Crown Court and HM Customs and Excise ex parte Sorsky Defries* [1996] Crim. L.R. 195 where it was alleged that one of the partners had been involved in advising as to money laundering.
131. CO/1759/98 QBD.
132. This is the primary remedy under Schedule 1. A warrant should be applied for only when a production order has not been complied with or where giving notice of application for an order may seriously prejudice the investigation; see chapter 4.
133. Sect. 8(3) and Schedule 1 paras. 12 and 14.

4   Particular Searches under PACE

Searches not Authorised by Section 8 Warrants

Certain searches for evidence, although falling within PACE, are not legitimated by the warrant process under section 8. This chapter deals with two PACE searches of very different kinds. One category of search involves documents or records and the other the taking of bodily samples. Although the authorisation procedures are very different in respect of the two categories, both involve searches of a confidential or intimate nature. The first category of search is that concerning special procedure or excluded material. This must take place under the procedure set out in Schedule 1 of PACE. There is analogous power to conduct searches for documentation under provisions in other statutes where the purpose is to disclose profits made from drug trafficking or other crime and these will be briefly mentioned by way of comparison. The second category concerns the package of powers, existing under sections 61-65 of PACE,[1] to take fingerprints or samples from a suspect in order to confirm his involvement with an offence. These latter powers require no judicial authorisation, perhaps because, in England and Wales, the procedure is regarded as being one confirming identity rather than as one involving a search, albeit that 'evidence' is seized as a consequence of the procedure.

It has already been seen that certain material is excluded from search and seizure under magisterial warrant.[2] The Royal Commission on Criminal Procedure[3] took the view that a 'compulsory power' to search for evidence would only be necessary in 'rare circumstances' and recognised that where information was held on a confidential basis, the holder might be 'unwilling to disclose it for fear of being sued for breach of duty'. The Commission therefore recommended that a compulsory power to search for evidence should have two stages. The first would be an order requiring the person to whom it was addressed to allow the police to inspect or to provide access to the items specified in the order. Upon proof of deliberate refusal to comply, or where notice of the order would lead to the destruction of evidence, a warrant could be issued. This proposal was, thus, intended to apply to *all* searches under warrant. In fact, it applies, under PACE, only to those searches that require the authorisation of a circuit judge because the nature of the material sought is regarded as too confidential or sensitive for a magistrate to make any decision legitimating police entitlement to rights of entry, search and seizure. This material is divided into three classifications. The first is legally privileged material and this class of material is totally excluded from *any* legitimate power of search and seizure. The second and third categories are special procedure and excluded material. Legally privileged material is exempt, even from any authority exercised by a circuit judge ordering its production, but the exact scope of the privilege is not without controversy. It is therefore necessary to identify those situations where documents are privileged and to differentiate them from those where they are not. It is possible that, if material fails the privilege test, it will fall within the definition of special procedure material.

Legally Privileged Material

The common law concept of legal privilege attaches to communications passing between a lawyer and his client so far as those communications relate to advising the client on the conduct of legal transactions, including litigation. The privilege also extends to communications between a lawyer, or his client, and a third party. However, in this second situation, the dominant purpose of the communication must be to enable the lawyer to conduct litigation.[4] The privilege does not extend to communications where the intent of either lawyer or client is to facilitate crime or fraud. In the case of *R v Cox and Railton*[5] it was said that, in such circumstances, there was neither professional confidence, nor professional employment. This principle has been affirmed more recently in *R v Leeds Magistrates' Court ex parte Dumbleton*[6] where a warrant was issued under the Forgery and Counterfeiting Act 1981 to search for evidence concerning the alleged forgery of documents used to support a fictitious claim to assets by a debtor company. The legal adviser to that company contended that, because he was acting for the company, legal privilege applied to him. It was held that the material specified in the warrant was not legally privileged because the documents sought were forged or were made with the object of furthering a criminal purpose.[7] It was said that parliament 'cannot have intended to protect forged documents on the grounds that they were forged by a solicitor or supplied to him by a fraudulent client'.

It is clear, therefore, that, a criminal cannot gain protection from search by depositing forged documents with his solicitor, even where the solicitor is acting on his behalf. In *R v Justice of the Peace for Peterborough ex parte Hicks and ors*[8] it was held that, in such a situation, the solicitor 'can assert in respect of its seizure no greater authority than the client himself or herself possesses'. The 'criminal communications' exception to solicitor client privilege is also recognised in Canada. In *Descouteaux v Mierzwinski and Attorney-General of Quebec*[9] the issue arose in respect of a warrant issued to search the offices of the Legal Aid Bureau in Montreal for an allegedly fraudulent legal aid application. Lamer J. stated that those parts of the communications, containing false financial information, were 'criminal in themselves' and therefore did not benefit from the protection of privilege. The other information contained in the application was privileged. In all the cases considered above, either the solicitor or the client had a criminal or fraudulent purpose and the claim of privilege would have shielded such purpose. More controversial is the situation where neither lawyer, nor client, has such a purpose, but a third party involved in the transaction may do so. This issue has arisen in the context of attempts by the courts to construe section 10 of PACE and to reconcile it with the common law privilege discussed above.

Section 10 is thought to set out in statutory form the pre-existing common law. Subsection 10(1) states that the following fall within the definition of 'items subject to legal privilege'

(a) communications between a professional legal adviser and his client or any person representing his client made in connection with the giving of legal advice to the client;

(b) communications between a professional legal adviser and his client or any person representing his client or between such an adviser or his client or any such representative and any other person made in connection with or in contemplation of legal proceedings and for the purpose of such proceedings; and

(c) items enclosed with or referred to in such communications and made–

(i) in connection with the giving of legal advice; or

(ii) in connection with or in contemplation of legal proceedings and for the purpose of such proceedings, when they are in the possession of a person who is entitled to possession of them.

The single statutory exception is contained in subsection 10(2). This exception relates to 'items held with the intention of furthering a criminal purpose'.[10] It is the scope of this exception, rather than the positive description of legal privilege that has caused controversy. It was originally held that the 'intention' that furthered the criminal purpose had to be that of the person holding the items sought.[11] Thus a legal aid application was privileged when held by the Law Society notwithstanding that it may have contained false information.[12] However, in *Francis and Francis v Central Criminal Court*,[13] the concept of the criminal communications exception was significantly extended by the House of Lords. The police had obtained an order under the Drug Trafficking Offences Act 1986[14] to require a firm of solicitors to produce all files within their possession relating to one of their clients. The documents sought related to the purchase of business premises by the client. It was not alleged that either the solicitor or the client was purchasing the property with any criminal purpose in mind. However, the mortgage that was used to fund the purchase was allegedly to be paid from the proceeds of drug trafficking. In essence, it was contended that a member of the client's family was engaged in money laundering through the client, albeit that the client was unaware of the situation. A 'purposive' approach was taken toward the interpretation of subsection 10(2) and it was considered that the 'intent' referred to in the subsection was that of *any* person *including* the holder.

It was considered that such an interpretation would materially assist in achieving the purposes of the Act and 'would prevent the principle of legal privilege being used to protect the perpetrators of serious crimes'.[15] It was clear that their Lordships were of the view that a narrower construction of the subsection would mean that

> almost all applications to have access to documentation held in a solicitor's office are likely to be unsuccessful for it is only in rare cases that solicitors will be a party to the crime.[16]

It was also stated that there would be considerable practical difficulties in limiting intent to that of the holder and that the existence of the privilege would then depend on who possessed the document at the time of search. Newbold (1990) argues that the decision was made on the mistaken premise that there was no other way at common law that the material could be obtained. In fact, a solicitor could be requested to produce information. The power of search and seizure existed in a more extreme circumstance, that where the holder had a criminal purpose, for instance where the solicitor was dishonest. The judicial interpretation given to subsection 10(2) therefore reduces the scope of the privilege and authorises police search in situations that would not have been permitted at common law. The significance of this reduction is now greatly increased by the fact that the Police Act 1997, in dealing with electronic search, adopts the PACE concept of legal privilege. The power of search, whether for tangible or intangible information, now arises whenever one individual with criminal or fraudulent intent is connected, even indirectly, with an otherwise innocent transaction between lawyer and client. It is debatable whether such an interpretation will survive Article 8(2) as being an infringement of privacy that is necessary in a democratic society. A request to the legal adviser to produce the information sought would be a more proportional measure.[17]

Even if legal privilege is lost, it does not mean that the material sought is not protected by confidentiality. Thus in *R v Guildhall Magistrates' Court ex parte Primlaks Holdings Co. (Panama) Inc.*[18] it was stated that pre-existing documents that are not made in connection with the giving of legal advice might none the less be held in confidence under an express or implied undertaking and thus be special procedure material. This alternative finding cannot apply where the material sought is criminal in itself.[19] However, even where lawyers are themselves suspected of crime, any warrant issued must be sufficiently specific to prevent the search for and seizure of items that are genuinely within the scope of privilege. Thus in *R v Southampton Crown Court ex parte J and P*,[20] warrants were so widely drawn that they covered all the firm's accounting records without limit of time or specification of clients. The warrants were quashed as being defective. Only those transactions giving rise to files and records relating to allegations of theft from one particular client should have been specified in the application. It is probable that where an item that is subject to legal privilege is obtained by unfair or deceptive means, the evidence will be excluded under section 78 of PACE since, in civil proceedings, an injunction would have been available to preclude its usage at trial.[21]

Excluded and Special Procedure Material

Assuming that the material is *not* subject to legal privilege, then application may be made to search for evidence even though it is held in confidence. Subsection 9(1) and Schedule 1 of PACE allow a constable to obtain access to such material by applying to a circuit judge. By subsection 9(2), all pre-existing authority to search for such material is repealed.[22] The access conditions pertaining to this material are somewhat complex and depend upon the type of the material sought. An analysis of the two categories (excluded and special procedure material) therefore precedes any discussion of the criteria to be satisfied on application by a constable. Excluded material is defined in section 11 of PACE as consisting of the following

    (a)   personal records which a person has acquired or created in the course of any trade, business, profession or other occupation or for the purposes of any paid or unpaid office and which he holds in confidence;

    (b)   human tissue or tissue fluid which has been taken for the purpose of diagnosis or medical treatment and which a person holds in confidence;

    (c)   journalistic material which a person holds in confidence and which consists-
        (i)   of documents; or
        (ii) of records other than documents

By virtue of subsection 11(2), a person holds material, other than journalistic material, 'in confidence' if it is held under an express or implied undertaking to hold it in confidence, or there is a statutory restriction on disclosure or other obligation of secrecy. Journalistic material must satisfy the additional requirement that it has been so held continuously since its acquisition or creation for the purposes of journalism. The confidential material that falls within section 11 is therefore of three kinds, personal records, human tissue or tissue fluid and journalistic material.

The term 'personal records' is further defined by section 12 as meaning documentary or other records concerning an individual (whether living or dead) who can be identified from them. The records must relate to that individual's physical or mental health, to spiritual counselling or assistance given to him, or to other counselling or assistance for the purposes of his personal welfare. Counselling may be by a voluntary organisation or by a person who, by reason of his office, occupation or order of the court, has responsibility for the welfare of the individual. Thus medical and psychiatric records held by doctors and nurses are clearly 'excluded material'. In addition, the records held by practitioners not recognised by the British Medical Association such as alternative therapists would fall within section 12. The holder of the records need not have any recognised medical qualification. Spiritual counselling covers not only the records of priests, but also those of organisations such as the Samaritans and even those of 'new age' religions, since there is no statutory limitation in PACE on those recognised as capable of administering spiritual assistance. The final category of personal records is that relating to an individual's personal welfare. This category embraces the pastoral records held by educational institutions in respect of their students and records kept by the Marriage Guidance Council and other voluntary agencies dealing with familial issues. Those records kept at legal advice centres, which are not subject to legal privilege, are within the section as are those of court appointed officers such as probation officers.

Human tissue or tissue fluid is not excluded material unless it is taken for the purpose of diagnosis or medical treatment. Thus, if an individual has supplied blood in order to test whether he is HIV positive, the sample and the test results will be excluded material. It is a moot point whether the same would be true of a blood donation. The blood is being taken for the purpose of treatment, but not the treatment of the person from whom it has been taken. It is important to remember that section 11 deals with pre-existing bodily samples. If the police wish to obtain a sample of blood for the purpose of confirming or disproving that person's involvement in an offence, they may do so under section 62 of PACE with his consent.[23] Even if the suspect does *not* consent, a DNA analysis may be made from a non-intimate sample.[24] It is less likely with advances in DNA technology that the state will be precluded from making an appropriate forensic analysis because samples already in existence are classified as excluded material. Even where intimate samples are required to prove involvement in an offence, such material may be voluntarily surrendered by the holder and it is then admissible against an accused as evidence obtained through a consensual search. Thus in *R v Singleton*,[25] a dentist handed over to the police dental records and the dental impression of a tooth taken from one of his patients. The patient was a murder suspect and the evidence assisted in convicting him because the dental impression matched the bite marks made on the victim. Lord Justice Farquharson made the following comment

> Plainly the object of the Act is to protect disclosure of such confidential personal records. It seems equally clear that the person to be protected from disclosure is not the suspect in any particular case, but the person who has acquired or created the record. Accordingly, if that person voluntarily discloses the record he does not seek or require the protection given by the Act to that class of record.

Ultimately, therefore, the decision about whether the police can gain access to a pre-existing intimate sample taken from a suspect rests not with that suspect, but with the medical practitioner holding the excluded material. It is the misfortune of the person under investigation that he has previously sought medical assistance and that the practitioner concerned has made a moral judgement in favour of disclosure to the police.[26]

The final category of excluded material is journalistic material. In the House of Lords' case of *British Steel Corporation v Granada Television Ltd.*[27]

the concept of a journalistic immunity, prohibiting the right to compel disclosure of sources, was rejected as placing journalists 'in a favoured and unique position as compared with priest-confessors, doctors, bankers and other recipients of confidential information'. The Contempt of Court Act 1981 section 10 attempted to assuage the disquiet caused by this apparent rejection of confidentiality. It provides that no court may require a person to disclose the source of information contained in a publication for which he is responsible unless the court is satisfied that disclosure is necessary in the interests of justice, national scurity, or for the prevention of disorder or crime. The case of *Goodwin v UK* [28] has established that these three exceptions are not to be given a wide interpretation. Clearly the enforcement of private legal remedies will not always satisfy the necessity principle in respect of Article 10(2). Freedom of speech, in the context of civil disclosure, is a paramount concern.

In the context of criminal investigation, the necessity for disclosure may be justified by the need to prevent disorder or crime.[29] However, even where it is so justified, section 11 of PACE prevents police from seeking documents or records held in confidence (whether containing the names of sources or other information) other than under the procedure available for excluded material. The material must have been acquired or created for journalistic purposes and this would clearly include interviews and other investigative activity. It would also include photographs or tapes produced by a citizen and handed to the press to use for publication. 'Document' has the meaning attributed to it by the Civil Evidence Act 1968 section 10 and therefore includes a map, photograph, disk, tape or film.[30] Should the material fail to be excluded material, either because it is not held in confidence, or because there has been a break in the continuity of the initial confidential holding, it may none the less be special procedure material.

Special procedure material is of two kinds. The first is journalistic material, other than excluded material.[31] It is unlikely that, given the wide definition of 'document', material will fail to be contained in a document or record and for that reason be special procedure rather than excluded material. However, the material may not satisfy the confidentiality requirements discussed above. The second kind of special procedure material is that created in the course of a trade, business or profession and held in confidence.[32] This is a fairly wide ranging category and includes business records held by banks, building societies and accountants. Because the person acquiring or creating the record may be the holder of a paid or *unpaid* office,[33] it also includes records kept by clubs, local societies and voluntary groups.

Obtaining Access to Excluded and Special Procedure Material

Subsection 9(1) of PACE provides that a constable may obtain access to excluded or special procedure material by making an application to a circuit judge under Schedule 1. Code B2.4 states that such an application must be made by an officer of at least the rank of a superintendent. Under Schedule 1 paragraph 7, the application for a production order is made *inter partes*. This contrasts with the application for a warrant under paragraphs 12 and 14 which is made *ex parte* in accordance with usual warrant procedure. However, the fact that the application for a production order is *inter partes*, does not mean that the individual suspected of criminality is entitled to notice of the application. In *R v Crown Court at Leicester, ex parte Director of Public Prosecutions*,[34] it was stated that the only parties referred to in the Schedule 'are the police who make the application and the person or institution in whose custody the special procedure material is thought to be'. The Schedule made no reference to a 'suspected person or to a person who has been charged'. Although this interpretation can be defended on a literal construction of PACE, it is also clear that this was a policy decision. Lord Justice Watkins agreed with the argument put by the Crown Prosecution Service that the material sought might be destroyed or disposed of by persons or corporate bodies succumbing to 'threats' or to the 'influence' of suspected persons. This attitude displays a substantial lack of faith in the integrity of the holder of the material, but the judgment was approved in the later case of *Barclays Bank PLC v Taylor*.[35] The Court of Appeal confirmed that a bank had no contractual obligation to notify its client of the application nor to resist it, since this could hinder the investigation. Such protection as does exist for the client arises from the judicial control exercised by the circuit judge in assessing the application.[36] Thus, despite the confidential and possibly sensitive nature of the material sought, a suspect is in no better position to contest an application for a production order than he would be in were the application to be made for a warrant.

It is true that pre-PACE powers in respect of the investigation of financial crime were grossly inadequate. The police could not search bank accounts under the Bankers' Books Evidence Act 1879 unless criminal proceedings were already in existence (Graham and Walker, 1989). Further, that statute did not extend to correspondence between the bank and the client. However, Zuckerman (1990) points out that it is fallacious to rely on possible hindrance to the investigation as a reason not to notify 'the person most affected by the order'. He argues that the second procedure for obtaining confidential material, that of applying for a warrant under paragraph 12, deals with the problem of potential prejudice to pre-trial investigation. The consequence of the interpretation given by the courts to the notification procedure is that law enforcers have 'almost all the advantages of *ex parte* proceedings' without having to justify the need for secrecy.[37] Indeed, it could be said that they have *greater* advantages, since, under section 8 of PACE, a suspect is aware that a search under warrant has taken place. Zuckerman (1990:447) makes the trenchant observation that

> There is something disturbing and objectionable in the possibility that the state should be able to gain access to a person's confidential information without such person finding out, either before or after the event, that the confidentiality has been breached and that the state is in possession of his confidential information.

It is likely that the practice of notifying the holder of the information, rather than the suspect, will be challenged under Article 8 of the European Convention. However, in *Klass v Federal Republic of Germany*,[38] the European Court of Human Rights accepted that it was not feasible in all cases to notify a suspect affected by surveillance activities, even after the cessation of such surveillance. Article 8(2) would permit non-notification where it was necessary 'for the protection of the democratic society as a whole'. Whether the current procedure for obtaining a production order would satisfy the proportionality principle will depend upon the facts of the particular case. In cases of organised and ongoing financial crime, it may be that the interests of society override those of individuals. In other situations, such as a search for personal records held by a voluntary organisation, the invasion of privacy may well be insufficiently counterbalanced by the public interest in the detection of crime.

Before a judge can make a production order, he must be satisfied that one or other of the two sets of access conditions specified in the Schedule is made out. Excluded material may only be obtained if the second set of access conditions, contained in paragraph 3, is made out. These are that

(a) there are reasonable grounds for believing that there is material which consists of or includes excluded material or special procedure material on the premises specified in the application;

(b) but for section 9(2) above a search of the premises for that material could have been authorised by the issue of a warrant to a constable under an enactment other than under this Schedule; and

(c) the issue of such a warrant would have been appropriate.

The effect of this rather convoluted drafting is that no order can be made under PACE unless a warrant could have been issued under a statute in force prior to the implementation of PACE.[39] If such a statute, for instance the Theft Act 1968, provides a basis to search for documents or records no additional criteria need be satisfied beyond those in the pre-existing statute. However, if no relevant statute existed prior to PACE, then no order can be made to produce excluded material. Thus in *R v Central Criminal Court ex parte Brown*[40] the Divisional Court set aside an order for the production of the medical records of a person suspected of murder. The records could not have been obtained under any enactment prior to PACE. They were therefore immune from seizure under Schedule 1.

In respect of special procedure material there may be two options open to the police. The combined effect of subsection 9(2)(c) and Schedule 1 paragraph 3 is that, where the special procedure material is comprised in a document or record, it may be applied for under the second set of access conditions discussed above. Where this applies, it frees the police from the necessity of demonstrating that the detailed requirements in respect of the first set of access conditions apply and, in particular, does not limit applications to investigations involving serious arrestable offences. Where special procedure material is not in documentary or recorded form, or where, as is much more likely to be the case, no pre-PACE warrant could have been issued, the first set of access conditions must be complied with. The conditions are very similar to those requiring the grant of a warrant under section 8 of PACE, save that the judge must also be satisfied that it is in the public interest to grant the order.

Paragraph 2 of Schedule 1 states that these are fulfilled where

    (a) there are reasonable grounds for believing–
        (i)   that a serious arrestable offence has been committed;
        (ii) that there is material which consists of special procedure material or includes special procedure material and does not also include exclude material on premises specified in the application;
        (iii) that the material is likely to be of substantial value (whether by itself or together with other material) to the investigation in connection with which the application is made; and
        (iv) that the material is likely to be relevant evidence;
    (b) other methods of obtaining the material–
        (i)   have been tried without success; or
        (ii) have not been tried because it appeared that they were bound to fail; and
    (c) it is in the public interest, having regard–

    (i)   to the benefit likely to accrue to the investigation if the material is obtained; and

   (ii) to the circumstances under which the person in possession of the material holds it, that the material should be produced or that access to it should be given.

It is no bar to an application under paragraph 2 that the material includes other material that is not special procedure material. However, the judge must be satisfied that the conditions are met or the order will be quashed on review.

In *R v Maidstone Crown Court ex parte Waitt*,[41] the Divisional Court emphasised the necessity for careful consideration of applications made under the Schedule. It was said that the procedure was a 'serious inroad' into the liberty of the subject and that the 'responsibility for ensuring the procedure is not abused lies with circuit judges'. It was of 'cardinal importance' that judges should discharge this responsibility scrupulously. In the case of *R v Crown Court at Lewes ex parte Hill*,[42] Lord Justice Bingham again asserted the necessity for careful judicial scrutiny and said that a judge should not make an order under the Schedule unless he was satisfied that the application was 'substantially the last resort'. This requires a judge 'to be satisfied that other practical methods of obtaining disclosure have been substantially exhausted without success'. Paragraph 2(b) introduces the 'last resort' principle into *inter partes* procedure. If the material can be obtained consensually, or, presumably, under other more draconian powers,[43] it is not appropriate for an order to be made. However, once all the conditions *are* made out, there is no 'discretion' vested in the judge to refuse to make the order simply because he regards the procedure as a 'sledgehammer to crack a nut'.[44] This is despite the permissive language in paragraph 1 stating that the judge 'may' make an order.

Even if the police are investigating a serious arrestable offence, and even if the material otherwise satisfies paragraph 2, the judge must refuse an order if the material sought is subject to legal privilege. It has been pointed out above that the distinction between legally privileged material and special procedure material is nor necessarily clear-cut. This lack of clarity becomes more pronounced when it is the legal advisers who are themselves under investigation. In *R v Leeds Crown Court ex parte Switalski*,[45] it was stated that warrants (or orders) issued under Schedule 1 should contain an express provision excluding items of legal privilege. On the exceptional facts of the instant case, however, items that were *prima facie* privileged (such as proofs of evidence and letters to clients) were the very subject of the criminal investigation for fraud and conspiracy to pervert the course of justice. It was not possible to tell in advance which particular set of documents were held with 'the intention of furthering a criminal purpose' within subsection 10(2) of PACE. It remains a nice point which particular documents are subject to this privilege, even when wrongdoing is not alleged against the legal adviser. The instructions given by a client (criminal purpose apart) will be protected. However, notes relating to a firm's management of its practice, for instance appointment dates, charging schedules and fee earners' sheets, will be special procedure material and not privileged material. In *R v Manchester Crown Court ex parte Rogers*,[46] it was even thought proper for the police to seek production of an attendance note where such production was sought purely to establish the date and time of a suspect's visit to his lawyer. It was said that any part of the attendance note that contained legal advice could be 'covered up, blacked out or obliterated'.

The only judicial discretion that does exist is the implied one contained within the 'public interest' condition. It is clear that this implied discretion must not be used capriciously.[47] However, there is little reported case law where the assessment of the public interest criterion has been considered in any detail. An exception is the case of *R v Bristol Crown Court ex parte Bristol Press and Picture Agency Ltd.*[48] The Divisional Court here considered an application for the production of journalistic material. The police wanted to see photographs, taken by an employee of a news agency, of disturbances in the St. Paul's area of Bristol. The agency provided photographs to the local and national press. The police believed that the photographs were likely to assist them in identifying persons who had committed offences and in showing details of offences in respect of which no one had yet been charged. The press agency argued that to seek production of the photographs, without linking them to a specific crime or crimes, was too wide an application and could not be said to demonstrate any 'substantial value' to the investigations. This argument was rejected by the Court. Lord Justice Glidewell agreed with the view of the circuit judge that there was 'no reason to suppose that the photographers confined their attentions to groups of docile people or law-abiding citizens'. So far as the balancing exercise in relation to public interest was concerned, there was acknowledgement that there was a public interest in the press 'being free to report and to photograph' as much as they can of what is happening in the deprived areas of cities. It was also conceded that there was an additional public interest in the press being able to carry out that activity in safety. The news agency had expressed concern that journalists would not be able to go about their job in safety if production were ordered in this type of situation. None the less, taking account of all the relevant considerations, it was held that the circuit judge had been correct to make the order.[49]

Concern has been expressed by journalists over the use made by police of video tapes recorded for use in broadcasting.[50] Such tapes are relied upon to gather information concerning criminal activity, particularly in connection with public order offences. In Canada, similar concerns have arisen over police applications for search warrants in respect of videotapes taken by journalists during the commission of group offending. The Supreme Court has made it clear that in every case the justice of the peace must exercise discretion, taking into account the need to balance the competing interests of the state in investigating and prosecuting crime, the privacy interests of the individual and the effect on innocent third parties. There should be a 'demonstrated necessity' to obtain the information.[51]

In the United States, a related issue has arisen where journalists have claimed that a requirement to name their informants is an infringement of the First Amendment. In *Branzburg v Hayes*[52] the Supreme Court accepted that the press has the right not to publish all the information that it has obtained, but considered that the right to withhold relevant information from a grand jury was another matter. The private restraint on the flow of information did not override all other public interests. This was so even if an undetermined number of informants might refuse to talk to the press if they felt that they might later be identified in an official investigation. The Court could not

> seriously entertain the notion that the First Amendment protects a newsman's agreement to conceal the criminal conduct of his source, or the evidence thereof, on the theory that it is better to write about crime than to do something about it.

It is true that *Branzburg* involved issues of confidentiality, which clearly did not occur in the *Bristol Press Agency* case. It is also true that confidential journalistic material is protected to a greater degree in England and Wales since it is likely to be excluded material. However, so far as special procedure material is concerned, the general principle seems clear. Public interest in the suppression of crime trumps the right of journalists to withhold their information on the basis that disclosure might be detrimental to their safety or to the trust of their informants.

Of course a circuit judge can only make a properly balanced decision whether or not to grant an application for a production order if sufficient information has been presented to the court. In *R v Acton Crown Court ex parte Layton*[53] it was emphasised that the police must be open handed and set out all the material in their hands, whether it assisted in the application under Schedule 1 or militated against it. The requirement of sufficiency of information is no different from that arising in relation to warrants issued by the magistracy, but at least, in the case of a production order, the hearing is on notice.[54] Even though the hearing does not require 'absolute compliance' with the strict rules of evidence, the applicant must not make 'statements which have no substance' and which are 'to the prejudice of the party who is the object of the order sought'.[55] Further, information that is served on a court must also be served on the party against whom the order is sought, though not necessarily in advance of the hearing.

In those situations where even the requirement of giving notice would hinder the investigation, a warrant may be applied for in respect of excluded or special procedure material. It must be appreciated that the warrant conditions are *in addition* to the last resort principle contained in paragraph 2 of the Schedule. Thus it cannot be argued, in respect of a warrant applied for under the first set of access conditions, that consensual or co-operative means to obtain the material have been tried without success or are bound to fail.[56] In those circumstances, a production order should be applied for. This in itself should preserve the evidence sought since, under paragraph 11, service of notice of an application prevents concealment, destruction or disposal of the material without police or judicial permission. If a production order has been obtained under the second set of access conditions, but not complied with, a warrant may be issued under paragraph 12(b).[57] Paragraph 14 lists certain further conditions that may entitle the police to a warrant as opposed to a production order. The first is the impracticability of communicating with a person entitled to grant access to the premises or to the material. There is no statutory definition of what is 'practicable'. Presumably something more than a temporary absence from the premises is required in respect of the person from whom permission to access the material is sought. Equally, something more than initial lack of response to a request to effect a consensual search is required. Such failure to respond could be dealt with by way of an application for a production order. If there is a subsequent deliberate failure to respond to such application, this would, arguably, justify the issuance of a warrant. The second condition in paragraph 14 is that service of the notice of an application may 'seriously prejudice the investigation'.[58] Here the police should satisfy a circuit judge that evidence might be lost or destroyed if an *inter partes* procedure is used. In *R v Southampton Crown Court ex parte J and P,*[59] the use of *ex parte* procedure against a firm of solicitors (albeit a firm under investigation) was said to be 'a cause for concern'. The police had already obtained a good deal of evidence, the firm's accounts had already been seen by the Law Society and the police already had copies of some ledger sheets. The privacy of the firm's clients, as well as that of the solicitors, was infringed by the grant of the warrant. It appears that Code B2.7 of PACE was not properly complied with. This requires that the police indicate to the circuit judge *why* it is believed that the service of notice of an application for a production order may seriously prejudice the investigation. Finally, the third condition under paragraph 14 is that material is held under a statutory obligation of secrecy or restriction on disclosure and that it is likely to be disclosed if a warrant is not issued. Obviously, this last situation is likely to arise in the case of offences under the Official Secrets Act 1989. This is one of the statutes mentioned below.

Statutes Providing Analogous Search Powers

Certain post PACE statutes have echoed the PACE search provisions. Searches under the authority of these statutes are governed by similar, if not identical, criteria to those taking place under section 8 or Schedule 1 of PACE. The first of these descendant provisions is to be found in the Prevention of Terrorism (Temporary Provisions) Act 1989. Section 17 of that Act gives power to obtain 'information for the purposes of terrorist investigation'. Terrorist investigation is then further defined to include investigations into the commission, preparation or instigation of acts of terrorism, or into acts done 'in furtherance of' or 'in connection with' acts of terrorism. Acts of terrorism are those connected with the affairs of Northern Ireland, or acts of international terrorism, in other words, those that are not connected solely with the affairs of the United Kingdom.[60] Certain other offences may also be investigated under section 17. These include membership of or contribution to proscribed organisations and contributing finance towards acts of terrorism.[61] Schedule 7 governs the use of power under section 17. The definitions of legal privilege, special procedure material and excluded material have the same meaning as in PACE.[62] Magisterial warrants may be obtained for material that is not within these categories.[63] In virtually all respects, the conditions for the issuance of magisterial warrants replicate those under section 8 of PACE. However, a warrant is applied for on the basis that a terrorist investigation is being carried out, not on the basis that a serious arrestable offence has been committed.

Where material does consist of excluded or special procedure material, an application can be made to a judge, *ex parte* under Schedule 7, for a production order. However, the criteria for making the order differ somewhat from those under PACE. In the first place, the material (as with magisterial warrants under this Act) must be sought for the 'purposes of a terrorist investigation'. Secondly, any order made applies not only to persons having possession of material, but also to those having 'custody or power' and to government departments as well as to individuals.[64] Thirdly, the order may apply to material which is not yet in existence or in the possession of the relevant person, but which is expected to become so within 28 days of the order.[65] Most significantly, orders in 'urgent cases' may be made by a police officer of at least the rank of superintendent if that officer has reasonable grounds for believing that the case is one of great emergency and that, in the interests of state, immediate action is necessary.[66] An authorisation given in these circumstances includes the right to search for all material other then legally privileged material. It therefore entitles the police to make a warrantless, non consensual search for material, including excluded and special procedure material, should the interests of state so require. Whether this power can be justified within Article 8(2) is debatable, particularly as the terms 'emergency' and 'interests of state' are not further defined. It is therefore unlikely to be sufficiently certain.[67] Whilst it is true that the POT(TP) Act 1989 deals with planned offending as much as with offences that have already been committed, the proportionality principle is likely to be applied fairly strictly to any statutory provision that does away with the need for neutral and detached scrutiny of a search power. It seems even more likely that there will be challenge following the incorporation of Article 8. There is, additionally, power under paragraph 5 of Schedule 7 to issue a warrant to search for excluded and special procedure material. One basis for the grant of a warrant is that the investigation would be 'seriously prejudiced' unless a constable can 'secure immediate access to the material'. Comparison can be made with the power of the Secretary of State who may make an order under paragraph 8 in relation to investigation into financial assistance towards terrorism. It is of importance that the situations and conditions for the issuance of this order are statutorily circumscribed and that the relevant offences are specified.[68] Otherwise, the powers are unlikely to be 'in accordance with the law' under Article 8(2).

The question has arisen, in this extremely sensitive area of police operations, just how much information has to be given to a circuit judge. Since the application is *ex parte*, he is in the same guardianship position as if he were issuing a warrant. Whilst there is a right to apply to discharge or vary an order once made,[69] it is obviously far harder to set aside a *fait accompli* than to challenge the order in the first place and even more difficult if there is no access to the information upon which the order was obtained. In *R v Crown Court at Middlesex Guildhall ex parte Salinger and anor.*[70] an order was granted in respect of journalistic material. The journalist in question had interviewed those suspected of the Lockerbie bombing in Libya and had recorded the interviews on videotape. An application to discharge the order was refused and the matter came before the Divisional Court. Two questions arose in this case. The first was the sufficiency of information given to the judge and the second the sufficiency of information given to the subject of the order. The Divisional Court considered that there might be occasions, in terrorist investigations, 'when the nature and identity of the source of the information and perhaps also the information itself' is such that it would not be appropriate to disclose it 'even to the judge'. The judge should be given a written statement of the material evidence upon which the constable wishes to rely in support of the application. This statement should not normally disclose the identity and source of the information if, as is likely to be the case, it is sensitive. However, it should normally contain the nature of the information, unless this too 'is secret and should not be disclosed'. It was said that even if the identity and source of the information were disclosed to the judge, it would rarely be appropriate or necessary to disclose it to the recipient of the order.[71] The recipient should be given as much information as he 'properly can' as to the grounds upon which the application is made.

Ex parte Salinger purports to lay down guidelines on the information flow under the POT(TP) Act, but succeeds only in establishing general principle. This is that the judge holds the crucial role of determining whether an order should be made and, if it should, what information should be served with the order itself. The judge is also responsible for controlling the questions put on any discharge application. However, although a controlling role resides in the judge, it is to be noted that the judge himself is not necessarily in receipt of all the relevant information. The systemic dependence of the judiciary upon information supplied by investigators applies with even more force in this situation and challenges the whole notion of neutral and detached supervision.

Certain statutes utilise PACE by incorporating it directly rather than by borrowing from it. The Official Secrets Act 1989 creates criminal liability in respect of the disclosure, without lawful authority, of matters relating to security, intelligence, defence or international relations. It applies principally to those who are working, or who have worked, for the government and are therefore bound by confidentiality agreements.[72] The pre-existing power to issue search warrants under section 9 of the Official Secrets Act 1911 applies to offences under the 1989 Act. Section 11 of the 1989 Act incorporates section

9(2) and Schedule 1 paragraph 3(b) of PACE. The combined effect of all of this is to give power to search for excluded or special procedure material under the second set of access conditions in Schedule 1.

Similarly, the Criminal Justice (International Co-operation) Act 1990 does not borrow from PACE. It directly applies it. The Act gives power to obtain evidence in other jurisdictions for use in the United Kingdom and also to obtain evidence in the United Kingdom for use overseas. The statute deals with the taking of statements and the gathering of documents under 'letters of request'. In addition, under section 7(1), it is stated that PACE powers of search and seizure 'shall have effect' in relation to the investigation of offences committed outside the United Kingdom. They must be serious arrestable offences as defined within domestic criminal law. Section 8 and Schedule 1 of PACE apply to these investigations. The Secretary of State must direct that an application for a warrant or order be made.[73] Such a direction may be made in response to a request from another jurisdiction and any evidence seized shall be furnished to the Secretary of State for onward transmission overseas. If the offence committed outside the United Kingdom would only be an 'arrestable offence' under PACE,[74] then a warrant may be obtained from a magistrate under section 7(2) of the 1990 Act. The magistrate must be satisfied that criminal proceedings have been instituted against an individual outside the United Kingdom, or that a person has been arrested in the course of a criminal investigation taking place abroad. The justice must also be satisfied that that there are reasonable grounds for suspecting that there is on premises, occupied or controlled by that person, evidence relating to the offence (other then items of legal privilege).[75] Although the main purpose of this statute was to deal with the growth of international crime, it can equally apply to medium level offending where there is some domiciliary or personal nexus between the offender and the United Kingdom.[76]

Finally, there is statutory provision that has echoes of PACE, but which contains fewer safeguards for the citizen. There are statutes that deal with investigations necessary to trace the proceeds of crime in order to give effect to confiscation orders. This legislation does not govern an investigation into *offending*, because criminal activity, upon which the confiscation order depends, has already been proved to the court. Sections 93H to 93J of the Criminal Justice Act 1988, as amended by the Proceeds of Crime Act 1995, provide that a person may apply to a circuit judge for a warrant, or for an order, in respect of material disclosing the extent or whereabouts of proceeds of crime. This material must be of substantial value to such an investigation or to an investigation into whether a person has 'benefited from any criminal conduct'.

In *R v Crown Court ex parte Bowles*[77] Simon Brown L.J. observed, at the Divisional Court hearing of the case, that there were four differences in respect of applications under this Act from those made under PACE. Firstly, applications under the Criminal Justice Act 1988 can be made *ex parte*. Secondly, there is no requirement under that Act that applications relate to a 'serious arrestable offence'. A third distinction is that there is a different threshold test for probable cause. PACE requires that there be 'reasonable grounds for believing' that an offence has been committed. The Criminal Justice Act 1988 only requires that there are 'reasonable grounds for suspecting' that a person has benefited from any criminal conduct. The final difference is that PACE applications are limited by the 'last resort' principle in paragraph 2(b) of Schedule 1, but this principle does not apply to the Criminal Justice Act 1988.

It therefore might seem an attractive option to the police to rely on the Criminal Justice Act rather then upon PACE on the basis that, on its literal wording, an investigation into 'whether any person has benefited from criminal conduct'[78] might include an investigation into suspected, but as yet unproven, financial crime. However, in *ex parte Bowles*, the House of Lords, affirming the view of the Divisional Court, held that sections 93H to 93J cannot be relied upon in an investigation as to whether a person has committed a crime which has benefited him. The wording of section 93H is to be read in the context of that part of the statute which is headed 'Confiscation Of The Proceeds Of An Offence'. Further, the wording is tightly bound in with the confiscation order provisions of the Act as a whole. Thus, the House held that the police could not rely on section 93H in order to investigate a criminal offence involving the obtaining of money or other property. However, should the police find evidence of crime as an 'incidental consequence' of a genuine search for the proceeds of crime, that evidence would be admissible in subsequent criminal proceedings.[79] The Criminal Justice Act 1988 does not deal with the search for and confiscation of the proceeds of drug trafficking. The Drug Trafficking Act 1994 sections 55-57 deals with such investigation and echoes Schedule 1 of PACE, although there are some differences which largely mirror those existing between PACE and the Criminal Justice Act 1988.[80] Thus the application is *ex parte*.[81] The applicant need show only reasonable suspicion that a person is involved in drug trafficking and that the material is likely to be of substantial value to the investigation.[82] Special procedure material is given no separate status, although excluded and legally privileged material cannot be applied for.[83] Since the decision in *ex parte Bowles*, it is clear that this statute cannot be used to investigate an offence of importation of drugs. It can only be relied upon to trace the proceeds of proven offending.

Bodily Samples and Compelled Search and Seizure

In England and Wales, bodily samples and fingerprints are regarded as identification evidence. Indeed, Code D of PACE, the Code dealing with identification of suspects, includes 'identification by fingerprints'[84] and 'identification by body samples and impressions'[85] in its provisions. It is, of course, true that, by confirming or disproving a suspect's involvement in an offence, this scientific evidence may identify the suspect as an offender, but it is not qualitatively the same as witness identification evidence. It is only available to investigators through the use of procedures that involve an intrusion into bodily autonomy to a greater or lesser degree. The intrusion may be slight, as in the case of taking fingerprints, or it may be more serious in that it would, if done in other circumstances and without consent, amount to an assault. This is true of the taking of blood samples or the taking of a swab from a body orifice. The fact that such procedures involve an intrusion upon the person is recognised in the United States and Canada where they are evaluated in the context of whether or not there has been an unreasonable search and seizure.[86] Thus the compulsory taking of samples is only legitimate if either the Fourth Amendment or section 8 of the Canadian Charter has not been violated by the process.

Apart from the right to privacy, a second human rights issue that arises is that of the privilege against self-incrimination. The classic definition of this privilege is considered to be that given by Lord Justice Goddard in *Blunt v Park Lane Hotel Ltd.*[87] His Lordship stated that no one was bound to answer a question if that answer would 'have a tendency to expose the deponent to any criminal charge, penalty of forfeiture'. He also considered that this privilege applied to the discovery of documents and thus to the compelled production of evidence in written form.[88] In England and Wales, prior to PACE, it was regarded as also applying to the taking of samples through trickery or even through reliance upon a misunderstanding of the suspect, absent illegality.[89] Indeed, it was more likely that such evidence would be excluded for impropriety on the part of investigators than other kinds of real evidence because it was regarded as being in virtually the same category as a confession or admission in that it was evidence obtained from the accused in person after the offence.[90] However, it will be seen that PACE has statutorily overridden the privilege to a substantial degree. The link between searching an individual and depriving that individual of his right not to incriminate himself is an intriguing one and was, at one time, expressly recognised by the Supreme Court of the United States. In *Boyd v US*,[91] a statute compelling the production of incriminating documentation was regarded as being in breach of the Fifth Amendment. The Amendment provides that no person shall be compelled to be a witness against himself in a criminal case. This breach was in addition to any violation of the Fourth Amendment. Justice Bradley commented that the 'Fourth and Fifth Amendments run almost into each other' in the protection of the right to personal liberty and property.[92] It has been pointed out that the broad construction given to the Fifth Amendment in *Boyd*, would lead to an extension of the privilege against self-incrimination to *any* tangible evidence (O'Brien, 1979:119). However, the courts in the United States have gradually, on a case by case basis, retreated from this position and have now clearly rejected the application of the privilege to non testimonial evidence and, hence, to bodily samples.[93] On the other hand, in Canada, there is still the possibility of arguing that the evidence would not have come into existence but for the improper conduct of the investigators.[94] The right, under section 7 of the Charter, not to be deprived of life, liberty or security of person, except in accordance with the principles of fundamental justice, runs in tandem with the protection from unreasonable search.

There are strong policy reasons why governments should want the compulsory taking of fingerprints and samples to have constitutional validity. The evidence that results therefrom is extremely probative. Indeed, continuing scientific advances mean that such evidence is one of the most powerful weapons in the fight against crime. Whilst there may be some controversy about the statistical niceties of 'random occurrence ratios' in DNA analysis[95] and about the necessary number of similar ridge characteristics per digit in fingerprinting,[96] the reliability of this kind of evidence far exceeds that of witness testimony or identification evidence. It is unlikely that courts are going to strike down statutory provisions, permitting the compulsory obtaining and subsequent use of this evidence, as being a violation of an individual's right to privacy or right not to incriminate himself.

Statutory Provisions Authorising the Taking of Samples

PACE section 61 gives the police the right to take fingerprints without consent. Firstly, authorisation may be given by an officer of the rank of superintendent or above if a person has been detained on suspicion of having committed a 'recordable offence'.[97] The authorisation must be based upon reasonable grounds for suspicion as to the involvement of that person in a criminal offence and reasonable grounds for belief that the fingerprints will tend to confirm or disprove his involvement. Secondly, fingerprints may be taken, in any event, where a person has been charged with a recordable offence, but has not previously had his fingerprints taken.[98] Fingerprints may also be taken when a person has been convicted of a recordable offence.[99] Reasonable force may be used to effect the procedure, but the suspect must be told the reason for their being taken and also told that the prints may be used in a 'speculative search'.[100] A speculative search involves checking the prints against those already held on the police database. If a person is not charged, or if he is acquitted after trial, his fingerprints will be destroyed.[101] If a person is convicted, his fingerprints remain on the database and form part of the increasing body of police information that is held not as evidence of current offending, but because it may be of potential utility in the solution of undetected or future criminality.[102]

In Canada, the compulsory taking of fingerprints is not in violation of the Charter if that person is arrested on reasonable and probable grounds. In *R v Beare, R v Higgins*,[103] La Forest J. stated

> It seems to me that a person who is arrested on reasonable and probable grounds that he has committed a serious crime, or a person against whom a case for issuing a summons or warrant, or confirming an appearance notice has been made out, must expect a significant loss of personal privacy. He must expect that incidental to his being taken into custody he will be subjected to observation, to physical measurement and the like. Fingerprinting is of that nature. While some may find it distasteful, it is insubstantial, of very short duration and leaves no lasting impression. There is no penetration of the body and no substance is removed from it.

In consequence, it was held that statutory provision for fingerprinting as an incident of being taken into custody did not violate the principles of fundamental justice. However, where the arrest that precedes the compulsory fingerprinting is itself unlawful, the subsequent fingerprinting may be a violation of the Charter. In *R v Feeney*,[104] the Supreme Court held that a variety of Charter breaches concerning the search of the accused's premises prior to his arrest, rendered the arrest itself unlawful. This being the case, the fingerprinting that then took place was 'a violation of section 8 of the Charter, involving as it did a search and seizure related to the appellant's body'. In the United States, a similar approach has been taken toward fingerprint evidence obtained in the course of an illegal detention. In *Davis v Mississippi*,[105] fingerprints were originally taken from a rape suspect in the course of a wide ranging police 'sweep' during which at least 24 suspects were rounded up and later released. A second set was taken following the subsequent arrest of the petitioner which, the State conceded, was supported neither by warrant nor by probable cause. This constituted a violation of the Fourth Amendment, notwithstanding the reliable nature of fingerprint evidence and the fact that the process of taking prints constituted 'a much less serious intrusion upon personal security than other types of police searches and detentions'. Surprisingly perhaps, this decision was followed in the later case of *Hayes v Florida*.[106] It was however, stated that it was the forcible removal into custody for the purpose of fingerprinting that breached the Fourth and Fourteenth Amendments. The Court left open the possibility that a 'brief detention in the field for the purpose of fingerprinting where there is only reasonable suspicion' might be permissible.

In England and Wales, it was held in the case of *R v Nathaniel*,[107] that sample evidence should have been excluded under section 78 of PACE where it had been retained wrongly in respect of a previously acquitted defendant. This is a rare instance of judicial exclusion of highly probative evidence of serious crime. The decision should apply to fingerprints as well as to bodily samples, but it is so atypical of the exercise of judicial discretion by the courts that a way to confine it to its facts will surely be sought. It is unlikely that, in the future, evidence will be suppressed because a prior arrest was without reasonable grounds, or even because the sample is taken, at that stage, without reasonable grounds for suspicion concerning the person's involvement in the offence. The probity of the evidence, particularly if the crime is a heinous one, may impel a court to condone the breach of PACE (Sharpe, 1998a).

Bodily samples are classified by PACE as either 'intimate' or 'non-intimate samples'. The significance of this classification might be thought to turn on the degree of intrusion into personal autonomy arising from the taking of each category of sample. To some extent this is the case. Thus, intimate samples are defined in section 65 of PACE[108] as being blood, semen or any other tissue fluid, urine, pubic hair, a dental impression and a swab taken from a body orifice other than the mouth. It will be seen that whilst the taking of blood or of a dental impression may involve an intrusive search, the taking of urine will not do so. However, crucially, the sample of urine cannot be supplied without consent. In chapter 2, it was pointed out that the correlation between intimate searches and intimate samples is not an exact one. Section 65 defines an intimate search as one consisting of an examination of body orifices other then the mouth. Whilst some intimate samples may thus be the product of an intimate search, there are many intimate samples that are not so obtained and also, conversely, evidence that is not even a bodily sample (such as packets of prohibited drugs) may be found as the result of an intimate search. The more crucial distinction between intimate and non-intimate samples is the level of compulsion that may be used in their obtainment.

Intimate samples may only be taken with the consent of the suspect.[109] This requirement is in addition to that of authorisation by an officer of the rank of superintendent or above. The authorisation may be given, as in the case of fingerprints, if there are reasonable grounds for suspecting the involvement of the person in a recordable offence and that the sample will tend to confirm or disprove his involvement. The suspect's consent must be given in writing.[110] An intimate sample, other than a sample of urine, must be taken by a registered medical practitioner, or where appropriate, a dentist. The same provisions apply to speculative searches and to the creation of a police database of information collected from the samples of convicted persons.[111] This means that, given the wide coverage of recordable offences, virtually all medium level to serious offending can justify the taking of an intimate sample and, if conviction results, the information derived therefrom will be retained. The refusal of the suspect to allow such a sample to be taken cannot be directly overridden, but there is a sanction for refusal 'without good cause'.[112] Subsection 62(10) provides that, in determining 'whether that person is guilty of the offence charged', a court or jury may

> draw such inferences from the refusal as appear proper; and the refusal may, on the basis of such inferences, be treated as, or as capable of amounting to, corroboration of any evidence against the person in relation to which the refusal is material.

This provision predated the parallel drafting of sections 34-38 of the Criminal Justice and Public Order Act 1994. These sections allow for the drawing of 'proper' inferences in respect of silence in the face of questioning under caution, or where there is a refusal by a defendant to testify on his behalf. There has been challenge to the permissibility of drawing such inferences. However, in *Murray v United Kingdom*,[113] the European Court of Human Rights held that there was no violation of Article 6 so long as the conviction was not based solely or mainly on the accused's silence or refusal. The exact scope of this decision may still be subject to debate,[114] but it seems highly unlikely that section 62 will be struck down under Article 6 of the Convention on the basis that the defendant has not received a fair trial as a consequence of such inferences being drawn.[115]

Non-intimate samples are listed in section 65 of PACE. It is notable that the list has been extended by CRIMPO 1994 section 58. Thus a wider range of searches now fall within the non-intimate category. Several non-intimate samples involve virtually no bodily intrusion. Thus footprints, or other bodily impressions, apart from finger or palm prints, are within this category. A sample of nail, or one taken from under a nail, and samples of body hair, other then pubic hair, are also classified as non-intimate. In these cases there is a bodily intrusion, but not a particularly severe one. It can, of course, be painful to have body hair or head hair plucked. In *R v Cooke*,[116] the appellant tried to argue that if hair included the sheath, it became an intimate sample. The Court of Appeal rejected this argument and stated that even if the living 'root' of the hair is removed it is still a non-intimate sample. PACE Code D, in Notes for Guidance paragraph 5C, provides that the suspect should be given 'a reasonable choice' as to the part of the body from which he wishes the hair sample to be taken. This choice only applies to samples taken for DNA analysis rather than those taken in order to make a visual match. The Code and section 63A(2) of PACE state that where hairs are plucked, they should be plucked individually and that no more should be taken than is reasonably necessary for a sufficient sample. The other types of non-intimate samples are saliva and a swab taken from a person's mouth. The original intention of including mouth swabs in the list of non-intimate samples may have been to extend the possibility of DNA testing to those situations where the suspect refused to provide a sample. However, with scientific advances, it is now possible to obtain DNA from human hair. The consequence of this reclassification and of scientific progress is that samples for DNA analysis may be taken by compulsion.

Compulsion is an option where a suspect does not consent in writing to the search, he is being held in police custody and an officer of the rank of superintendent or above gives authorisation. The authorisation may be given for exactly the same reasons as those justifying compulsory fingerprinting. Reasonable force may be used to effect the search.[117] This power of compulsion gives the police the right to effect warrantless bodily searches. The power is not limited to the immediacy of a pre-charge investigation. Section 63A of PACE[118] authorises the police to require a person to return to a police station to have such a sample taken if he has been charged with a recordable offence, but has not yet had a sample taken, or if he has been convicted of such offence.[119] Failure to attend will result in a warrant being issued. The objective of such a power is not the investigation of the instant offence, but the storage of information by the police. The shift in police methodology, from the seeking of evidence to the seeking of information, is exemplified in these provisions. In the final chapter the impact of this part of PACE on the obtaining and retention of data by law enforcers is considered in more detail.

Human Rights, Due Process and Non Consensual Samples

The case of *Saunders v UK*[120] did not specifically deal with bodily samples; it dealt with the compelled questioning of the applicant by the Serious Fraud Office. However, in the course of the judgment, the European Court delivered an assessment of the nature of the privilege against self-incrimination and its lack of applicability to bodily samples taken for the purposes of criminal investigation. The applicant had been questioned under section 2 of the Criminal Justice Act 1987.[121] Subsection 2(2) entitles the Director of the SFO to require a person 'whose affairs are to be investigated' to 'answer questions or otherwise furnish information with respect to any matter relevant to the investigation'. The section also enables the Director to call for the production of documents and, in default of production, a warrant may be applied for. Subsection 2(3) imposes a criminal penalty for failure 'without reasonable excuse' to comply with the requirements of section 2. Although any information obtained through the use of this procedure cannot be led in evidence against the provider, it could be used by way of impeachment should this person give any inconsistent evidence in subsequent criminal proceedings.[122] Mr. Saunders claimed that this use of compelled evidence violated his right to a fair trial under Article 6(1). The European Court upheld this claim. In doing so, however, a limitation was set upon the privilege against self-incrimination. It was said to be primarily concerned

> with respecting the will of an accused person to remain silent. As commonly understood in the legal systems of the Contracting Parties to the Convention and elsewhere, it does not extend to the use in criminal proceedings of material which may be obtained from the accused through the use of compulsory powers but which has an existence independent of the will of the suspect such as, *inter alia*, documents acquired pursuant to a warrant, breath, blood and urine samples and bodily tissue for the purpose of DNA testing.

The evidence of the applicant in the instant case was testimonial. Whilst the preparatory investigation was not, of itself, an infringement of the privilege, the use made of the relevant statements at the applicant's criminal trial did violate Article 6. However, no such argument could be put forward in respect of sample evidence because of its non-testimonial character.

This decision validates the PACE provisions so far as they permit compelled incrimination. It also validates earlier statutory provisions now contained in the Road Traffic Act 1988. Section 6 of that Act enables a constable in uniform to require a specimen of breath for a breath test. The constable must have reasonable cause to suspect that the driver has excess alcohol in his body, or that he has committed a traffic offence, or been involved in an accident. It is an offence to fail to produce a specimen 'without reasonable excuse'. By section 7 of the same Act, a constable investigating offences of driving whilst unfit through drink or drugs, or driving with excess alcohol, may require the suspect to provide two specimens of breath or a specimen of blood or urine for a laboratory test. The qualitative difference between this statute and PACE is that the sample is directly relevant to whether an offence has been committed *at all*, not as to whether it is the suspect who has committed it. No issue has as yet been taken either under the RTA 1988 or under PACE as to whether the sample provisions could constitute statutory authorisation for unreasonable searches or seizures. In Canada, however, both road traffic samples and samples taken in the course of investigation into other crimes have been subject to challenges on this basis.

It was in the context of road traffic legislation that the debate about compulsory search and seizure of bodily samples and the compatibility of such a practice with section 8 of the Charter first arose. In *R v Dyment*,[123] a blood sample from a free-flowing wound was taken by a physician whilst the accused, who had been involved in a road accident, was suffering from concussion. The intention of the doctor was to use the sample for medical diagnosis. He later handed it over to a police officer and, when analysed, the sample showed that excess alcohol had been consumed by the accused.[124] The Supreme Court of Canada accepted that there had been a violation of section 8 of the Charter in that an unlawful search and seizure had taken place. There was no urgency nor any other reason justifying such a seizure without a warrant, even assuming that the police officer could show reasonable cause. La Forest J. acknowledged that claims to privacy must be 'balanced against societal needs, and in particular law enforcement'. However, the charter guaranteed the privacy of the individual against unjustified state intrusion and this guarantee went far beyond the protection of property and extended to 'a violation of the sanctity of a person's body'. Indeed, he stated that

> If anything, when the search and seizure relates to the integrity of the body rather than the home, for example, the standard [of probable cause] is even higher than usual.[125]

Thus *R v Dyment* confirmed that the taking of a body sample was a search and was covered by the requirements of probable cause.[126]

More recently, in *R v Bernshaw*,[127] the Supreme Court restored a conviction for driving with excess alcohol that was based on a roadside screening test administered pursuant to section 254(2) of the Criminal Code. The argument of the accused that the officer had failed to exclude the possibility of the presence of alcohol in the mouth, and thus that the search was unlawful, was rejected. Notwithstanding the decision on the facts before the Court, the possibility of excluding such evidence for a Charter breach was acknowledged.[128] Thus even a breath test may come within the scope of section 8. The degree of intrusion into bodily autonomy is, of course, far greater when a blood sample is taken than when a breathalyser test is administered. In *Knox v The Queen*,[129] the more intrusive nature of a blood sample was recognised. In this case, on the facts, the taking of a blood sample was thought not to bring the administration of justice into disrepute. Yet, the failure of the police officer to assure the accused that the procedure would be undertaken by a registered medical practitioner, who was satisfied that taking the sample would not endanger the health or life of the suspect, did amount to a breach of sections 7 and 8.

The view that the taking of bodily samples must comply with the constitutional prohibition on unreasonable searches and seizures extends to samples taken for DNA analysis. Section 487 of the Criminal Code has now extended warrant provisions to enable the non-consensual taking of samples for such analysis and the taking of bodily impressions. Prior to these DNA warrant provisions, the case of *Stillman v The Queen*[130] held that, at common law, conscripted evidence (hair samples, teeth impressions and a bucal swab) should be excluded from the prosecution case. Significantly, the rationale for the exclusion of this evidence did not depend solely on the fact that a warrantless search had been undertaken. This was so even though the search was 'so unreasonable and constituted such a serious violation of section 8 that to admit the evidence obtained from the search would bring the administration of justice into disrepute'.[131] The decision was also based on the fact that there had been a violation of section 7 in that the principle against self-incrimination had been overridden. It was said that

> the unauthorised use of a person's body or bodily substances is just as great an invasion of the essence of the person as is compelled "testimony" that could render the trial unfair as a compelled statement.[132]

However, if the compelled search falls within sections 487.05 to 487.09 of the Criminal Code, there is no violation of Charter rights.[133]

These sections permit the court to issue a DNA warrant where satisfied that

104 Search and Surveillance

(1)   there are reasonable grounds to believe that
    (a)   a designated offence has been committed;[134]
    (b)   a bodily substance has been found at the crime scene;
    (c)   a person was a party to the offence (the "suspect");
    (d)   forensic DNA analysis of a bodily substance from the suspect will provide evidence about whether the crime scene sample was from the suspect. And
(2)   where satisfied that it is the best interests of the administration of justice to issue the warrant.

In *Re F (S) and the Attorney General for Canada et al*[135] it was decided that the minimisation requirements inherent in the sections, the necessity for probable cause to be shown and the requirement for judicial authorisation, which was to be given only in the interests of justice, together ensured that the legislation did not offend against the Charter.

Self-incrimination is not an issue in the United States since the evidence obtained from a bodily sample fails the 'testimonial communications' requirement laid down in *Doe v US*.[136] None the less, the Fourth Amendment *does* apply to the taking of bodily samples or to intimate searches.[137] The intrusiveness of the procedure is relevant when considering whether an unreasonable search has taken place. In *Cupp v Murphy*,[138] a bodily search was incidental to detention based on probable cause to believe that the suspect had committed a murder. The 'very limited intrusion' involved in taking scrapings from the suspect's fingernails and the 'highly evanescent' nature of the evidence justified the warrantless search. Where the search involves a highly intrusive procedure, it requires judicial scrutiny. Thus, in *Winston v Lee,*[139] the State sought an order compelling a suspect to undergo surgery under an anaesthetic in order to remove a bullet which, it was alleged, could provide evidence of guilt or innocence. The Supreme Court affirmed that such an order would violate the Fourth Amendment. It was stated that

> The reasonableness of surgical intrusions beneath the skin depends on a case by case approach in which the individual's interests in privacy and security are weighed against society's interests in conducting the procedure. In a given case, the question of whether the community's need for evidence outweighs the substantial privacy interests at stake is a delicate one admitting of few categorical answers.

Thus, no single principle governs judicial authorisation of bodily searches. Certain factors will, however, be relevant. These are the level of interference with bodily autonomy, the likelihood that the search will produce the desired evidence, the risk of injury to the suspect and the availability of alternative evidence (Rogers, 1987).

As discussed above, in England and Wales, there is no necessity for a warrant and thus no judicial scrutiny. There is no probable cause requirement, merely a requirement of reasonable grounds for 'suspecting' involvement in offending and a belief that the analysis may 'tend to confirm or disprove' such involvement. A sample is thus justified if taken to clear an individual of suspicion rather than because an officer has probable cause sufficient to satisfy a warrant application. Indeed, it need serve no immediate investigative function since it may be taken after charge, or even after conviction. Samples may be taken in respect of a wide range of criminality including *all* imprisonable offences. The fundamental difference in approach is that such evidence is not considered to have been *seized* as a consequence of a *search*. Thus, the implementation of the Human Rights Act notwithstanding, until there is an acceptance of this wider concept of search, there is no likelihood of procedures under PACE being challenged under Article 8 of the European Convention. Whilst intimate samples may not be taken under PACE without consent, the current provisions may be criticised for failing, in every case, to satisfy a test of evidential necessity and thus of proportionality. The provision of samples has proved to be a very potent weapon in effecting crime control, however, and it is likely that the derogation provision contained in Article 8(2) will be applied flexibly to legitimate existing procedures.

Notes

1. As amended by CRIMPO 1994.
2. Subsect. 8(1)(d) of PACE.
3. Cmnd. 8091 (1981) at paras. 3.41-3.42.
4. *Waugh v British Railways Board* [1980] AC 521. The 'dominant purpose' test was the majority view. Lord Denning (dissenting) considered that, for a claim of privilege to exist, the document must have been brought into existence wholly or mainly for the purpose of litigation or legal advice.
5. (1884) 14 QBD 153.
6. [1993] Crim. L.R. 866.
7. Neither was it special procedure material because it could not have been acquired or created in the course of his profession as a solicitor. There was 'no confidence in iniquity' and the documents could therefore not be held under an implied undertaking to hold them in confidence.
8. [1978] 1 ALL ER 225. Cp. *Fisher v US* (1976) 425 US 391.

9.   (1982) 141 DLR (3rd) 590.
10. In Canada and the U.S. a public safety exception applies where there is an imminent risk of serious bodily harm or death to an identified person or group of persons; see *Tarasoff v Regents University of California* (1976) 551 P 2d 334. In England and Wales, this exception has also been applied in respect of third parties such as psychiatrists; see *W v Egdell* [1990] 1 ALL ER 835.
11. *R v Crown Court at Snaresbrook ex parte DPP and anor.* [1988] 1 ALL ER 315.
12. It would have been disclosable in a prosecution by the Law Society under the Legal Aid Act 1974, but not otherwise. Cp. *Descoutreaux v Mierzwinski and Attorney General of Quebec* (above) and *R v Littlechild* (1979) 108 DLR (3rd) 340.
13. [1989] 1 AC 346.
14. Now the Drug Trafficking Act 1994 and outlined below.
15. Per Lord Brandon at 381.
16. *Ibid* per Lord Griffiths at 383.
17. Cp. *Niemietz v Germany* (1990) 16 EHRR 97. For a general discussion of judicial incursions into legal privilege see Passmore (1999).
18. [1990] 1 QB 261 and see *R v Maidstone Crown Court ex parte Rogers* [1999] 1 WLR 832, the record of time of attendance of a client is special procedure material, but not subject to legal professional privilege.
19. *R v Leeds Magistrates Court ex parte Dumbleton* [1993] Crim. L.R. 866. In that case the forged material could not have been acquired or created in the course of the profession of a solicitor.
20. [1993] Crim. L.R. 962. See also *Shumiatcher v A.G. Sask* (1960) 129 CCC 267.
21. *Ashburton (Lord) v Pape* [1913] 2 CH 469; *Goddard v Nationwide B.S.* [1986] 3 ALL ER 264; *IBM Corp. v Phoenix International Computers* [1995] 1 ALL ER 413.
22. This subsection also repeals any pre-existing statutory authority to search for legally privileged material.
23. See below for a discussion of the taking of bodily samples. Inferences may be drawn from a refusal to provide an intimate sample.
24. *E.g.* saliva or head hair, see below.
25. [1995] 1 Cr. App. R. 430.
26. Compare the public safety exception in legal privilege, see note 10 above.
27. [1981] AC 1096 at 1171 per Lord Wilberforce.
28. (1996) 22 EHRR 123.
29. This exception overrides the First Amendment right to freedom of speech and of the press; see *Branzburg v Hayes* (1972) 408 US 665.
30. Sect. 118(1) of PACE.
31. PACE subsect. 14(1)(b) and see above.
32. PACE subsects. 14(1)(a) and 14(2).
33. Subsect. 14(2)(a).
34. [1987] 3 ALL ER 654 DC.
35. [1989] 3 ALL ER 563 CA.
36. *R v Crown Court at Manchester ex parte Taylor* [1988] 2 ALL ER 769.
37. Zuckerman (1990:475).
38. [1978] 2 EHRRR214
39. These restrictions do not apply to post PACE statutes, unless the statute so states.
40. CO/0881/92, The Times 7th September 1992. Cp. *R v Worth* (1989) 54 CCC (3d) 215 and 223.

41. [1988] Crim. L.R. 384.
42. (1991) 93 Cr. App. R. 60, see also *R v Crown Court at Southwark ex parte Bowles* [1998] 2 Cr. App. R 187.
43. For instance under the Criminal Justice Act 1987; see below.
44. *R v Crown Court at Northampton ex parte Director Of Public Prosecutions* (1991) 93 Cr. App. R. 376 at 380.
45. [1991] Crim. L.R. 599.
46. [1999] 1 WLR 832.
47. See *R v Crown Court at Northampton ex parte Director Of Public Prosecutions* (1991) 93 Cr. App. R.376.
48. (1987) 85 Cr. App. R. 190.
49. See also *Re an Application under section 9 of the Police and Criminal Evidence Act 1984* The Independent 27th May 1988.
50. The Times 4th October 1990; report of a statement made by the then Deputy Director of the BBC.
51. *Societe Radio Canada v Nouveau-Brunswick* (1991) 67 CCC (3d) 544 per Cory J. and see *Societe Radio Canada v Lessard* (1991) 67 CCC (3d) 517.
52. (1972) 408 US 665.
53. [1993] Crim. L.R. 458.
54. The need for accurate and adequate information is even more crucial in those situations where the hearing is *ex parte*. See *The Crown Court at Southwark and ors. ex parte Gross* CO/1759/98 and chapter 3.
55. *R v Crown Court at Inner London sessions ex parte Baines and Baines* [1987] 3 ALL ER 1025.
56. Para. 2(b).
57. Para. 15 states that if a person fails to comply with a production order, that person shall be treated as if he had committed a contempt of court and may be dealt with accordingly.
58. Para. 14(d).
59. [1993] Crim. L.R. 962.
60. Subsect. 14(2).
61. Sections 2, 9 and 10.
62. Schedule 7 paragraph 1.
63. Para. 2 (1)(b) and 2A(1)(b).
64. Paras. 3 and 4, as amended by CRIMPO section 83.
65. Para. 3(3).
66. Para. 7.
67. Cp. *Malone v UK* (1985) 7 EHRR 352 and *Camenzind v Switzerland* (1998) EHRLR 352.
68. Paras. 2–5 must be complied with and there is an additional requirement concerning prejudice to the capabilities of the Royal Ulster Constabulary or the safety of other persons if application were made to a justice or judge.
69. Para. 4.
70. [1993] 2 ALL ER 310.
71. *Ibid* at 318–319.
72. The statute repeals section 2 of the Official Secrets Act 1911. That section was controversially wide in its application. Certain offences relating to unauthorised disclosure can be committed by persons other then Crown servants or government contractors.

73. Subsect. 7(4).
74. *I.e.* one carrying up to 5 years' imprisonment and certain other offences listed in section 24(2) of PACE.
75. Subsect. 7(2)(c).
76. See *The Crown Court at Southwark and ors. ex parte Gross* (above).
77. [1998] 2 Cr. App. R. 187.
78. Criminal Justice Act 1988 section 93H(1).
79. *Ex parte Bowles* (above) at 198.
80. See above.
81. Subsect. 55(6).
82. Subsect. 55(4).
83. *Ibid.* Further, Code B does not apply to this Act.
84. Code D para. 3.
85. Code D para. 5.
86. *Cupp v Murphy* (1973) 412 US 291; *Winston v Lee* (1985) 470 US 753; *R v Borden* (1991) 119 DLR (4th) 74; *Stillman v The Queen* (1997) 144 DLR (4th) 193 and *Re F (S) and Attorney General for Canada et al* (1997) 155 DLR (4th) 315.
87. [1943] 2KB 253 at 257.
88. But see the Criminal Justice Act 1987 section 2 and the discussion below of *Saunders v UK* (1996) 23 EHRR 313. See also Sharpe (1998).
89. *R v Payne* [1962] 1 ALL ER 848; *R v Court* (1960) 44 Cr. App. R. 242; *R v Sang* [1980] AC 402.
90. See Lord Diplock in *R v Sang* (above).
91. (1886) 116 US 616.
92. The 'property' based rationale of the Fourth Amendment has now been replaced by one of privacy. See chapter 5.
93. *Schmerber v State of California* (1966) 384 US 757; *Doe v US* (1988) 487 US 201.
94. *Stillman v The Queen* (above); *Re SF and Attorney General for Canada et al* (above).
95. See *R v Doherty and Adams* [1997] 1 Cr. App. R. 369; *R v Gordon* [1995] 1 Cr. App. R. 290 and Redmayne (1995). The Crown has started to use a 10 point test (as opposed to a 6 point test) with effect from the end of 1999.
96. *R v Buckley* 30th April 1999 CA no. 9802835/Y2.
97. Recordable offences are those for which convictions may be recorded in national police records; PACE subsect. 27(4). The list of these offences may be added to by statutory instrument. At present, it includes *all* offences that are imprisonable and certain non imprisonable offences such as having a bladed article in a public place under CJA 1988 sect. 139(1).
98. Subects. 61 (3) and (4).
99. Subsect. 61(5).
100. Subsect. 61(7)A, as inserted by CRIMPO Schedule 10 para.56(a).
101. Code D para. 3.4 and sect. 64 of PACE.
102. See chapter 7 for a further discussion.
103. (1988) 55 DLR (4th) 481 at 501.
104. (1997) 146 DLR (4th) 609 at 642-643.
105. (1969) 394 US 721.
106. (1985) 470 US 811. The members of the Supreme Court in this case have not frequently been noted for their support of due process rights.

107. [1995] 2 Cr. App. R. 565.
108. As amended by CRIMPO 1994 sects. 58 and 59.
109. Subsect. 62(1)(b) of PACE.
110. Subsect. 62(4) of PACE. If under 17 years, the consent of a parent or guardian is required.
111. Sects. 63, 63 A and 64 of PACE and chapter 7 below.
112. This has been given a very narrow meaning in respect of the parallel CRIMPO provisions; see *R v Cowan* [1995] 4 ALL ER 439; *R v Argent* [1997] 2 Cr. App. R. 27 and *R v Daniel* [1998] 2 Cr. App. R. 373. Legal advice, unsupported by the reasons therefore, will not prevent inferences being drawn.
113. (1996) 22 EHRR 29. Challenge was made under the similarly worded Criminal Evidence (Northern Ireland) Order 1988.
114. The Court in *Murray* was a Diplock court and hence a reasoned judgment was given. In England and Wales. Under the Contempt of Court Act 1981, it is still impermissible to go behind a jury verdict.
115. This is particularly so in view of the ECHR dicta in relation to compelled bodily samples. See *Saunders v UK* (1996) 23 EHRR 313 and below.
116. [1995] 1 Cr. App. R. 318.
117. PACE section 117.
118. Inserted by CRIMPO sect. 56.
119. This includes situations where a sample was taken but was 'unsuitable' or 'insufficient'.
120. (1996) 23 EHRR 313.
121. There is also legislation which is aimed primarily at financial investigations and is made for regulatory purposes, but which allowed compelled answers to be given in evidence in subsequent criminal proceedings; see Companies Act 1985 sects. 434–436; the Insolvency Act 1986 section 236 and *Re Arrows Ltd. (no. 4) v Naviede* [1995] 1 Cr. App. R. 95. The use of this evidence in subsequent criminal proceedings against the provider is now prohibited by section 59 and Schedule 3 of the Youth Justice and Criminal Evidence Act 1999.
122. Subsect. 2(8). This has now been amended by the 1999 Act (above).
123. (1988) 55 DLR (4th) 503.
124. Cp. *R v Apicella* (1985) 82 Cr. App. R. 295.
125. At p. 521.
126. Although consent to the taking of samples is no longer required, compliance is required and a sample cannot be taken forcibly; see *R v Knox* (1996) 139 DLR (4th) 1.
127. [1995] 1 SCR 254.
128. Per Cory J. and Sopinka J.
129. (1996) 139 DLR (4th) 1.
130. (1997) 144 DLR (4th) 193.
131. Per Cory J. at 229.
132. *Ibid* at 227. Cp. *Schmerber v California* (1966) 384 US 757.
133. See *Re S(F) and the Attorney General for Canada et al* (1997) 153 DLR (4th) 315. However, the compelled plucking of scalp hair did infringe section 8 as it will not yield usable DNA in 5–10% of the population.
134. These are serious indictable offences and mostly involve violence against the person and public safety.
135. Above.
136. (1988) 487 US 201. See also *Schmerber v California* (above) and *Fisher v US* (1976) 425 US 391; but cp. *Rochin v California* (1952) 342 US 165.

137. No clear distinction is made between these two procedures.
138. (1973) 412 US 291; see also *Breithaupt v Abram* (1957) 352 US 432.
139. (1985) 470 US 753.

5 Surveillance as Electronic Search

The advent of electronic technology has revolutionised police methodology in respect of the investigation of crime. Surreptitious monitoring may now take place of the actions and conversations of suspects. The focus has shifted from reliance upon custodial interrogation after a crime has been committed to targeting suspects prior to or during the commission of crime. There are many factors that may have contributed to this change in methodology. One is the undoubted difficulty in obtaining proof of 'victimless' crimes such as the importation or supply of prohibited drugs. Another factor, in England and Wales, may well be the substantial due process protections afforded to a suspect detained for formal questioning under PACE and Code C thereunder (Sharpe, 1994:802). These protections can be evaded if covert surveillance provides evidence of offending. An important bonus for law enforcers is that electronically recorded evidence provides incontrovertible proof. There is no room for argument over whether a particular act was done or certain words were spoken. Any defence to resultant criminal charges must be based on external considerations such as entrapment, abuse of process or the violation of due process rights.[1] Surveillance may be effected through the bugging of persons, the bugging of premises, or the interception of communications (for instance a telephone conversation). In the United States and in Canada such surveillance is regarded as an integral aspect of search powers.[2] In England and Wales, until very recently, no theoretical or systemic relationship was acknowledged to exist between searches for tangible evidence and the use of covert surveillance. The incorporation of the European Convention on Human Rights has finally led to some recognition that the acquisition of 'intangible' information may fall within the purview of Article 8 and that any prosecution that relies upon such evidence might be challenged under Article 6, should there be an unreasonable interference with privacy rights.[3] This chapter examines the piecemeal powers that exist in relation to surveillance in England and Wales and compares them with the more principled and integrated approach that exists in North America.

The Wiring of Individuals

The wiring of persons was, probably, the first use of electronic surveillance in respect of criminal investigation. Certainly the earliest cases on the adduction of evidence from electronic recordings concern the wiring of individuals co-operating with the police in obtaining admissions and, forty years ago, concern was expressed over the use of such an investigative technique.[4] It is axiomatic that such surveillance cannot be undertaken without the co-operation of at least one party to the conversation or transaction that is being recorded. This is in contradistinction to all other forms of electronic search.[5] The practice of listening into private conversations conducted between citizens is an effective tool of crime control, essentially because it *is* covert. The target of the eavesdropping is unaware that law enforcement officers, or agents acting on their behalf, are monitoring and recording information and potential evidence upon which to base a criminal charge. It is the false sense of privacy that is created that leads the target to reveal matters that would never voluntarily be disclosed to the police or government interrogator. The creation of an environment of misplaced confidence may be the only 'deceptive' practice employed by the police. Alternatively, there may be positive inducements to the target to incriminate himself. In these more extreme situations, the co-operating participant may attempt to lead the target into making admissions and may have a personal interest in doing so. This personal interest may emanate from deals done with law enforcers over criminal activity on the part of the participant or from payments receivable by an individual who is an accredited police informant.

The relationship between the use of persons as covert recording devices and the use of persons as informants, and even as *agents provocateurs*,[6] is a close one. The use of paid informants has a lengthy historical origin and predates the establishment of professional police forces (Sharpe, 1994). The re-emergence of deals made with criminals, whether as to payment from public funds, or as to preferential or lenient treatment, is now a normative feature of current day policing (Maguire and Norris, 1993). In part, official endorsement of this practice[7] has been because of its efficacy in controlling crime. Once the participant is wired, or carries a concealed recorder, the electronically preserved statements and actions cannot be refuted in court. They are, in that sense, as probative as tangible incriminating evidence found as the result of a physical search. In England and Wales, the evidence obtained through such subterfuge is treated purely as confession evidence. There has never been any argument that, because of an invasion into the privacy of the target, the authorities have conducted an unreasonable search. Section 82 of PACE defines a confession as 'any statement wholly or partly adverse to the person who made it, whether made to a person in authority or not and whether made in words or otherwise'. This encompasses all evidence obtained through electronic eavesdropping. Because challenge is historically confined to the admissibility of any resultant confession, arguments have centred on two specific issues. The first of these is the level of deception involved and whether the suspect has been effectively entrapped.[8] The second is whether there has been a deliberate evasion of Code C of the PACE Codes of Practice in that statutory safeguards attaching to interrogation under PACE have been evaded.[9] Both these issues will be discussed in the following chapter.

There are, at present, no statutory provisions governing the wiring of individuals as part of a criminal investigation. The National Criminal Intelligence Service, in conjunction with the Association of Chief Police Officers and HM Customs and Excise, has issued a *voluntary* set of Codes dealing with various aspects of covert investigative techniques.[10] One Code deals with the 'Use Of Informants' and another with 'Undercover Operations'. The objective of the Codes is to make the activities of investigators Convention 'compliant'. However, apart from the fact that the Codes have no greater status in law than the Home Office Guidelines that preceded them,[11] the authorisation and control of such operations remains vested in the police or other relevant agency.[12] There is therefore no external control over when the wiring of individuals may take place. Reform proposals, discussed below, will not change this situation. The rhetoric of the Codes is to apply the principle of proportionality to all covert policing activity. Code 2.3, relating to informants, states that the use of an informant may only be authorised if the authorising officer is satisfied that such use 'is likely to be of value in the prevention or detection of crime, in the maintenance of public order or community safety' and that 'the desired result of the use of the informant cannot reasonably be achieved by other means'. Where the use is likely to result in the acquisition of knowledge of 'confidential material',[13] including legally privileged material, the authorisation may only be given in the case of investigation into 'serious crime'.[14]

Authorisation for the use of undercover officers should only be given where the use is 'proportionate to the seriousness of the crime being investigated and the history and character of the individual(s) concerned'.[15] The 'serious crime' limitation applies to the use of undercover officers when knowledge of 'confidential material' is likely to be acquired.[16] Equally, the deployment of such officers is only justified where the desired result 'cannot reasonably be achieved by other means'.[17] However, these provisions are not as stringent a control on the use of covert operations as may appear from the assertions of principle that precede the detailed substance of the Codes. The necessity principle is fairly generously interpreted. The meaning of 'cannot reasonably be achieved by other means' is not that all other methods have been tried and failed; it is enough that 'such other means would not be practicable or would be unlikely to achieve what the action seeks to achieve within a reasonable time or to a reasonable standard'.[18] In other words, the Codes sanction the use of covert evidence gathering if such use will yield a speedier and more probative result than would overt policing. Such a provision legitimates expediency and does not adequately restrict speculative search in respect of prospective offending, so long as the end is found to justify the means. The definition of 'serious crime' is also quite generous to law enforcers. It mirrors the definition contained in the Interception of Communications Act 1985 and the Police Act 1997[19] and encompasses much medium level offending such as burglary, assault occasioning injury, or a breach of a prohibition on trespassory assembly.

An absence of legislative control and an absence of jurisprudence concerning possible due process violations inherent in these investigative practices marks out the wiring of individuals as one of the least regulated tools of police investigation in England and Wales. In the next chapter, the approach of the courts to the reception of such evidence is considered. It will be seen that since the inherent deception involved in such practices does not detract from the reliability of the evidence, judges refuse to allow deceptive practice to militate against admissibility (Ashworth, 1998). The wiring of persons has been debated in the United States and in Canada on a two-fold basis. The first consideration is whether or not the common law privilege against self-incrimination has been breached. The second is whether there has been a violation of privacy rights and hence an unreasonable search.

So far as the privilege against self-incrimination is concerned, the courts will determine whether the practice offends against the common law right of silence. In the United States, the issue is whether there has been a deliberate elicitation of material by the informant and whether this has taken place after charge. Thus in *US v Henry*,[20] a previous inmate of a prison, who had acted as a police informer, revealed to a government agent admissions made to him in prison by the accused. The informant had been paid for his information on a 'contingent fee basis'. Here the accused was in custody at the time of the conversation[21] and the government intentionally created a situation 'likely to induce Henry to make incriminating statements without the assistance of

counsel'. The Sixth Amendment right of the accused was therefore viol
However, such a right would not have arisen had the government _____
'undercover agents to obtain incriminating statements from persons not in
custody but suspected of criminal activity prior to the time charges are filed'.
Even if the accused has been charged and his Sixth Amendment right to counsel
has been activated, there will be no violation of the privilege against self-
incrimination where the informant simply listens to freely volunteered
admissions. In *Kuhlman v Wilson*,[22] Chief Justice Burger stated that there
was a 'vast difference between placing an "ear" in the suspect's cell and placing
a voice in the cell to encourage conversation for the "ear" to record.' A similar
approach is taken in Canada. It is only if the monitoring takes place after
charge and if there is more than 'passive surveillance' of the accused, that the
privilege against self-incrimination is violated.[23]

This distinction between 'passive surveillance' and the active elicitation
of information does not take account of the fact that there are many stages in
between the two positions. Ruses, such as using a trusted friend to speak to
the suspect,[24] or allowing an informant to give the impression that he is a
suspect when he is not,[25] may subtly influence the accused and encourage
him to confide when he would not otherwise do so. Observations on the state
of the case against the suspect and 'expressions of solicitude'[26] may also
exert a psychological influence on the suspect. The courts in North America
will not find that the right to silence has been violated except in the narrowest
of circumstances, that is an effective interrogation of the accused after he has
been charged. Participant monitoring in all other circumstances is fair game.

The second issue that has arisen is whether this practice infringes the
Fourth Amendment or section 8 of the Canadian Charter. Electronic search
that involves the interception of private communications, of whatever kind,
requires authorisation in the United States and in Canada.[27] There is systemic
harmonisation in respect of the covert recording of acts or words whether the
search is by wiring individuals, installing secret recording devices in premises,
or by intercepting telephone conversations or other electronic communications.
As a matter of fact, however, it is unlikely that arguments to the effect that
there has been an unreasonable search will be raised, or if raised upheld,
where one of the parties to the conversation participates in the activity. This is
surprising in view of comments made in the case of *R v Herbert*.[28] The
Canadian Supreme Court was considering the admissibility of incriminating
statements that had been made by an accused whilst he had been detained in
a cell with an undercover police officer. In restoring the appellant's acquittal,
the Court held that section 7 of the Charter[29] had been violated. Sopinka J.

drew a distinction between 'passive surveillance' and the deliberate elicitation of admissions after arrest. In considering this distinction, he conceded that 'in cases of electronic search through "participant surveillance" different constitutional issues arise pursuant to section 8 of the Charter'.[30] Reference was made to the case of *Duarte v The Queen*,[31] a case concerning the consensual bugging of premises, where La Forest J. asserted that prior judicial authorisation was required in respect of participant surveillance. The consent of the informer or agent was insufficient to override the right to be secure against unreasonable searches enshrined in section 8. None the less, cases, in which the person of the participant (as opposed to the premises) is wired, appear to be argued on the basis of section 7 of the Charter,[32] despite the fact that there is clearly scope for a secondary argument under section 8.

In the United States, the position is somewhat different.[33] The courts have been unwilling to hold that a violation of the Fourth Amendment has occurred, even though privacy rights attach to 'people not places',[34] because a person who mistakenly confides in another does not have a reasonable expectation of privacy in the communication. It was stated in *US v White*[35]

> However strongly a defendant may trust an apparent colleague, his expectations in this respect are not protected by the Fourth Amendment when it turns out that the colleague is a government agent regularly communicating with the authorities.

There is therefore no legitimate interest to be protected. Misplaced trust does not give rise to a privacy right, even when such trust results in the conversation being electronically recorded and/or transmitted. The suspect has assumed a risk and must take the consequences. Mr. Justice Harlan, dissenting in *White*, considered that a rule of law that 'permits official monitoring of private discourse limited only to the need to locate a willing assistant' would restrict the spontaneous discourse 'that liberates daily life'. The view, that freedom of speech and of correspondence is adversely affected, has not received majority consensus. However, the argument in favour of granting the protection of the Fourth Amendment to participant monitoring is strong. It has been stated that it is 'rather too late to dispute that that privacy includes the privacy of communicative relationships with others; Mr. Katz was in a telephone booth not a water closet' (Amsterdam, 1974:407).

The consequence of judicial interpretation of the Fourth Amendment is that it only begins to bite where there has been no assumption of risk by the suspect, thus where there is no awareness that his words or deeds are being observed even by confidants. This unawareness is likely to arise both in the bugging of premises and in the interception of messages. However, where the undisclosed monitoring of a conversation, whether held on private premises or over the telephone, is undertaken with the *consent* of the other conversant, it is difficult to see a qualitative difference between tapping a telephone and wiring an informant. The only distinction is that in the latter situation the parties are face to face with one another. Amsterdam makes the point succinctly by stating that the distinction is between being 'afraid to talk to anybody in you office over the phone' or simply being 'afraid to talk to anybody at all' (Amsterdam, 1974).

The Bugging of Premises in England and Wales

In England and Wales, the installation of covert recording devices in private premises was previously regulated only by Home Office Guidelines.[36] These provided a comprehensive code on the criteria for police authorisation of surveillance techniques, but they did not have the force of law, since they were no more than administrative directions to senior police officers. Further, the Guidelines were not readily available for consultation by the targets of the surveillance, nor even by practising solicitors. It is not surprising, therefore, that in an era of greater awareness of the potential of the European Convention on Human Rights to shape domestic law, challenge should be made to surveillance carried out under such authority. In the case of *R v Khan (Sultan)*[37] the House of Lords was faced with such a challenge. The appellant was suspected of being a party to the importation of prohibited drugs. He visited the home of another man to whose house, unbeknown to the appellant and to the occupier, a listening device had been attached. The device was fixed to an outside wall and the police conceded that there were elements of civil trespass outside the building and that a certain amount of criminal damage had taken place through affixing the device. As a consequence of conversations recorded at these premises, the appellant was convicted of importing heroin. He challenged his conviction, arguing that the combination of civil trespass, criminal damage and the intrusion upon his privacy under Article 8 of the Convention, required the trial judge to exclude the recordings under section 78 of PACE.[38]

Both the Court of Appeal and the House of Lords rejected this argument. The evidence was admissible. There were two related reasons for this conclusion. The first was that there was, at the time that the case was heard, no right of privacy in English law and no requirement that evidence be excluded for a violation of Article 8. The Human Rights Act 1998, incorporating the Convention, had not then been passed. Lord Nolan asserted that if evidence obtained in breach of privacy were inadmissible, then 'privacy too would become a defence to a criminal charge where the substance of the charge consisted of acts done or words spoken in private'.[39] He considered that such a proposition did not 'bear serious examination'. The position post the Human Rights Act 1998 is different in that an infringement of privacy would inevitably accompany an improper intrusive search. Whether the resultant evidence would be excluded is another matter. The second reason for disallowing the appeal was that, even taking account of the rights enshrined in Article 8, there was nothing to suggest that the right to a fair trial had been affected by the admission of the evidence. There is no automatic exclusionary rule in respect of improperly or illegally obtained evidence and it was considered that the trial judge had been right to admit this relevant evidence. The evaluation of judicial discretion will be revisited again in the next chapter.

From the point of view of the development of the law, perhaps the most important pronouncements to come from the case related to judicial astonishment at the absence of any statutory system governing covert surveillance.[40] In the Court of Appeal, Lord Taylor thought it to be 'at least worthy of consideration' that 'the circumstances in which bugging a private home by the police can be justified should be the subject of statutory control'. Such comments and the acknowledged disparity between the interception of telephone communications, where a statutory regime does exist, and the bugging of premises where it did not, impelled the government to legislate. There is no doubt that had the government not done so, legislation would have been forced upon them. The European Court of Human Rights has declared Mr. Khan's contention that Articles 6 and 8 had been violated to be an admissible application.[41] The government's argument that the Home Office Guidelines were public and accessible and provided constraints within which surveillance was limited to the investigation of serious crime is to be determined by the full Court.[42] Sections 91 to 108 of the Police Act 1997 now provide for a statutory framework of authorisation in respect of listening devices.

It is important to note that not all electronic surveillance is covered by the legislation. It does not govern the wiring of persons, nor the consensual bugging of property. Where the occupier consents to the installation of the device, the Act does not bite. The Police Act does not cover any form of surveillance that does not require a physical entry onto or interference with premises or interference with wireless telegraphy. Thus, despite a large amount of media generated concern when the Bill passed through parliament, advances in technology are likely to make the provisions less and less significant as remote surveillance becomes a feasible option for the police. It is not surprising that, given the embryonic nature of privacy rights in England and Wales, the Police Act should be couched in proprietary terms and that trespass should be required to activate its protections.

In the United States, the Fourth Amendment was, at one time, interpreted so as to affect only those searches involving physical trespass. In *Olmstead v US*,[43] the Supreme Court held that telephone tapping that involved no trespass upon any property of the defendants was not an unreasonable search. The Chief Justice stated that Federal decisions that had been put before the Court supported the principle that a defendant could not rely upon the Fourth Amendment

> unless there has been an official seizure of his person, or such a seizure of his papers or his tangible material effects, or an actual physical invasion of his house 'or curtilage' for the purposes of making a seizure.

This interpretation did not survive the radical reappraisal effected in *Berger v New York*[44] and *Katz v US*.[45] In *Berger*, Mr. Justice Clarke, delivering the opinion of the Court, stated that authorities subsequent to *Olmstead* had held that a 'conversation' was within the protection of the Fourth Amendment 'and that the use of electronic devices to capture it was a "search" within the meaning of the Amendment'. The Supreme Court confirmed that this was now the law and reaffirmed this opinion in *Katz* a few months thereafter. There is therefore no longer any necessity for an invasion of proprietary interests before constitutional safeguards bite. This single conceptual advancement has perhaps done more to synthesise the law relating to search and seizure than any amount of detailed legislation. It allows for privacy rights to develop in line with new technological advances, freed from literal and narrow constraints that are founded in the historical roots of trespassory entry.

In England and Wales, this conceptual leap forward has not yet been achieved. The Police Act is still grounded in physical entry and deals only with specific forms of surveillance. Section 92 provides

> No entry on or interference with property or with wireless telegraphy shall be unlawful if it is authorised by an authorisation having effect under this Part.

It is to be noted that this section is drafted in negative terms. It remains to be seen how the courts will treat evidence that has not been obtained with the proper authorisations and, thus, unlawfully. The evidence will, none the less, be relevant and highly probative and may therefore be admitted in any event.[46] Apart from certain limited exceptions, authorisations under the Act are granted by the police and customs officers, not by judicial officers.

Section 93 contains a detailed list of senior officers, such as Chief Constables, Police Commissioners and the Director of the National Criminal Intelligence Service, who may give authorisations. The officer must believe

    (a)   that it is necessary for the action specified to be taken on the ground that it is likely to be of substantial value in the prevention or detection of serious crime, and

    (b)   that what the action seeks to achieve cannot reasonably be achieved by other means.[47]

These provisions would seem to conform to the proportionality principle inherent in Article 8(2). It is to be noted that the definition of 'serious crime' is culled from the earlier Interception of Communications Act 1985 (hereinafter IOCA). Subsection 93(4) states that a crime is serious if

    (a)   it involves the use of violence, results in substantial financial gain or is conduct by a large number of persons in pursuit of a common purpose, or

    (b)   the offence or one of the offences is an offence for which a person who has attained the age of twenty-one and has no previous convictions could reasonably be expected to be sentenced to imprisonment for a term of three years or more.

As discussed above,[48] such a definition encompasses much 'middle range' offending such as aggravated assault, theft whilst in a position of trust, mortgage fraud or public order offending engaged in by a large number of people. There may be occasions where the level of the intrusion into privacy is not justified as being 'necessary in a democratic society' and each case will have to be evaluated on its own facts.

The concept of necessity also appears in the requirement that the evidence sought 'cannot reasonably be achieved by other means'. However, this is a less stringent requirement than that prescribed in Schedule 1 of PACE,[49] or even by the previous Home Office Guidelines. PACE provides that a circuit judge may only make a production order where other methods of obtaining the information 'have been tried without success' or 'have not been tried because it appeared that they were bound to fail'.[50] Since the wording in the Police Act is identical to that in the NCIS Codes,[51] it is likely that the same interpretation will be given to the expression. The practicability of other means, including the time taken to achieve police objectives through other investigative methods, will be determinative. The statutory Code of Practice, entitled 'Intrusive Surveillance' and laid under section 101, does not give much guidance on the interpretation of these words. In fact, this Code, the only statutory Code governing electronic surveillance, does little to flesh out the substance of the Act.[52] It is made clear that the Act is not to be used to circumvent IOCA.[53] Thus, if the same objective can be achieved by overhearing speech transmitted via a public telephone system, the police should not forcibly enter private premises and install a listening device therein. However, the Code of Practice also states that the 'use of a surveillance device should *not* be ruled out simply because it may incidentally pick up one end of a telephone conversation'.[54] Apart from this one specific example, the Code does not elucidate on the meaning of 'cannot reasonably be achieved by other means' and the expression will, no doubt, be further considered judicially.

In order that the intrusion should be no more extensive than is necessary, there are requirements in paragraph 2.15 of the Code as to specificity. These are similar to the 'minimisation' requirements contained in Title 18 section 2518 of the United States Code. The application for authorisation should specify, *inter alia*, the identity or identities of those to be targeted (where known), the property to be affected, the identity of any known persons who are likely to be affected by collateral surveillance, details of the offence planned or committed and details of the intrusive surveillance involved. Under section 95, authorisations normally last for a maximum period of three months. Where, due to the absence of an authorising officer, the authorisation is given by an assistant chief constable or commander, the authorisation only lasts for 72 hours. Renewal for a maximum of three months is permitted under subsection 95(3). The section also incorporates another aspect of the minimisation principle in that the authorisation must be cancelled if the authorising officer is satisfied that the surveillance is no longer necessary.

The one major weakness of the statute, so far as compliance with Article 8 is concerned, is the absence of any requirement, in the majority of situations, for judicial authorisation *prior* to surveillance. A Chief Commissioner and a number of other Commissioners are appointed by the Prime Minister to oversee surveillance activities under the Act. The Commissioners are senior judges. Notice of all authorisations granted must be given in writing to a Commissioner.[55] The Chief Commissioner is also responsible for receiving complaints made under the Act[56] and is empowered, under section 103, to quash an authorisation if he is satisfied that it was not granted on a proper basis. Where he does quash an authorisation, he may also order the destruction of any records relating to information obtained by the authorisation other than records required for pending criminal or civil proceedings.[57] There is thus no requirement to destroy material that has become evidence against a defendant, even though the authorisation to bug his premises may have been wrongly granted. In the Parliamentary debates prior to the Act, great concern was raised over the absence of any prospective judicial control. Lord Rodgers, at the Committee Stage of the Bill,[58] proposed an Amendment substituting a circuit judge as the 'authorising officer' in lieu of law enforcement officers. The government had resisted this alteration at the Second Reading, claiming that it was not right to involve judges in the investigation of crime.[59] Persisting in his attempt to change the substance of the Bill, Lord Rodgers stated

> If the Bill remains unaltered its powers will be unusual in the western world. Among the countries requiring judicial authorisation for bugging are the United States, Germany, Canada, Australia, New Zealand, France and others. I believe that the Committee may reasonably ask the Minister why we should be the odd man out. What is it about our system of administration that makes it unnecessary for us to use a provision that is found desirable elsewhere?

Lord Browne-Wilkinson[60] returned to basic principles and pointed out that *Entick v Carrington*[61] required state intrusion onto private property to be justified by the issuance of a judicial warrant. It has never been considered undesirable for members of the judiciary to issue ordinary search warrants, or that this pre-trial function compromises their independence. After some debate, the Amendment was withdrawn to allow for further consideration.

The compromise that was eventually agreed by the government was that prospective authorisation by a Commissioner should be required in respect of certain intrusions. Subsection 97(2) of the Police Act distinguishes between the property under surveillance and the information likely to be acquired. However, in many cases *both* the property bugged and the information likely to be acquired will justify this extra protection. The premises specified in subsection 97(2)(a) are those used wholly or mainly as a dwelling, or as a bedroom in a hotel and office premises. The protected information is set out in subsection 97(2)(b) and consists of matters subject to legal privilege, confidential personal information and confidential journalistic material. Concern had been expressed that the Police Bill did not provide any exception in respect of legally privileged communications. The intention of the original drafters of the legislation was to prevent criminals consulting lawyers 'for the sole purpose of furthering their illegal activities and frustrating the purpose of the Bill'.[62] It is debatable that such communication would be legally privileged[63] and it is also debatable whether more than a small percentage of criminals 'are such important clients of lawyers that the lawyers will visit their homes and offices'.[64] In the event, public concerns, not only about the lack of judicial control over the acquisition of knowledge relating to legally privileged material, but also about intrusion into private homes and doctors' surgeries, forced the government to make concessions.[65]

It is obvious that heavy reliance has been placed on PACE. The definition of legally privileged material replicates, with the necessary amendments, the wording of section 10 of PACE.[66] The definitions of 'confidential personal information' and 'confidential journalistic material' replicate those contained in sections 11 and 12 of PACE. Thus the concept of 'excluded material' is resurrected in the context of electronic search.[67] The Code, in paragraph 2.4, states that whereas spiritual counselling is a situation requiring the prior approval of a Commissioner, confessionals are not to be subject to surveillance. As a general principle, paragraph 2.5 emphasises that 'collateral intrusion is a matter of particular concern, especially in the case of premises used for any form of medical or professional counselling or therapy' and that 'particular thought' should be given to such operations. Notifications to a Commissioner should include an assessment of any collateral intrusion. There is one substantial difference between powers of surveillance under the Police Act and powers of search under PACE. Sections 8, 19 and Schedule 1 of PACE do not allow for the seizure of legally privileged material. The Police Act does so allow. It merely puts constraints on the way in which privileged information may be acquired. The fact that this information may not itself be admissible in court in the course of any subsequent criminal trial,[68] is cold comfort to a suspect who may be convicted as a result of derivative evidence obtained as a consequence of the surveillance. It is of even less comfort to those innocent clients of lawyers whose business is no longer private because their legal adviser has become a target through advising suspected criminals. The failure to exempt legally privileged material from surveillance activities is also a feature of the voluntary Codes.

In situations of 'urgency' subsection 97(3) permits the police to bug protected premises without prior judicial authorisation. Paragraph 2.13 of the Code makes clear that the 'urgency provisions should not be used routinely'. The Code states that 'there may be exceptional circumstances, for example where it is impracticable in the time scale needed to carry out the operation, to obtain prior approval of a Commissioner'. It may be questioned whether, in the absence of any guidance as to the meaning of 'urgency' in the primary legislation, the exemplar in the Code is, in reality, likely to curb a fairly frequent use of the emergency power. In many situations it may be possible to argue that a tip off was received at short notice; that the target was only likely to be at the venue for a limited period of time (as in the case of a hotel bedroom); or that the target is likely to make only one visit to his lawyer's office or to the home of an accomplice. A safeguard, such as it is, resides in the obligation under section 96 to notify a Commissioner in writing of the authorisation and to specify the grounds on which the case is believed to be one of urgency.[69]

The Police Act does go a long way toward providing compliance with Article 8. Its major weakness, that in the majority of cases prior authorisation is by law enforcers, is a weakness common to the majority of surveillance activities carried out in England and Wales. Where the Act does not apply, there is no control over authorisation other than the voluntary NCIS Code on 'Surveillance'. This Code is, in many respects, similar to the statutory Code, but there are certain significant differences. One of these is that where consent to bugging is given, or where no physical trespass occurs, surveillance may be undertaken in the 'detection of crime'.[70] It is not necessary that the investigation concerns serious crime. The only stage at which the limitation of 'serious crime' becomes operative is when the investigation is likely to result in any person acquiring knowledge of 'confidential material'.[71] Confidential material covers legally privileged material, confidential personal information and confidential journalistic material as defined in the Police Act.[72] Further, authorisation is always by a police or custom's officer. There is no requirement of prior judicial authorisation even in those situations of intrusive surveillance where there is likely to be acquisition of knowledge of confidential material. In this latter event, the authorisation must be given by a more senior official.[73] Consent therefore relieves officers from seeking judicial approval. Consent need only be given by one party to the conversation and, not infrequently, where the law enforcement agency is the occupier of the premises that are being bugged, the consent of neither conversant is necessary. Thus, where police bug their own cells to record the conversations of inmates, the detainees may be unaware that they are being covertly recorded.[74] Even if one of the detainees is aware of the subterfuge, he may have an interest in persuading another to take responsibility for offending.[75] When carrying out 'sting' operations undercover officers may be renting and occupying the premises that are under surveillance.[76] In these circumstances, those being recorded are totally unaware that they are confiding in a police or custom's officer. The evidential implications of these deceptions are considered in the next chapter.

Another substantial difference between the voluntary Code and the Police Act 1997 is that the former also covers the surveillance of public places. Paragraph 3 provides for a system of authorisation with more senior level authority required when the target is specified than when he is not.[77] However, the rank of officer (superintendent or inspector) is, in any event, lower than that required to grant surveillance authority in respect of private premises. The Code only bites where observation in public places is to 'meet a particular law enforcement need' or is targeted 'against specified individuals'. It does not regulate the observation of those members of the public coming to the notice of police officers 'in the normal course of duty' as a result of conduct giving rise to suspicion of offending.[78] Thus, surveillance of a particular street in which the police suspect that drug-trafficking occurs would require authorisation under the Code. A watch on an individual who is thought to be responsible for a series of robberies in an area would require authorisation, even though that individual is to be observed and recorded walking around a shopping centre. If, however, the police are watching an airport as part of their normal law enforcement duties and, whilst doing so, become suspicious that an individual may be stealing passengers' property, the continued observation of that individual would not fall within the Code. The temporary surveillance of private premises, following on from a previously authorised surveillance of public places, is authorised in paragraph 2.5 of the Code. This may last as long as is necessary to fulfil the described purpose, but not for more than 24 hours without further authorisation from an appropriate officer. If the police are watching a suspect robber, in the example given above, and that person leaves the shopping area to enter a flat above one of the business premises, observation may continue for up to 24 hours without the need for additional authority.

The discussion above has been concerned with surveillance aimed at specified individuals and certain locations. The increased indiscriminate use of Closed Circuit Television (CCTV) in public places and in business premises, as a form of security and criminal deterrence, may have substantial civil liberties implications, even though such systems are not set up solely in order to investigate crime.[79] However, the use of CCTV is unlikely to infringe a reasonable expectation of privacy if it is confined to areas to which the public have access and is not installed with the purpose of filming inherently private events.[80] Thus, even when the police seek stills of camera recordings in order to prevent or detect crime,[81] it is unlikely that the subsequent use of such photographs in evidence will violate Article 6 or Article 8 of the European Convention. The information gathering exercise is legitimated in the public interest and the evidence acquired has not been obtained by any deceptive practice. The position in the United States and in Canada in relation to electronic bugging and in relation to the interception of communications, since the processes are governed by the same principles, is considered later in this chapter.

Telephone Interception in England and Wales

The interception of communications sent by post or by a public telecommunications system is now governed by the Interception of Communications Act 1985. This statute was passed in direct response to a complaint made by a British national to the European Court of Human Rights. The case of *Malone v United Kingdom*[82] decided that the previous system of authorisation, based upon warrants issued, as a matter of practice only, by the Secretary of State was not 'in accordance with the law' under Article 8(2) and therefore violated the right to 'respect for private life and correspondence'. The Court stated that 'it cannot be said with any reasonable certainty what elements of the powers to intercept are incorporated in legal rules and what elements remain within the discretion of the excutive'.[83] The government's response was to introduce legislation to give a clear framework, but an essentially limited one. Despite the recommendation of the Royal Commission on Criminal Procedure[84] that surveillance activity in general (including bugging) should be subject to statutory control, IOCA only regulates the transmission of communications through a carrier. Further, the Act is currently limited to interceptions of the *public* telecommunications system and that is proving to be an increasingly insupportable restriction in view of the fast growing use of mobile telephones.[85] It is also to be noted that the Act does not deal with electronic communications.[86] The fact that IOCA is insufficiently adaptable to deal with the advances of new technology has not gone unnoticed. A Home Office Consultation Paper has been issued and draft legislation introduced with a view to covering these communications.[87]

The protections afforded by IOCA have been described as a 'minimalist interpretation' of the United Kingdom's obligations under the Convention (Cameron, 1986:149). Whilst they have passed muster in subsequent challenge under the Convention,[88] this has been on the basis that the information obtained may only be used 'as a starting point from which to gather admissible evidence'.[89] The statute is *par excellence* a legitimisation of information gathering, of covert knowledge acquisition by the executive or law enforcement agencies. There are two major criticisms of IOCA. The first relates to the fact that authorisations are given by the executive and that judicial scrutiny of such authorisations is purely retrospective. The second centres upon section 9 of the Act, a section that prohibits challenge to the legality of any interception that has occurred.

Section 1 of IOCA provides that a person who intentionally intercepts a communication in the course of its transmission by post, or by means of a public telecommunications system, commits an offence. There is an exemption from criminal liability in respect of interceptions under warrant issued by the Secretary of State and interceptions where the interceptor 'has reasonable grounds for believing' that either the person to whom, or the person by whom the communication has been sent has consented to the interception.[90] Subsections 2(2) and 2(3) provide

(2) The Secretary of State shall not issue a warrant under this section unless he considers that the warrant is necessary–
    (a) in the interests of national security;
    (b) for the purpose of preventing or detecting serious crime;
    (c) for the purpose of safeguarding the economic well-being of the United Kingdom.[91]
(3) The matters to be taken into account in considering whether a warrant is necessary as mentioned in subsection (2) above shall include whether the information which it is considered necessary to acquire could reasonably be acquired by other means.

Thus, the issuance of a warrant under the Act is *not* a judicial function. Further, the definition of the necessity principle that is apparently adopted in subsection 2(3) is closer to that incorporated into the Police Act than that adopted in PACE.[92]

The Act is not solely concerned with crime and is as much aimed at the regulation of state security investigations, since the 'interests of national security'[93] is a criterion within section 2, even if no specifically unlawful conduct is involved. A perceived need to protect the country from threat caused by terrorism, espionage or major subversive activity is not necessarily based on objective evidence that a criminal offence is being planned (Cameron, 1986:136).[94] Following IOCA, the Security Service Act 1989 has placed MI5 on a statutory footing and adopted the structure of IOCA so far as the issuance of warrants involving trespassory entry is concerned.[95] The government then passed the Intelligence Services Act 1994, regulating the Secret Intelligence Service (M16) and the Government Communications Headquarters (GCHQ). The combined effect of IOCA, the Security Service Act 1989 and the Intelligence Services Act 1994 is that a warrant from the Secretary of State may authorise telephone interception, the bugging of premises or the interference with wireless telegraphy whenever a matter of national security is considered to be in issue.

However, the investigation of crime and the protection of national security are not always clearly distinguishable. The functions of the police and of the Security Service have become further blurred by the enactment of the Security Service Act 1996. That statute empowers the Service 'to act in support of the activities of police forces and other law enforcement agencies in the prevention and detection of serious crime'.[96] PACE does not govern the activities of the Security Service and grave concerns must exist about the empowerment of such an organisation to investigate national crime.[97] The provisions of IOCA enable the executive to authorise and to control telephone interception and to do so with relatively little accountability. The supposed safeguard that exists is the retrospective review of telephone interceptions conducted by a Commissioner appointed under IOCA section 8. The Commissioner must be a past or present holder of 'high judicial office' and his remit is to keep under review the functions carried out under the Act by the Secretary of State and to assist the Tribunal, established under section 7, to investigate breaches of the Act. The Tribunal has a somewhat limited function, because in most instances, under section 9, no evidence may be raised in chief or questions asked in cross-examination as to whether an offence has taken place under the Act or as to whether a warrant has been issued.[98]

The Commissioner's Report contains information which, for security reasons, is not available to the general public. The published Annual Report for 1999[99] states that the Commissioner had access to all relevant files and appropriate documentation. Having inspected a sample of warrants from a complete list, he was satisfied that all the 'serious crime warrants' concerned offences 'which would rank as serious crime by any reckoning'. The Commissioner was also satisfied that a distinction had been 'faithfully observed' between the powers of the Secret Intelligence Service in respect of IOCA and their more proactive powers under the Intelligence Services Act 1994. Despite listing certain errors made by Public Telecommunications operators, the Security Service, Secret Intelligence Service, GCHQ, NCIS and Customs and Excise, the Commissioner stated that he continued to be 'highly impressed with the general standard of efficiency and dedication' displayed at all levels.[100] Such an uncritical response does little to foster faith in retrospective judicial review as an effective curb on the wide discretionary powers of the executive. The number of warrants issued under IOCA has grown from just over one thousand in 1993 to just over two thousand in 1998.[101] This hundred per cent increase over a period of only five years indicates that the Article 8(2) requirement of necessity in respect of derogation from privacy rights is a flexible one.

A main difficulty in testing the validity of the derogation in Article 8(2) is that section 9 prevents any challenge to the legality of interceptions that may have occurred. In the vast majority of cases, the interceptions will not form evidence in any subsequent criminal trial. In *R v Preston and ors.*[102] the House of Lords confirmed that the correct interpretation of IOCA was that 'neither the existence of a telephone intercept under warrant nor the result thereof are to be disclosed in evidence'.[103] The express wording of IOCA therefore undermines the normative rules about the disclosure of unused evidence in criminal proceedings.[104] The European Commission upheld this position stating that there was no arguable complaint under Article 6 or Article 8.[105] A major factor in this conclusion was that

> the defence and prosecution are in the same position from the outset of the criminal proceedings since neither can make use of the material.

This equality of position did not apply where the interception took place *other* than under a warrant issued under section 2. Thus where the interception was alleged to have been made on reasonable grounds to believe that one participant to the conversation consented to monitoring taking place,[106] the intercept was admissible in evidence. In *R v Rasool, R v Choudhary*,[107] the Court of Appeal confined the statements in *Preston* to warranted intercepts and held that recordings that had been made, allegedly with the knowledge of the informer, were admissible against the accused. This was despite the fact that, under section 9 of IOCA, no challenge could be made to test whether, in fact, there were reasonable grounds to believe in consent when the recording was made. Perhaps surprisingly, the European Court, in *Choudhary v United Kingdom*,[108] held that the complaint of Mr. Choudhary that his privacy rights were violated was inadmissible. Further, his right to a fair trial and, specifically under Article 6(3)(d), to examine and to cross-examine witnesses had not been infringed. The Court, adopting its usual rather passive position in respect of the factual findings of domestic judges, considered that there was no reason to enquire further into the finding of the trial judge that reasonable grounds for belief in consent existed. Arguments concerning the implicit deception involved in obtaining evidence in this way were also rejected. They will be considered in the next chapter.

In *R v Owen, R v Stephen*,[109] the issue of consent arose with respect to a telephone call made whilst in custody. The accused had telephoned his wife from a prison call box. He made incriminating admissions in this conversation. It was claimed that prisoners were informed that their conversations were liable to be listened to and recorded. The Court of Appeal held, following *Rasool*, that no question could be asked about the prison officers' reasonable belief as to whether either conversant consented to the intercept. Equality no longer exists between prosecution and defence when evidence can be adduced, but not challenged. In the later case of *Morgans v DPP*,[110] Kennedy, L.J. commented in the Divisional Court.

> It is a somewhat astonishing state of affairs if intercepted material on which the prosecution wishes to rely is to be excluded when a warrant has been obtained even if the defence want to see it admitted, but not when the material has been obtained illegally, that is to say by one of the persons identified in section 9(2) of the 1985 Act committing an offence.

In the House of Lords, this criticism was taken on board and acted upon. In *Morgans*, their Lordships overruled both the Court of Appeal decision in *Rasool* and that in *Owen*. Lord Hope expressed the view that, on a proper construction of *Preston*, there was

> no room for the drawing of a distinction between interceptions under warrant, which are undoubtedly lawful, and those whose lawfulness will depend on whether or not they can be shown to be consensual.

The 'integrity of the system would be put at risk' if the prosecution could adduce intercepted evidence and yet could not be challenged as to the method by which it was obtained. The House of Lords have, therefore, prevented the Crown from adducing evidence of intercepts of public systems in criminal trials save perhaps, in the narrow situation postulated by Lord Mackay, where both the prosecutor and the accused 'were agreed that the interception had been consented to'.

The European Court of Human Rights looks to the formality of the monitoring process rather than its substance. Thus, in those countries where, under an inquisitorial system, interception may only be authorised by a judge, failure to comply with the requirement of judicial authorisation will give rise to a violation of Article 8. In *A v France*,[111] police intercepted a telephone conversation and made recordings at the request of an informant. This procedure was held to violate Article 8 because there had been no order from an investigating judge and therefore the intercept 'had no basis in domestic law'. In the European Court, the clarity and detail of national statutory provisions appears to matter more than the 'quality' of due process protection enshrined therein, despite rhetoric to the contrary.[112]

The irony is that law enforcement agencies were aware of the deficiencies in English surveillance legislation earlier than the government. The package of voluntary NCIS Codes includes one that specifically covers the Interception of Communications and Accessing Communications Data. This encompasses forms of interception that are not within IOCA. Under the Code, an interception made under the Wireless Telegraphy Act 1949, that is the interception of radio waves, should only be sought where largely the same criteria apply as are required for the interception of a message sent via a public material communications system.[113] The interception of messages sent via pagers may now have greater protection under this Code, even though authorisation is still to be given by a member of the executive.[114] It is to be noted that *interference* with wireless telegraphy (jamming) is still within section 92 of the Police Act 1997. The interception of communications sent via private telephone systems is also now within paragraph 5 of the Code and the Code covers another lacuna in the legislation in that it governs consensual telephone tapping.[115] Inevitably, authorisation is by the police or by officers of Customs and Excise. Thus consent still removes the need for external executive authorisation, as does the intercepting of a private rather than a public system.[116] However, the authorising officer must be satisfied that the interception is necessary within the framework of the Code. The general scheme of IOCA is adopted in that authorisation is only justified in the interests of national security, for the purposes of detecting serious crime[117] or for the purpose of safeguarding the economic well-being of the United Kingdom. The principles of proportionality[118] and necessity are incorporated into the Code, although again the wider concept of necessity, that the desired result cannot reasonably be achieved by other means, is adopted.[119] The minimisation principle is acknowledged by a statement in para.1.7 that

> Applications for the interception of communications or accessing telecommunications data must specify any risk to intrusion into the privacy of persons other then the specified target (collateral intrusion) to allow the

authorising officer to take account of this when considering the application. Measures will be taken whenever practicable to avoid collateral intrusion.

It is a nice point whether, in view of the fact that interceptions may not generally be disclosed in evidence, such a principle can be enforced.

Electronic Search in the United States

In the United States, the problems associated with a piecemeal evolution of surveillance powers has been avoided by applying the Fourth Amendment to such situations, not in a proprietary way, but in a way that respects rights of privacy upon which an individual has 'justifiably relied'.[120] This recognition that the Amendment 'protects people not places' has enabled the development of legislation that governs nearly all forms of electronic search and applies consistent principles, whether the search is by interception of telephone calls, by the bugging of premises or by accessing data held in computers. Title 18 USC sections 2510 to 2520 control the authorisation of such searches. Section 2510 defines three different types of communication falling within Title 18. The first is a 'wire communication'. This means an 'aural transfer made in whole or in part through the use of facilities for the transmission of communications by the aid of wire, cable or other like connection between the point of origin and point of reception'. The Electronic Communications Privacy Act 1986 deleted any 'common carrier' requirement. The interception of private telephone systems is thus governed by the authorisation requirements. It was recognised, much earlier than in England and Wales, that the growth of private telephone systems required this amendment. Cellular telephones are also within this category.

The second type of communication covered by statute is an 'oral communication'. This is any utterance by a person 'exhibiting an expectation that such communication is not subject to interception under circumstances justifying such expectation'. Thus bugging falls within the same authorisation provisions as telephone interception. However, unaided overhearing does not, since the term 'intercept' is limited to the acquisition of the contents of a communication 'through the use of any electronic, mechanical or other device'. The definition does include at least some cordless telephones (Sundstrom, 1998:208). These have been included since 1994 (at least where the system incorporates security devices demonstrating a reasonable expectation of privacy) by virtue of the Communications Assistance for Law Enforcement

Act. There is some uncertainty whether voice pagers are included. They are not 'wire' communications as they are transmitted by radio waves. Any argument that the use of radio waves to communicate evinces no reasonable expectation of privacy on the part of the target has been substantially met by the inclusion of cordless telephones into the definition of 'oral' communication. However, since voice pagers do involve an oral transfer, this would exclude them from the category of 'electronic communication', and unless they do fall within the concept of oral communication, they are outside the authorisation provisions (Rutgers, 1987:500).

The final type of communication is an 'electronic communication'. Here there is less clarity as to the forms of communication encompassed by the expression, but it is, none the less, far more extensive than the range of communications covered by the statutory regime in England and Wales. Such a communication means

> any transfer of signs, signals, writing, images, sounds, data or intelligence of any nature transmitted in whole or in part by a wire, radio, electromagnetic photoelectronic or photooptical system that affects interstate or foreign commerce, but does not include–
> (A) any wire or oral communication;
> (B) any communication made through a tone-only paging device;
> (C) any communication from a tracking device (as defined in section 3117 of this Title);
> (D) electronic funds transfer information stored by a financial institution in a communications system used for the electronic storage and transfer of funds.

The definition includes computer communications, data pagers, electronic mail[121] and digital transmissions. It clearly excludes tone-only pagers. The interception of these pagers merely informs the interceptor that the paging company has notified a customer of the existence of a message. It also excludes tracking devices,[122] since they emit a tone, but are not 'electronic communications'. There are other similar interceptions that fall outside section 2510, for instance, pen registers and toll records.[123] In *Smith v Maryland*,[124] it was confirmed by the Supreme Court that there was no reasonable expectation of privacy in respect of the numbers being dialled from the telephone of the subscriber, as opposed to any conversation taking place from that telephone.

Those communications that do fall within section 2510 are protected to the extent that the authorisation requirements of sections 2516 to 2518 apply. Failure to comply with these will render the 'intentional' interceptor liable to prosecution,[125] the evidence will be suppressed at trial[126] and an 'aggrieved person' may claim damages.[127] The basis of authorisation is judicial order. By section 2511, an order is not required when at least 'one of the parties to the communication has given prior consent to such interception'. Thus participant monitoring gives law enforcers in the United States the same freedom from constraint that it does in England and Wales; but perhaps the advantages are greater because, if no consent is given, the surveillance application must receive detached and neutral scrutiny by a judicial officer. Other exemptions from judicial order are cases involving the acquisition of intelligence information by the United States Government[128] and certain emergency surveillance, although in this latter case the exemption is only from *prior* judicial authorisation under section 2518(7). The situations justifying emergency surveillance are that there is an immediate danger of death or serious physical injury to a person, or that there is a conspiracy threatening national security or one involving 'organised crime'. The emergency power lasts for 48 hours unless renewed by a judge.

Section 2516 provides that either a State Court judge or a Federal Court judge may authorise interception. However, in the case of orders made by a Federal judge, a distinction exists between wire and oral communications, on the one hand, and electronic communications on the other. The interception of wire and oral communications is permitted only to obtain evidence of specified offences. The list, though fairly compendious, limits such surveillance to more serious crimes. Any authorisation for interception granted by a State Court judge, pursuant to State legislation, is also limited to a specific list of offences that is even more restrictive than that pertaining to applications made to a Federal judge.[129] However, where the order sought from a Federal judge is one authorising the interception of an electronic communication, the evidence to be obtained may relate to 'any felony'.

The matters of which a judge must be satisfied in hearing an application for an order echo those that are relevant to applications for warrants to search for tangible property. The safeguards of specificity, sufficiency of information, probable cause and necessity are all represented in the information requirements set out in section 2518. An application must provide 'a full and complete statement of the facts and circumstances relied on' including details of the relevant offence, the nature and location of the interception, the type of communication to be intercepted and the identity of the person, if known, whose communications are to be intercepted. However, this last requirement is not crucial. In *US v Donovan*,[130] it was stated that the precise identification of each party to an intercepted communication is not required, but a description of the general class, or classes, which they comprise is essential to enable the judge to determine whether additional information is necessary for a proper evaluation of the interests of the various parties.[131] Even though, in this case, the Government failed to comply with the test, the warrant was not suppressed. It was considered that the identification of the targets did not play a substantial role in the judicial authorisation. The view that the particular identification of targets is less important than the identification of the locations at which the intercept is to take place, is in direct contrast to the 'roving surveillance' provisions contained in section 2518(11).

Roving surveillance enables law enforcement officers to monitor criminals who continuously and frequently change telephone line usage and move the location of meetings. The Electronic Communications Privacy Act 1986 incorporated into section 2518 removes the need to specify the nature and location of the facilities from where the communication is to be intercepted. Although this would, at first sight, appear to be a draconian provision enabling electronic search to go far beyond the normal limitations of a search warrant, it has been pointed out that in focusing on the target, rather then on the premises, a roving surveillance order may be more protective of innocent third party rights. Orders that specify only places may permit all conversations that occur at the designated premises to be intercepted. There must be some limit on the validity of roving surveillance authorisations. Once the application extends beyond a few locations, there may be some difficulty in establishing probable cause in respect of each location (Goldsmith, 1987).

The principle of necessity is reflected in the requirement that there must be a full and complete statement as to whether or not other investigative procedures have been tried and failed, or why they reasonably appear unlikely to succeed if tried, or to be too dangerous.[132] In *US v Girodano*,[133] and *US v Khan*,[134] it was emphasised that this requirement is 'designed to assure that wiretapping is not resorted to in situations where traditional investigative techniques would suffice to expose the crime'. Electronic surveillance should not, therefore, be a routine part of criminal investigation. It should also not be used for expediency in order to obtain results more quickly since, unlike the situation in England and Wales, there is no reference to the practicability of other means and achieving the desired objective within a 'reasonable time'. The minimisation principle resides not only in those requirements relating to specificity of location and target, but also in the time limitation contained in section 2518(5). The maximum period of authorised surveillance (unless renewed) is 'no longer than is necessary to achieve the objective of the authorisation' or 'no longer than thirty days' whichever is the shorter period.

It is to be noted that this period, although it may be renewed, is much shorter than that applying to initial authorisations granted in England and Wales.[135] Any lack of an equivalent provision in a State statute is likely to fall foul of the Fourth Amendment.[136] It will ultimately be the objective reasonableness of the actions of investigators that is crucial, not their subjective intentions concerning minimisation.[137]

There are certain situations where the specificity and minimisation requirements of section 2518 may be said to be less stringent. One of these is the power to effect roving surveillance. Another is the power of officers, under section 2157(5), to use intercepted communications 'other than those specified in the authorisation'. This enables an application of the 'plain view' doctrine. This doctrine was recognised to be applicable to searches for tangible property in the case of *Coolidge v New Hampshire*.[138] Providing that an officer has prior justification to effect surveillance and the discovery is inadvertent, serendipitous evidence obtained from the electronic search may be used by the police. It has been argued that this provision is rendered unnecessary by *Coolidge* (La Due, 1990). However, there are certain conditions attached to electronic plain view search that do not apply in the case of other searches. An application to 'amend' the surveillance order must be made to a competent judge as soon as practicable. The judge may then approve the use of the evidence obtained where it has been found that the conversation was 'otherwise intercepted' in accordance with statute. This relaxation of the specificity requirement has been further expanded by judicial interpretation that supports crime control at the expense of due process rights. There is no need to rely upon retrospective authorisation when the evidence obtained is deemed to be of a similar offence or an integral part of the suspected offence. By widening the parameters of the original investigation, a court justifies a finding that the original application was not a subterfuge.[139] In another swipe at the restrictions imposed by section 2517, courts have also held that if there is mention of the plain view interception in renewal applications, or even in a judicial report, that there exits an implied authorisation; a kind of incorporation by reference theory therefore applies.[140] As reliance on covert policing to combat serious crime increases, the courts in the United States, as in England and Wales, are finding justifications to admit probative evidence despite there being some arguable illegality in the way that it was obtained.

A major difficulty in constraining the use of electronic search is that it is more difficult to draw a clear line concerning expectations of privacy when remote intrusions are concerned. The *Katz* paradigm has been criticised for not identifying those factors that might indicate when a reasonable expectation

of privacy exists. It has been said to resemble an Inland Revenue Code w
states 'pay whatever you think is fair, subject to a *post hoc* jud
determination that you have paid a fair tax, with penalties for bad guesses'
(Power, 1989:56). It is made additionally difficult to define and maintain
justified privacy expectations when the very nature of electronic eavesdropping
dictates that 'all communications are presumed pertinent and are therefore
monitored – until agents decide otherwise' (Goldsmith and Balmforth, 1991).
If the same rule were applied to physical search, police would be able to
ransack homes and offices to search for information or for evidence and would
only be obliged to return items seized if they proved to be irrelevant. It is
much easier to be specific about a document or file that is being sought than
about a conversation that has yet to take place. For this very reason, it has
been said that electronic eavesdropping is 'more penetrating, more
indiscriminate, more truly obnoxious to a free society' than ordinary searches
and 'makes the police omniscient'.[141]

Electronic Search in Canada

The Protection of Privacy Act[142] predated the Canadian Charter in recognising
that a right to privacy existed in respect of communications and in attempting
to effect a balance between the often 'antagonistic purposes' of law enforcement personnel, armed with sophisticated eavesdropping devices, and citizenry
'whose privacy was so zealously guarded by other aspects of the legislation'
(Watt, 1979). Electronic search in Canada is now governed by sections 183 to
196 of the Criminal Code. These sections provide a complete code for the
interception of 'private communications'. 'Private communications' cover
the same range of communications that are protected from unauthorised
interception in the United States. In addition, the installation and monitoring
of tracking devices is governed by section 492.1 of the Criminal Code. If the
police place a beeper in a car without first obtaining a warrant, the search will
be an unreasonable one under section 8 of the Charter. However, in *R v Wise*,[143]
the Supreme Court held that such an unauthorised search was only minimally
intrusive. There was a lower expectation of privacy in a car than in an office[144]
and, despite the Charter breach, the admission of the evidence would not
bring the administration of justice into disrepute. The use of a pager appears
to be a controversial method of communication in all jurisdictions. In *R v
Lubovac*,[145] the Court of Appeal in Alberta held that messages sent by pagers
were not private communications since the pager simply broadcast a message

to 'those who may happen to hear –or to overhear it'. It is necessary to examine each paging system on its own merits since some pagers broadcast messages on a discrete frequency that can be received only by a receiver set to that frequency. As in the United States, the real question is whether there has been a violation of a justifiable expectation of privacy.

Assuming that a communication is within the Criminal Code, an application for authority to intercept must be made in writing to a judge. The application must be signed by a provincial Attorney-General or Solicitor-General, or a designated agent. It must be accompanied by a sworn affidavit based on the 'information and belief' of a law enforcement officer. The affidavit must depose to matters that would support an application for a warrant to search for physical items and there are substantial similarities with United States' legislation. Sufficiency of information is required. The affidavit must set out the facts justifying belief that the authorisation should be granted and the particulars of the offence. In *R v Garofoli*,[146] it was stated that *Hunter v Southam Inc.*[147] applied equally to electronic search and that, if there were not reasonable grounds to believe that a specified crime had been committed and that the interception would afford evidence of this, there would be an unreasonable search. The basis of a reasonable grounds finding is, however, the 'totality of circumstances' test as propounded in *Illinois v Gates*[148] and a tip off from an informant may play a significant part in establishing probable cause.

Specificity and minimisation of intrusion requirements are incorporated. The affidavit must state the type of private communication to be intercepted, the names, addresses and occupations, if known, of all targets and a general description of the nature and location of the place where the interception is to occur. The manner of interception to be used must also be stated.[149] It may be that greater specificity is required in respect of private premises than in respect of places to which the public have access. In *R v Thompson*,[150] the appellants had been charged with a conspiracy to import a controlled drug. The Crown's case rested principally on intercepted communications. The authorisations had permitted interceptions at the specified addresses of certain individuals and also at locations 'elsewhere in the Province of British Columbia resorted to' by these persons. The affidavit revealed that the police intended to intercept public pay telephones. The police installed equipment in residences, hotel rooms and pay booths. Subsequent applications extended the range of public pay phone bugging and, on some occasions, tape recorders were installed and were left on 'automatic play mode' throughout the night. As a consequence, the conversations of innocent third parties were also intercepted. The majority of the Supreme Court held that the authorisations complied with the Criminal Code. There were limitations contained in the warrants and they did not permit the interception of communications of 'anyone anywhere in the province'. The failure to list the pay telephones targeted did not invalidate the authorisations, even though a more specific description could have been given. There was criticism, however, of any use of indiscriminate recording 'in the hope that the target comes along'. There should be probable cause to believe that a target is using the telephone before a listening device is activated. In contrast, interception obtained by means of surreptitious entry onto private residential premises, that were not specifically mentioned on the face of the authorisations, was said to violate section 8 of the Charter.[151] The result of *Thompson* is that there is some parity with the 'roving surveillance' provisions applied in the United States.

However, even in places which are accessible to the public, albeit by invitation or licence only, a reasonable expectation of privacy exists. Thus, in *R v Wong*,[152] police, with the permission of the hotel management but without any judicial authorisation, bugged a hotel room which they had cause to believe had been used for gambling activities. The Supreme Court held, without any doubt, that the surreptitious video recording, even though it did not intercept a conversation but recorded presence at a location, was a 'search' and, if it was unauthorised, it was unreasonable under section 8 of the Charter. La Forest J. stated

> I am firmly of the view that if a free and open society cannot brook the prospect that the agents of the state should, in the absence of judicial authorisation, enjoy the right to record the words of whomsoever they choose, it is equally inconceivable that the state should have unrestricted discretion to target whomsoever it chooses for surreptitious video surveillance.

The Court also considered that, although those who engaged in meeting others with common interests cannot expect their presence to go unnoticed,

> it is no part of the reasonable expectations of those who hold or attend such gatherings that as a price of doing so they must tacitly consent to allow agents of the state unfettered discretion to make a permanent electronic recording of the proceedings.

The fact that the room was being used for an illegal purpose was not determinative in deciding whether a reasonable expectation of privacy existed. It was said that if it were otherwise, *ex post facto* reasoning would enable the police to validate any unauthorised search that had revealed criminality on the part of the target. Therefore, the fact that criminal proceedings result from the search cannot influence an assessment of whether a justifiable expectation existed at the time that the surveillance was carried out.

Specification of the identity of the target is also a less than absolute obligation. In *Grabowski v The Queen*,[153] the Crown sought to adduce intercepted conversations where authorisation had been given in respect of the caretaker of premises where drugs were allegedly being manufactured. The warrant also named 'certain other persons whose identity is at present unknown, but who have acted or are acting, or may act in concert or in collusion with [the caretaker] or with a person found at one of the places named' in the authorisation. Charges against the caretaker were later withdrawn. The Supreme Court held that this did not mean that the use of his name was a fiction designed to ensure the granting of the authorisation. The very wide location description that also appeared on the face of the warrant[154] was deleted and the remainder of the authorisation was thereby validated on the basis that interceptions in fact only took place from a named location.

The judge hearing the application must satisfy himself that it would be 'in the best interests of the administration of justice' to issue a warrant and that 'other investigative procedures have been tried and failed, or are unlikely to succeed, or the matter is so urgent that it would be impractical to carry out the investigation of the offence using other investigative procedures'. Thus the principle of necessity receives statutory recognition in a form that combines both the narrower and the wider last resort approaches. Practicality does enter in as a valid consideration, but only when urgency is involved. Thus expediency has only a limited part to play. In *R v Rowbotham*,[155] it was said that eavesdropping must be more than 'just a useful tool' and that the court should be apprised of the nature, progress and difficulties of the investigation.

In England and Wales and in the United States,[156] consent to eavesdropping, even by one party only, removes the need for judicial authorisation. The position is less clear in Canada. Although it was thought prior to the enactment of the Charter that the Criminal Code expressly permitted consensual monitoring without judicial control (Watt, 1979), this cannot remain the case in the light of *Duarte v The Queen*.[157] In that case, an undercover officer and an informant had consented to the installation of recording equipment inside the wall of a flat that had been specifically leased for that purpose. Drug trafficking transactions were discussed in the flat and criminal charges brought on the basis of those conversations. The entire bugging operation had lasted for two years. La Forest J. queried whether the use of participant surveillance, even absent the need for statutory control, could leave the police free to 'conduct this type of surveillance on whom they wish, where they wish and for as long as they wish'. He determined that it could not. Rather than base this view on the 'assumption of risk' doctrine that exists in the United States,[158] he preferred to look at the issue in terms of the balance of rights between the individual and the State. It was said that

> No justification for the arbitrary exercise of state power can be made to rest on the simple fact that persons often prove to be poor judges of whom to trust when divulging confidences.

The need for authorisation was to protect all citizens from the unfettered discretion of the State and to protect a 'meaningful residuum' in the right to live life free from surveillance. However, as in the case of *Wong*, the ignorance of the police about the applicability of Charter rights to the monitoring that had been carried out and the fact that they had acted in accordance with the law as it had been for many years before the Charter, meant that the admission of the evidence would not bring the administration of justice into disrepute. That argument cannot now prevail, since officers can no longer claim that they acted on an 'entirely reasonable misunderstanding of the law'.

The Canadian experience is an instructive one. In the United States, eavesdropping legislation post-dated the Fourth Amendment. It was therefore necessary to redefine the protections granted by that Amendment in order to make them relevant to modern technologies. This led to a major shift in that people's private acts and utterances were protected even though no physical trespass had occurred. In Canada, statutory conditions in respect to interceptions existed before the general right to be secure against unreasonable searches was incorporated into the Charter. The courts thus had to reassess the validity of those statutory provisions in the light of the Charter. In much the same way, in England and Wales, an assessment will have to be made whether our surveillance legislation (and lack of judicial control) accords with the Human Rights Act 1998. As stated earlier, in Canada, legislation that is inconsistent with the Charter is 'read down' so that it no longer infringes basic rights. In England, it is not possible for judges to override primary legislation where there is a clear inconsistency with the Human Rights Act. There is merely an obligation, under section 3 to apply legislation in a way that is consistent with the Act 'so far as it is possible to do so'.[159] None the less, the potential for outlawing some current practices exists. Obvious areas of weakness are the lack of prospective judicial authorisation and of external accountability in the majority of surveillance activities. The impact of the Human Rights Act will depend, almost entirely, on the attitude of the English judiciary. A positive and pro-active approach to human rights enforcement might well result in a reformation of existing law. This has, by and large, been the approach adopted by the Canadian Supreme Court. A more conservative approach would mean that there will be little change in domestic legislation. Domestic law appears to be largely immune from effective scrutiny by the European Court of Human Rights on the basis that matters of procedure and evidence are for national courts (Sharpe, 1997). Further, the decision of a court that there has been an unreasonable search does not, of itself, have any impact on the admissibility of the fruits of that search in any subsequent criminal trial. Yet, the accused person is more concerned with whether the information or evidence obtained through an investigative search can be used against him, than with the often theoretical issue of whether his privacy and/or personal autonomy has been violated. In the next chapter the relationship between unlawful searches and trial evidence is considered.

The Future of Covert Investigation

On 9th February 2000, the Regulation of Investigatory Powers Bill was introduced in the House of Commons. It is claimed, in the explanatory notes accompanying the Bill, that the proposed legislation provides 'a new regime for the interception of communications' and 'goes beyond what is strictly required for human rights purposes'.[160] It is too soon to make any final evaluation of the truth of this claim since amendments will undoubtedly take place during its passage through Parliament. Further, much of the substance of the Bill is to be incorporated via regulations and codes of practice to be made by order of the Secretary of State.[161] However, the initial response to this proposed statute must be that, in most instances, protections for targets of electronic search will not be increased in any substantial way and, indeed in some cases, may even be diminished.

The Bill covers the interception and acquisition of communications, covert surveillance, the use of human intelligence sources (undercover agents and informers) and the decryption of encrypted data. Clauses 1–19 deal with the interception of communications and, to a large extent, replicate current IOCA provisions.[162] A distinction is still made between public and private telecommunications systems and services. A public service is one which 'is offered or provided to, or to a substantial section of, the public in any one or more parts of the United Kingdom'.[163] A private system is one which, though not itself a public system, is attached to a public system. Thus, an office network linked to a public system by a private exchange is a 'private system', but an entirely free standing system is not. The Bill provides regulation for the interception (not the jamming)[164] of both public and private systems. Clause 2(7) provides that coverage extends to the time when information is stored in the system for the intended recipient to collect or access. This covers electronic mail stored by a service provider or waiting pager messages.[165]

Interception is unlawful and a crime unless it falls within one of the legal justifications set out in clause 1(5) or, in the case of a private system, the person who has the right to control the system has given consent to the interception.[166] The justifications for interception largely replicate the existing situation. Interceptions based on reasonable belief in the consent of both parties to the communication, unsurprisingly, are lawful. Thus, the overt use of an answering machine is not a crime. Interceptions taking place by communications service providers and connected with the provision of such service are protected, as are interceptions under the Prison Act 1952 and the National Health Service Act 1977.[167] Three new provisions exist. One gives, in theory, somewhat greater protection to a target by providing that an interception is lawful if the consent of one party is obtained and also the interception is authorised as a surveillance activity by a law enforcement agency. Whilst tightening up the existing provision in subsection 1(2) of IOCA, it may make little difference in actuality because interceptions are unlikely to occur, even now, without the authorisation of a senior officer as required by the NCIS Code. The second new provision gives wide power to the Secretary of State to make regulations authorising the interception of communications where there are reasonable grounds to believe that the target is in a territory outside the United Kingdom. This power is to give effect to Article 17 of the European Draft Convention on Mutual Assistance in Criminal Matters.[168] The final new provision is that the Secretary of State may make regulations for interception effected as part of a 'legitimate business practice'. The remaining justification is that a warrant has been issued by the Secretary of State. The bases for the issuance of such warrants are widened to include not only the existing IOCA grounds, but also the additional ground of giving effect to any international mutual assistance agreement. The explanatory notes state that the necessity and proportionality principles of Article 8 are enshrined in the Bill with respect to the warrant provisions.[169] However, the necessity requirement in the proposed legislation does not differ one jot from the existing language of section 2 of IOCA, the effect of the Bill being, in this respect, a repackaging exercise. It is also made explicit that authorisation legitimates conduct incidental to the execution of the warrant. Significantly, the major objection, that the issuance of warrants is by the executive rather than by a detached judicial officer, remains.

There is a genuine attempt to ensure that the specificity requirements applying to warrants are fulfilled. Clause 8(1) states that the warrant must name the person or describe the set of premises from which interception will take place. The factors, such as addresses and telephone numbers that are to be used to identify the communications to be intercepted must also be stated. Alternatively, the Secretary of State may issue a certificate limiting the range of intercepted material that may be looked at or listened to under the warrant. However, this concession to due process protection has to be read in the context of clause 9 which provides for the duration of warrants. The period of interception under IOCA is two months, but the proposed legislation would provide for a period of three months (or six months if issued under the hand of the Secretary of State and justified by the need to protect national security or the economic well-being of the United Kingdom). Theoretically, the warrant must be cancelled if the ground for issuance no longer exists. The Secretary of State will put arrangements in place to 'ensure' that the disclosure and copying of data 'is limited to the minimum that is necessary for the authorised purposes'.[170]

The obvious problem from a human rights perspective is that these controls are systemically internal and are unlikely to be capable of challenge in the vast majority of cases. This is because it is unlikely that the intercepted evidence will be used at trial[171] and because public interest immunity protects this material from disclosure.[172] The prohibition on adducing intercepted communications as evidence in a criminal trial, that has so recently been expounded in *Morgans v DPP*,[173] is echoed in clause 16. Clause 16 virtually replicates the substance of section 9 of IOCA. Paragraph 132 of the explanatory notes states that clause 16(1) places a prohibition on the use of intercepted material in connection with court proceedings. It does this directly, by stating that the contents of the intercepted material and communications data may not be disclosed, and indirectly by prohibiting the disclosure of any suggestion that unlawful interception has occurred. However, the prohibition has certain exceptions. One is that a 'person conducting a criminal prosecution' may have disclosure of an intercept in order to fulfil his ethical duty to ensure that a prosecution is fair.[174] Disclosure may also be made to a judge at his request in 'exceptional circumstances' and when this is 'essential in the interests of justice'.[175] Such disclosure shall be to the judge 'alone' and may raise potential difficulties in immunity applications in respect of unused material. Clause 17(8) makes it clear that a judge *can not* order disclosure to the defence. He can only direct the prosecution to make such admissions of fact as he 'thinks essential in the interests of justice'. Even this power is only to be used 'in exceptional circumstances'.[176] Presumably, should the prosecutor not comply, a judge's only other option is to dismiss the prosecution. Since the European Court of Human Rights has consistently stated that the trial judge is in the best position to ensure the fairness of the proceedings before him, it is unfortunate that so many limitations are to be placed upon judicial control of the fact-finding process. A third exception to the prohibition on disclosure applies when interception is lawfully conducted without a warrant.[177] This exception is inconsistent with *Morgans* and proves that the Law Lords are more in tune with the realities of the inequality of arms that is inherent in an adversarial system than the drafters of the legislation or the judges of the European Court.[178]

Clause 25 sets up a statutory system of authorisation in respect of 'surveillance and covert human intelligence sources'. However, the impact of this provision is substantially reduced by clause 70. Clause 70 states that 'nothing in any of the provisions of this Act' shall be construed as making it unlawful to engage in any conduct of that description 'which would not be unlawful apart from this Act'. Nor does the Act prejudice 'any power to obtain information by any means not involving conduct that may be authorised by this Act'. The explanatory notes reiterate that

> the provisions themselves do not impose any requirement on public authorities to seek or obtain an authorisation where, under the Bill, one is available.

Law enforcement agencies may therefore 'take the risk' of proceeding without authorisation and put the onus on any target to challenge their actions under Article 8. This 'optional' statutory regulation applies to three separate types of surveillance. The first is 'directed surveillance'. By clause 25(2), such surveillance is covert but not 'intrusive'.[179] It is undertaken for the purpose of a specific investigation and in order to obtain information about or to identify a particular person, or to determine who is involved in the matter under investigation. Thus non-intrusive targeting is directed surveillance. It may also include telephone intercepts where one party consents to the interception.[180]

'Intrusive surveillance' is defined in clause 25 as being surveillance that is covert and

(a)   involves the presence of an individual, or of any surveillance device, on any residential premises or in any private vehicle;[181] or

(b)   is carried out in relation to anything taking place on residential premises or in a private vehicle by means of any surveillance device that is not present on the premises or in the vehicle.

Remote surveillance may thus be intrusive, but only if it consistently provides information of the same quality and detail as might be expected from a device placed inside premises or in a private vehicle.[182] The use of a tracking device is not intrusive surveillance.[183] However, the use of such a device might fall within the description of directed surveillance. It is interesting that the categories of specially protected locations have shrunk from those listed in the Police Act 1997 and the concept of specially protected information has disappeared.[184] The leitmotif of trespass and property protection appears again as the basis of protection. The final form of surveillance is 'covert human intelligence'. Clause 25(7) defines this as a relationship maintained for 'the covert purpose' of obtaining information, or providing access to any information to another person, or disclosing information obtained through the relationship. Informers and undercover officers are therefore within these provisions.

Conduct that is in accordance with an authorisation under the proposed Act is validated. Clause 26 states that such conduct 'shall be lawful for all purposes' and that no civil liability shall arise even for conduct 'incidental' to the activity. Much as warrants validate physical search, authorisation will preclude challenge to electronic search. Inevitably, the possibility of challenging whether conduct has been in accordance with proper authorisation may suffer from the same public interest immunity barrier that attaches, potentially, to all covertly obtained evidence.[185] The purposes for which direct surveillance or the use of human intelligence sources may be authorised are stated in clauses 27 and 28. The similarities with IOCA are evident, but the grounds are wider than those permitting interception. The prevention or detection of crime, or the prevention of disorder, is one ground, but there is no requirement that the relevant crime is 'serious'. The interests of public safety, the protection of public health and the assessing and collecting of taxes are also justifications. The Secretary of State may, by order, authorise further purposes beyond those set out in the Bill. Intrusive surveillance is dealt with in clause 30. This permits surveillance only on the grounds that justify the interception of communications.

A clear distinction is made, therefore, between the various categories of surveillance activity with much of such activity being justified on grounds wider than those existing under the current NCIS Codes.[186] Whilst the principles of proportionality and necessity are enshrined in clauses 27 and 28, only clause 30 provides any definition of necessity. This is the wider interpretation of the concept and requires that the information cannot 'reasonably' be obtained by other means. Expediency may therefore be a valid consideration. Authorisations are to be granted by law enforcers and not by the judiciary. Unless they are for intrusive surveillance, authorisations are not even to be reviewed by Commissioners.[187] The scheme of the Police Act is adopted as a paradigm, but the only situation that requires prospective authorisation by a Surveillance Commissioner is intrusive surveillance. Even this requirement does not apply where the situation is one of urgency.[188] A major defect in the Police Act 1997, that it does not, as a norm, require the police to obtain prior judicial authority, has not been addressed.

Intrusive surveillance carried out by the Security and Intelligence Services continues to be authorised by warrants issued by the Secretary of State or, in cases of urgency, by a senior official. Yet, there is still an overlap of functions between the police and defence services as warrants may be issued to the latter for the purpose of 'preventing or detecting serious crime'. The lack of accountability of the Intelligence and Security Services in the conduct of their criminal investigatory functions continues to be a matter of concern. The duration of authorisations for surveillance activity will depend upon the type of activity undertaken. Direct and intrusive surveillance authorisations will last for three months, unless they have been granted orally or in 'urgent' cases.[189] Authorisation for the use of a covert human intelligence source will last for twelve months. These relatively generous periods are capable of renewal on the same terms, though in the case of the use of human intelligence sources, an internal 'review' of the necessity for renewal shall take place.[190]

This first draft of the Bill is, in reality, little more than a formalisation in statute of rhetorical best practice under the voluntary NCIS Codes. It would set up a legal structure for covert investigatory activity, but would not permit prior judicial scrutiny, other than in the limited situation of intrusive surveillance conducted by law enforcers. It imposes no greater accountability on investigators than currently exists. Breaches of the legislation may well occur, but remain undiscovered or be incapable of discovery. To this extent, the codes of practice that are to be created under clauses 62 and 63 of the Bill may have a limited effect in ensuring compliance with Articles 6 and 8 of the Convention. The government obviously hopes that the reduction of current practice into statutory form will justify the widening of law enforcement powers with regard to the duration of authorisations and the purposes for which authorisations may be granted. The new power, to be granted to law enforcers and to intelligence agencies, to require the decryption of data that has been protected by encryption is a further example of the equivocal nature of this Bill.[191] It remains to be seen, assuming that no major amendments are made to the proposed legislation, how effectively these provisions will safeguard personal privacy and will allow challenge when such privacy is violated.

Notes

1.   The treatment by the courts of evidence obtained in breach of these rights, or by entrapment, or abuse is discussed in chapter 6.
2.   See chapter 1.
3.   The Police Act 1997 Part 3 and the NCIS Codes on Covert operations (1999) demonstrate a belated attempt to comply with Article 8. See below for a discussion of the provisions.
4.   See *On Lee v US* (1951) 343 US 747; *Lopez v US* (1963) 373 US 427; *Hoffa v US* (1966) 385 US 293.
5.   It will be seen that other forms of electronic search may be consensual or may be effected by authorisation and without the consent of any individual.
6.   An *agent provocateur* is one who 'entices another to commit an express breach of the law he would not otherwise have committed and then proceeds to inform against him in respect of such an offence', see The Royal Commission on Police Powers (1928).
7.   See for instance the Audit Commission Report (1993).
8.   In England and Wales, however, there is no substantive defence of entrapment and the courts have rarely held that conduct of the participant is such as to justify exclusion of the evidence against the accused; see chapter 6.
9.   *E.g.* the notification of the right to immediate and free access to legal advice and the administration of a proper caution.
10.   Issued May 1999.
11.   Home Office Circular no. 35/1986.
12.   NCIS Code on the Use Of Informants at paras. 2.6–2.17 and NCIS Code on Undercover Operations at paras. 2.5–2.16.
13.   The definition in para. 1.14.10 replicates the PACE definition of excluded material.
14.   Para. 2.4.
15.   Code on Undercover Operations para. 1.7.
16.   *Ibid* at para. 2.3.
17.   *Ibid* at para. 2.2.
18.   Notes for Guidance 2A. Cp. Schedule 1 of PACE which is much more restrictive.
19.   See below.
20.   (1980) 447 US 264.
21.   And thus his Sixth Amendment right to assistance of counsel attached.
22.   (1986) 477 US 436.
23.   See *R v Herbert* (1990) 57 CCC (3d) 1 and cp. *Broyles v The Queen* (1991) 68 CCC (3d) 308.

24. *Broyles v The Queen* (above).
25. *R v Pavic* (1998) 151 ALR 98.
26. *R v Pfenig (no.1)* (1992) 57 SASR 507.
27. See USC Title 18 sects. 2510–2520 and the Criminal Code of Canada sects. 183–196 and below.
28. (1990) 57 CCC (3d) 1.
29. Sect. 7 grants the right not to be deprived of life, liberty or security of person except in accordance with 'principles of fundamental justice' and this includes the right to silence.
30. At p. 16.
31. (1990) 65 DLR (4th) 240. See below for a fuller discussion.
32. The Court in *Duarte* (above) distinguished U.S. authority on this point.
33. *US v White* (1971) 401 US 745.
34. *Katz v US* (1967) 389 US 347.
35. See note 33 above.
36. Guidelines on The Use of Equipment in Police Surveillance Operations (1984). These Guidelines are now replaced by the NCIS Codes and the Code laid under the Police Act 1997.
37. [1996] 3ALL ER 289.
38. That to admit the evidence would have such an adverse effect on trial fairness that judicial discretion should be applied to exclude it; see chapters 1 and 6.
39. [1996] 3 ALL ER at 289.
40. Lord Nolan at 302 (HL) and Lord Taylor (1995) 1 Cr. App. R. 242 at 255 (CA).
41. *Khan v United Kingdom* Application No. 35394197, heard under the new Protocol 11 (1997) 27 EHRR CD 58.
42. The same arguments will be raised in the European Court's hearing of *Govell v United Kingdom* App. No. 27237/95.
43. (1928) 277 US 438.
44. (1967) 388 US 41.
45. (1967) 389 US 347.
46. See the next chapter.
47. Subsect. 93(2).
48. See the discussion of NCIS Codes on Undercover Operations and the Use of Informants.
49. See chapter 3.
50. Schedule 1 para. 2(b)(i) and (ii). There is also a 'public interest' requirement in para. 2(c).
51. See above.
52. Para. 1.1 states that the Code 'must be readily available' at police stations and public offices of HM Customs and Excise. As with PACE, the Code is admissible in evidence under sect. 101(10) of the Police Act, but a failure to comply with the Code does not, of itself, render a person liable to civil or criminal proceedings.
53. Notes for Guidance 2A; see also Lord McIntosh Hansard vol. 576 col. 233.
54. Notes for Guidance 1 A.
55. Sect. 96.
56. Sect. 102.
57. The order for destruction of records does not become operative until the period within which the authorising officer may appeal has expired; see subsect. 103(4) and sect. 104.
58. Hansard vol. 576 cols. 215–217.

59. *Ibid.*
60. *Ibid* at col.219.
61. (1765) 19 St. Tr. 1029 and see chapter 1.
62. Per Lord Mackay Hansard vol. 576 at col. 207.
63. See chapter 4 for a discussion of legal privilege.
64. Lord Mackay (above).
65. These areas replicate the 'constitutionally protected areas' that existed in the USA prior to *Katz*, see chapter 1.
66. See chapter 4.
67. See chapter 4.
68. It would always be possible to seek to exclude such evidence under sect. 78 of PACE.
69. Subsect. 96(3)(b).
70. Para. 2.1
71. Para. 2.3.
72. See above.
73. *Viz.* a Chief Constable or Commissioner rather than an Assistant Chief Constable or Commander.
74. *R v Bailey and Smith* (1993) 97 Cr. App. R. 365; *R v Ali* The Times Feb. 19th 1991.
75. This was arguably the case in *R v Roberts* [1997] 1 Cr. App. R. 217.
76. *R v Christou and Wright* (1992) 4 ALL ER 559; *Duarte v The Queen* (1990) 65 DLR (4th) 240.
77. Under para. 3.9 when the target is specified, authorisation must be by a superintendent or above, but under para. 3.10 when the target is not specified or urgent authorisation of a target in a public place is required, an inspector may so authorise.
78. Paras. 3.1 and 3.2.
79. One part of the purpose statement may be the 'detection, deterrence and prevention of crime' as well as the creation of a safe environment, assisting traffic movement and a reduction in the fear of crime.
80. The voluntary Code of Practice (A Watching Brief, 1999) adopted by local authorities makes clear that 'individual privacy will be safeguarded' and private and family life and the home respected. Chapter 11 also states that 'cameras must not look into private property'.
81. A Watching Brief (above) chapter 20 and see *R v Broadcasting Standards Commission ex parte BBC* The Times September 14th 1999.
82. (1984) 7 EHRR 14. The European Commission had declared the application admissible in 1981 and the government undertook to bring forward legislation.
83. Above at p. 45. The same view was taken of the arrangements to meter Mr. Malone's telephone calls.
84. Cmnd. 8092 at paras. 3.53 to 3.60.
85. *R v Ahmed* [1995] Crim. L.R. 246; *R v Effick* [1994] 3 ALL ER 458. In the United States a similar restriction in Title 18 USC 2510 was removed by the Electronic Communications Privacy Act 1986.
86. USC sects. 2510 to 2520 was amended to cover wire, oral and electronic communications, see below.
87. Interception of Communications in the United Kingdom. A Consultation Paper (1999) and the Regulation of Investigatory Powers Bill 2000.
88. See *Christie v United Kingdom* App. No. 21482/93.

89. *Preston v United Kingdom* App. No. 24193/94.
90. Subsects. 1(2)(a) and (b). There is also an exemption in subsect. 1(3) for interception for 'purposes connected with the provision of postal or public telecommunications services'.
91. The information in this category must relate to the 'acts or intentions of persons outside the British Islands'.
92. See above.
93. Lord Denning considered that these words were not capable of legal definition and should be left to the determination of the Secretary of State (Hansard vol. 464 col. 1869 HL).
94. Article 8 does not clarify this concept. See *Christie v United Kingdom* (above) and the Annual Report on IOCA (1999).
95. The unsatisfactory nature of the law prior to the 1989 Act is demonstrated by the case of *Hewitt and Harman v United Kingdom* App. No. 20317/92.
96. Security Service Act 1996 sect. 1.
97. The fusion of functions between the police and the Security Service is one matter that is outstanding in reaching European wide agreement on the Draft Convention on Mutual Assistance in Criminal Matters; see Statewatch (1999) vol. 9 (May/August) 3.
98. Evidence may be adduced where it relates to proof of a 'scheduled offence' (*viz* one under the Telegraph and Post Office Acts or under the Official Secrets Act) or relates to unfair dismissal proceedings for an alleged offence under sect. 1 of IOCA.
99. Cm. 4364. Lord Nolan is the current Commissioner.
100. At p. 10. Previous Annual Reports have been equally complimentary.
101. At p. 11.
102. [1993] 4 ALL ER 638 HL.
103. Per Lord Jauncey at 646 and see Lord Mustill at 667.
104. Lord Mustill at 668–9 and see the Criminal procedure and Investigations Act 1996, discussed in chapter 6.
105. *Preston v UK* App. No. 24193/94.
106. Subsect. 1(2)(b) IOCA.
107. [1997] 2 Cr. App. R. 190; see also *R v Effick* (1992) 95 Cr. App. R. 47(CA).
108. App. No. 40084/98, determined under the new Protocol 11.
109. [1999] 2 Cr. App. R. 59.
110. [1999] 2 Cr. App. R. 99 at 106. HoL decision 17th February 2000 Internet.
111. (1993) 17 EHRR 462.
112. *Kruslin v France* (1990) 12 EHRR 547; *Huvig v France* (1990) 12 EHRR 528; *Kopp v Switzerland* (1998) 27 EHRR 91.
113. Code paras. 3.1 to 3.6.
114. In the case of the police, this is 'an officer acting under the authority of the Secretary of State' and in the case of HM Customs and Excise, a Chief Customs Investigation Officer. Since the interception is not within the current terms of IOCA, sect. 9 would not apply and the evidence could be both admitted and challenged in court; see *R v Taylor-Sabori* [1999] 1 ALL ER 160.
115. Code paras. 4.1 to 4.14.
116. The Code in Notes for Guidance 4A and 5A provides that interceptions of this kind shall not be used a means of circumventing IOCA.
117. Defined as in IOCA. Note the difference between consensual bugging of premises and consensual interception. The former only requires as a purpose the detection of crime (not necessarily serious crime).

118. See para. 1.6. Actions should be 'proportionate to the seriousness of the crime being investigated and the history and character of the individual(s) concerned'. The IOCA warrant time limits of two months also apply.
119. See Notes for Guidance 1B; para. 3.6 and para. 4.4.
120. *Katz v US* (1967) 389 US 347.
121. Stored e-mail can be accessed under Title 18 USC sects. 2701 to 2703.
122. In *US v Karo* (1984) 468 US 705, the Supreme Court held that warrantless monitoring by a tracking device placed in a private location not open to visual surveillance violates the Fourth Amendment.
123. Sect. 2511(2).
124. (1979) 442 US 735.
125. Sect. 2511.
126. Sect. 2515.
127. Sect. 2520.
128. Sect. 2511(f).
129. *E.g.* murder, kidnapping, gambling, robbery, bribery, extortion, dealing in prohibited drugs and other crimes 'dangerous to life limb and property, and punishable with imprisonment for more than one year'.
130. (1977) 429 US 413.
131. Citing *US v Chunn* (1974) 503 F2d 533. See also *US v Chavez* (1974) 416 US 580.
132. Cp. The differing necessity standards in PACE and in the Codes to the Police Act and the NCIS Codes discussed above.
133. (1974) 416 US 505.
134. (1974) 415 US 143.
135. Two months under IOCA and three under the Police Act 1997.
136. *Berger v New York* (1967) 388 US 41.
137. *Scott v US* (1978) 436 US 128.
138. (1971) US 443 and see chapter 2.
139. *US v Watchmaker* (1985) 761 F2d 1459 (11th Cir.). There is a parallel development in England and Wales concerning the use of conspiracy charges to validate undercover operations; see chapter 6.
140. See *US v Tortorello* (1973) 480 F2d 764 (2nd Cir) and *US v Gambale* (1985) 610 F.Supp 1515 (DC Mass).
141. *Lopez v US* (1963) 373 US 427.
142. 1973–1974 c.50.
143. (1992) 1 SCR 527.
144. Cp. *US v Karo* (1984) 465US 705.
145. (1989) 52 CCC(3d) 551 (Alta. CA).
146. (1990) 60 CCC (3d) 161.
147. (1984) 11 DLR (4th) 641 and see chapters 2 and 3.
148. (1983) 462 US 213; see chapter 3 for a discussion of this issue.
149. Sect. 185 Criminal Code.
150. (1990) 2 SCR 1111.
151. See also *Lyons v The Queen* (1984) 14 DLR (4th) 482 (a pre-Charter case). It is implicit in authorisation to intercept a private communication that the police may trespass on private property to plant a listening device. The authority arises by 'necessary implication'.
152. (1993) 86 CCC (3d) 63.

153. (1985) 22 DLR (4th) 725.
154. *Viz.* 'any other place or locality' where the persons could be found.
155. (1993) 86 CCC (3d) 63.
156. A very few states, for example Massachusetts, require both parties to consent; see *Commonwealth v Blood* (1987) 507 NE 2d 1029.
157. (1990) 65 DLR (4th) 240 and above.
158. See *US v White* (1971) 401 US 745 and above.
159. Where inconsistency exists, the court may issue a certificate of incompatibility under sect. 3.
160. At para. 8 of the notes.
161. *E.g.* the codes of practice under clause 62, the rules of the new tribunal under clauses 56–60 and modifications to the descriptions of intrusive surveillance.
162. Almost all of IOCA is to be repealed.
163. Clause 2.
164. Clause 2(2).
165. Such information may be accessed under Schedule 1 of PACE.
166. A tortious action may lie against the controller of the system under clause 1(3), for instance by an employee against the employer controlling the system.
167. Clause 4. Secure mental hospitals and prisons are affected.
168. It is intended to allow operators of satellite communications systems to use a ground station in a member State to facilitate interception by using a service provider located in a member State. The interception and the service provider are required to be in the same member State.
169. Paras. 51 to 55 of the notes.
170. Clause 14(2). Clause 14(3) provides for the destruction of material when authorised grounds to retain it no longer exist.
171. See clause 16, below.
172. Public interest immunity is discussed in chapter 6.
173. HL 17th February 2000 and see above.
174. Clause 17(5).
175. Clause 17(5).
176. Clause 17(7).
177. Clause 17(3). Stored material is accessed through Schedule 1 of PACE.
178. See *Choudhary v United Kingdom* (above).
179. See below.
180. Clause 45(4).
181. A private vehicle is defined in Clause 45(1) as being any vehicle which is used primarily for the private purposes of the person who owns it or of any person otherwise having the right to use it.
182. Clause 25(5).
183. Clause 25(4).
184. *Viz.* hotel bedrooms and offices. Confidential material is also protected under the Police Act.
185. See chapter 6.
186. The NCIS Codes state that undercover officers and participating informants are to be used only in cases of 'serious' crime or where there is a 'significant' threat to public order or community safety.

187. There will be a Surveillance Commissioner, a Security Service Act Commissioner, a Covert Investigation Commissioner, an Intelligence Services Act Commissioner and an Interception of Communications Commissioner. The current Interception of Communications Commissioner will 'hold over' his post under the new legislation. See clause 53.
188. Clause 33(3) and 34.
189. In which case the period will be 72 hours as under the Police Act.
190. Clause 41(6).
191. Clauses 46 to 52 of the Bill.

6 Search, Surveillance and Fair Trials

A search (whether electronic or physical) is effected by investigators in order to obtain evidence against a person. Given that 'probable cause' must exist before a warrant is issued or an interception order made in respect of a target, the objective of the search is clearly to firm up that probable cause into a provable case against the suspect. The likely consequence of a search that results in the incrimination of the target is his conviction for offending, revealed or confirmed as an outcome of the search. To such a target, any incidental violation of his personal autonomy or privacy may well be of less significance than the utilisation of this evidence in proceedings against him. Thus, although any improper or illegal search may give rise to a theoretical claim that Article 8 of the Convention on Human Rights has been broken, or that there has been an unreasonable search and seizure under the Fourth Amendment or section 8 of the Canadian Charter, an accused is more concerned with whether the use of such evidence is adjudged to render his trial unfair. The debate therefore shifts from privacy to due process.

Article 6 of the European Convention gives the right to a 'fair and public hearing'. It also grants specific 'minimum' procedural rights within this general and over-arching protection. These include the right of an accused to be informed promptly 'and in detail' the nature of the charge against him,[1] the right to be legally represented[2] and the right to 'examine or have examined witnesses against him and to obtain the attendance and examination of witnesses on his behalf'.[3] The presumption of innocence is incorporated into Article 6(2), but this is a relative safeguard. It has already been pointed out[4] that in *Murray v United Kingdom*,[5] the European Court refused to hold that, as a matter of principle, the drawing of adverse inferences from silence or non co-operation in the face of police interrogation was incompatible with a fair trial. There is no 'absolute' right to silence. Such a finding may well have implications for participant monitoring and for arguments that centre on the privilege against self-incrimination. Although the subject of the argument is an induced adverse admission (the converse of silence), the issue is the same,

155

namely whether a suspect is being compelled to incriminate himself and the meaning and scope of compulsion. In the United States, the Fourteenth Amendment provides that no one shall be deprived of life or liberty except in accordance with 'due process of law'.[6] Section 7 of the Canadian Charter similarly provides that persons shall not be deprived of life and liberty 'except in accordance with the principles of fundamental justice'. The privilege against self-incrimination is constitutionally protected by the Fifth Amendment which provides that a person shall not be compelled 'to be a witness against himself' and by sections 11 and 13 of the Canadian Charter. Section 11(d) of that Charter preserves the presumption of innocence. The fact that these provisions are linguistically similar to Article 6 disguises a systemic divide between adversarial and inquisitorial systems. In the latter, principles of free proof and an absence of exclusionary evidential rules are supposedly counterbalanced by judicial control of the pre-trial process. The jurisprudence of the European Court of Human Rights can be said to demonstrate a lack of empathy with adversarial systems (Sharpe, 1997) and, to that extent, the decision making of the North American courts is of greater value in interpreting any future domestic application of the Human Rights Act 1998.

Even in adversarial jurisdictions these due process provisions do not necessarily lead to the exclusion of criminal evidence that has been obtained through impropriety. The analyses that judges undertake in order to determine whether or not evidence should be suppressed depend upon the statutory and constitutional imperatives that exist within each jurisdiction. However, the outcome of these different analyses is often similar in that crime control values trump due process arguments concerning police impropriety and a conviction is upheld. This chapter examines judicial approaches to the suppression of improperly obtained search evidence and also considers the related problem that exists when a defendant seeks to establish that such evidence may have been improperly obtained. The shield of public interest immunity or public policy allows law enforcers to withhold investigative information from the defence and frequently precludes challenge to prosecution evidence because the accused cannot establish the possibility that he may have been entrapped or have been the victim of a 'plant' by another.

The Admissibility of Criminal Evidence in England and Wales

There is no automatic rule of evidential exclusion in England and Wales. The primary rule of evidence is that all relevant evidence is admissible regardless of how it has been obtained.[7] Cross (1999:501) goes so far as to conclude that illegally obtained search evidence is admissible, provided that it involves neither a reference to an inadmissible confession, nor a contempt of court. This may be a largely accurate statement concerning the *exercise* of common law discretion to exclude real evidence, but it does not acknowledge the *existence* of a discretion to exclude such evidence, if illegally obtained, nor does it take account of the position in relation to electronic search. The discretion to exclude illegally obtained non confessional evidence was admitted to pre-PACE, though rarely applied. In *Kuruma v The Queen*[8] Lord Goddard did advert to the existence of a general discretion to 'disallow evidence if the strict rules of admissibility would operate unfairly against the accused'. He also went so far as to say that if a piece of evidence 'for instance a document' had been 'obtained from a defendant by a trick, no doubt the judge would properly rule it out'.[9] Yet, in the same judgment, his Lordship also made the contradictory assertion that the test of admissibility was simply one of relevance.[10] This ambiguity over whether there existed a residuary discretion to exclude evidence, other than self-incriminatory admissions, was perpetuated by case law that gave rhetorical acknowledgement to the discretion's existence, but continually failed to apply it in favour of defendants. In *Callis v Gunn*,[11] Lord Parker conceded that if there was any suggestion of the evidence, in that case fingerprints, having been 'obtained oppressively, by false representation, by a trick, by threats, by bribes, anything of that sort' the evidence would not have been admitted. Yet more than bare illegality was needed to exclude search evidence. In *Jeffrey v Black*,[12] Lord Widgery stressed that

> the simple unvarnished fact that evidence was obtained by police officers who had gone in without bothering to get a search warrant is not enough to justify the justices in exercising their discretion to keep it out.

The additional factor required was 'morally reprehensible' conduct on the part of investigators.

Heydon (1973) criticised this pre-PACE common law approach on the basis that it failed to make any distinction between the infringement of common law rules, statutory rules and constitutional rules. Thus, in *Kuruma*, a special statutory procedure was prescribed by emergency regulations and that procedure was not complied with. The search was carried out by an unauthorised officer, yet the evidence was deemed by the Privy Council to have been rightly admitted. This, as Heydon points out, substitutes a judicial view of constitutional legality for that imposed by Parliament. The issue is not of purely historical interest, since the statutory procedures governing electronic search may well be challenged in the future on the identical basis that an improperly authorised search has taken place. If the exclusionary philosophy of the common law survives PACE, there may be little prospect of successful challenge to such searches under IOCA 1985 or under the Police Act 1997, the Human Rights Act notwithstanding, and even less of a prospect where only a voluntary Code exists to govern the search.[13]

The only cases where the common law discretion was applied in favour of the person 'searched' were those where bodily samples were taken from suspects under a mistake.[14] It is significant that in these cases the evidence was regarded not as evidence obtained as a consequence of a search, but as a self-incriminatory admission obtained from the accused. Thus, it had similarities with confession evidence and fell within the narrow scope of evidence that, even before PACE, might be excluded if obtained oppressively or involuntarily.[15] The extent of the common law discretion to exclude non confessional evidence was never satisfactorily resolved, however. An attempt to do so by the House of Lords merely resulted in a further display of judicial discordance on the issue. The seminal case that featured this discordance was *R v Sang*.[16] It concerned the admissibility of evidence obtained through the entrapment of the accused by a fellow prisoner and by the police, who later arrested him at an arranged rendezvous. The House of Lords had two objectives in *Sang*. The first was to lay down guidance on residual judicial discretion to exclude non confessional evidence. The second objective was to prevent any defence of entrapment creeping in through the back door. Lord Diplock stated that any suggestion that the 'procedural device' of exclusion could be used to prevent the prosecution adducing evidence of the commission of an offence procured through entrapment did 'not bear examination'. Thus, the factual context of the case undoubtedly affected the tenor of some of the judgments.

The case is worth careful analysis because, although it was decided prior to PACE, reference has been made to it in Court of Appeal judgments post-PACE and its influence therefore survives the statutory discretion created by section 78 of that statute. Of the five Law Lords who delivered opinions, Lord Fraser was the most supportive of the existence of a general common law discretion. He considered that this should be exercised whenever it would ensure 'fairness' to the defendant[17] and that it was not confined to those situations where the prejudicial effect of the evidence outweighed its probative value. It was, according to Lord Fraser, not possible to lay down precise rules because the purpose of the discretion was to be wide and flexible enough to cover a variety of circumstances that may arise, but which could not be foreseen.[18] Lord Scarman also believed that there was 'one general discretion, not several specific and limited discretions'. He was prepared to concede that the prejudice versus probity evaluation was not a complete statement of this discretion and that it should be exercised to ensure that a fair trial had taken place.[19] Lord Salmon was the third Law Lord to state that the judicial duty to ensure a fair trial was not limited to excluding unduly prejudicial evidence.[20] Two members of the House took a more restrictive view of the unfairness discretion. Lord Diplock restricted it to those situations where evidence, tantamount to an incriminatory admission, was obtained from the accused in circumstances where the prejudice caused by adducing the evidence clearly outweighed its probative value.[21] Viscount Dilhorne went even further and, dismissing the dicta of earlier cases as incorrect, he refused to countenance the existence of any discretion to exclude evidence on the basis of unfairness or by reason of the use of trickery, deceit or threats.[22]

In the context of real evidence, the opinions of Lord Diplock and Viscount Dilhorne severely restricted the potential for exclusion. There is very little chance that real evidence can be 'prejudicial'. It exists or it does not exist. As a piece of proof, its validity and reliability is not affected by the way in which it has been discovered or obtained. It is only when wider issues such as the integrity of the criminal process enter in that arguments for exclusion merit consideration. Yet, the House was not inclined to take a wider view of the trial process. It was said that

> It is no part of the judge's function to exercise disciplinary powers over the police or prosecution as respects the way in which evidence to be used at trial is to be obtained by them.[23]

Thus the disciplinary principle, penalising police impropriety through the exclusion of prosecution evidence, was thought to have no place at common law. Another exclusionary principle, the protective principle, was not even considered in *Sang*. This principle is generally thought to encompass two elements. The first is the protection of the innocent from wrongful conviction and the second, of some relevance to evidence resulting from a search, is that the integrity of the criminal process be maintained.[24] This second limb of the protective principle is not so much concerned with the rectitude of the outcome, but with the moral harm that may emanate from a corrupt or brutal system of law enforcement (Ashworth, 1998a:51). Should such a system be condoned by the courts, an arguably greater harm would befall society as a whole, than would be inflicted by the wrongful acquittal of one accused. The principle has close links to a different judicial control mechanism, the power to stay proceedings for an abuse of process. This power is considered later in this chapter.

It is no surprise that in post PACE appeals, judges who wish to maintain convictions rely upon the narrower judgments of those in *Sang* who considered that the prejudice and probity equation defined the limits of discretionary power to exclude evidence at common law. Yet it should not be so. PACE created an entirely new regime, a statutory code of police powers and obligations and statutory provision in respect of the exclusion of investigative evidence. This new beginning should not be fettered by the harking back to pre-PACE orthodoxies that undeniably occurs (Sharpe, 1998a). Although is not possible to give a full account of the background to the PACE evidence provisions within the scope of this work,[25] it is important to understand the significance of the last minute Parliamentary amendment that became section 78 of PACE. The PACE Bill took two years to reach the statute book.[26] Throughout most of that two year period there had been only one clause containing a statutory exclusionary power. That clause was to become section 76. The section deals with confession evidence and only with confession evidence. It provides that the court must not allow a confession[27] to be given in evidence unless the prosecution can prove beyond reasonable doubt that it has not been obtained by 'oppression of the person who made it'[28] or 'in consequence of anything said or done which was likely, in the circumstances existing at the time, to render unreliable any confession which might be made by him in consequence thereof'.[29] Evidence resulting from a search can be categorised as confession evidence only when it comprises incriminatory statements made as a consequence of electronic search. Even when it does consist of admissions obtained through covert surveillance, the fact that these are electronically recorded will usually dispense with any claim based on 'unreliability'. Section 76 does not, therefore, have any real relevance to suppressing search evidence.

Had PACE not been amended at the very last moment, there would have been no further power to exclude evidence and illegally obtained non confessional evidence would have been admitted automatically, the only control on police investigation being internal regulation.[30] However, Lord Scarman introduced an Amendment at Committee Stage in the Lords. This proposed clause would have incorporated a 'reverse onus' exclusionary rule into PACE in respect of unlawful searches. It would have required the prosecution to prove beyond reasonable doubt that the search was in fact lawful, or that the illegality was not 'material' in the circumstances, or that the interests of justice required the admission of the evidence notwithstanding the illegality.[31] At Report Stage, Lord Scarman extended this clause to cover 'improperly obtained evidence' as well as that obtained in breach of statute[32] and made specific reference to 'fairness' as a criterion. This was to give judges the power to safeguard the 'fair administration of the criminal law' and to fulfil their 'duty to ensure a fair trial'.[33] The clause won support in the Lords and would have become the law, but for an eleventh hour intervention by the government when the Bill returned to the Commons for its final stage prior to the Royal Assent. Concerned that the clause, as it stood in the House of Lords, would lead to acquittals on technicalities and to protracted trials, a shorter and more general provision was substituted. This provision became section 78 of PACE. The reverse onus rule was scrapped. There was no longer any burden on the prosecution to prove that the evidence should be admitted despite illegality or impropriety. There was no distinction made between evidence of search and any other form of evidence. Section 78(1) of PACE, the full text of which is given in the first chapter,[34] merely refers to 'evidence' upon which the prosecution proposes to rely. With the stroke of a pen the government provided a general exclusionary discretion to be applied to all evidence. It no longer matters whether the evidence is a recorded conversation, documentary evidence, a bodily sample, or an object such as a knife. The only issue is whether the admission of this evidence would 'have such an adverse effect on the fairness of the proceedings that the court ought not to admit it'.[35]

The problem with section 78 is that it gives a totally unstructured discretion to the court. There is no guidance as to the meaning of fairness. Clearly the fairness in issue is that of the process itself, not the interests of one or other party to the proceedings. However fairness is an 'essentially contested concept' (Allen, 1990). The lack of concordance between prosecution and defence and the absence of express criteria within the section enables judges to exercise discretion according to a judicially desired outcome and without any need to justify their decision making (Zuckerman, 1987). The section therefore provides a *carte blanche* for exclusionary discretion to be exercised in support of crime control values and for such decisions to be upheld on appeal. It allows the court to focus narrowly on the trial hearing itself and on the probity of the evidence sought to be adduced. It enables the court to ignore the method by which search evidence came into the hands of the police so long as this has not adversely affected its factual rectitude. Inevitably, therefore, the case law that is analysed in the following pages demonstrates that judicial determinations are value laden and that police malpractice may have little impact on the subsequent admissibility of the evidence thereby obtained. To this extent, the overriding of Lord Scarman's Amendment may prove to be a serious loss to the development of the 'integrity principle' in the English criminal justice system.

The Bugging of Premises and Self-incrimination

Is it possible to argue that an unfair trial may result when the prosecution seek to adduce admissions that have been secretly recorded from premises and when the accused would never have made admissions if he had known of the recording device? There are two arguments for excluding such evidence. The first depends upon whether the recording has been made illegally in that the Police Act 1997 has not been complied with. Non compliance might occur where the authorisation has been given by an officer not qualified to do so,[36] or where the authorisation has been given on inadequate grounds,[37] or where a police authorisation has been given to bug a home or office in circumstances where there is no basis to believe that the matter is urgent.[38] The difficulty in establishing any of these matters is twofold. Firstly, justifications that rest on reasonable belief can be manufactured *ex post facto*. The second difficulty is that the veil of public interest immunity may prevent access to the information establishing that illegality has occurred. Case law prior to the Police Act indicates that the courts are unlikely to suppress evidence obtained through bugging even where there has been some level of impropriety.

The case of *Khan (Sultan)*[39] involved an admitted civil trespass and some, albeit relatively minor, damage to property resulting therefrom. None the less, as discussed in the previous chapter, the evidence was regarded as having been rightly admitted. Citing extensively from *Sang*, Lord Nolan referred to the narrower dicta of Lord Diplock who had considered that his discretion turned on whether prejudice outweighed the probity of the evidence sought to be adduced. He also affirmed Lord Diplock's view that 'save with regard to admissions and confessions and generally with regard to evidence obtained from the accused after commission of the offence', there was no discretion to 'refuse to admit relevant admissible evidence on the ground that it was obtained by improper or unfair means'.[40] Relying on Lord Diplock's assertion that there was no discretion to exclude evidence discovered as a result of 'an illegal search' and that there was only power to exclude confessional evidence that had been unfairly obtained from an accused,[41] Lord Nolan concluded that there had been no inducement to make the admissions that were recorded on tape. He considered that even if he was taking 'too narrow a view', there would be an exercise of discretion based on fairness and, although this was not expressly stated, the clear implication was that no unfairness could arise under the common law.

Whilst this may have been the position prior to PACE, it is unjustified to restrict the application of section 78 in this way. The section expressly includes investigatory malpractice within its scope by virtue of the words 'including the circumstances in which the evidence was obtained'. It clearly applies to *all* evidence, not simply to admissions. Indeed, it can be seen from the legislative history of PACE[42] that it was intended to apply to non confessional evidence and may extend to admissions as a consequence of inadvertent drafting rather then by virtue of Parliamentary intention. Ironically, the Court of Appeal has taken a robustly fresh approach to the interpretation of section 76 of PACE and has refused to define 'oppression' in accordance with pre-PACE decsisons.[43] It has been accepted that there is a need to 'examine the language of the statute and to ask what is its natural meaning uninfluenced by any consideration derived from previous case law'.[44] Yet, this is precisely what senior members of the judiciary are failing to do in respect of section 78. In turning to this new discretion, Lord Nolan dismissed its application to the facts of the case, emphasising that illegality on the part of law enforcers was significant only to the extent that it affected the 'fairness or unfairness of the proceedings'.[45] Thus, as in pre-PACE case law, more than mere illegality would be necessary to persuade a judge to suppress the evidence.

The later case of *Chalkley and Jeffries*[46] followed *Khan* in placing great emphasis on the common law. The case involved the installation of a listening device in the house of the appellant, C. C had been arrested by the police on a less serious matter and on which police enquiries had lapsed. This was in order to allow the police unhampered access to C's premises. The police used the opportunity to seize the appellant's car and to make a copy of the key to his house. They subsequently re-entered the premises by means of this duplicate key to renew the battery powered listening device. The Chief Constable (who did not give evidence) was probably aware of this stratagem. The appellants were charged with conspiracy to commit robbery on the basis of covertly recorded conversations. The trial judge took the view that, despite the stratagem involved, the arrest for the less serious matter was lawful and that the decision to install the device had been made in accordance with Home Office Guidelines.[47] He did hold that there had been a breach of Article 8 of the Convention, and of PACE, in the temporary seizure of the appellant's car and keys and in the installation of the device and the renewal of its batteries. Evaluating the public danger posed by undetected crimes of such seriousness, the trial judge admitted the evidence. Guilty pleas were then entered by those charged. The Court of Appeal affirmed the judge's view of the admissibility of the evidence. Auld L.J. made a straightforward integration between the statutory discretion and the dicta in *Sang*. He stated as follows[48]

> At first sight, the words in s.78 'the circumstances in which the evidence was obtained' might suggest that the means by which the evidence was secured, even if they did not affect the fairness of admitting it, could entitle the court to exclude it as a result of a balancing exercise analogous to that when considering a stay for abuse of process. On that approach, the court could, even if it considered that the intrinsic nature of the evidence was not unfair to the accused, exclude it as a mark of disapproval of the way in which it had been obtained. That was certainly not the law before the 1984 Act. And we consider that the inclusion of the words 'in the circumstances in which the evidence was obtained' was not intended to widen the common law rule in this respect as stated by Lord Diplock in *R v Sang*.

Thus, in a stroke, section 78 was reduced down to a restatement of the narrowest interpretation of the previously existing common law discretion to exclude improperly obtained evidence. The disciplinary principle was rejected out of hand.[49] This reactionary application of the PACE provision does nothing to promote the principle of maintaining the moral integrity of the process (Paciocco, 1991:316) and is an inadequate response to the legislative background that gave birth to section 78.

Another issue that may arise in bugging cases is not illegality, but the question of whether the target has been induced to incriminate himself. This occurs when police not only take advantage of the implicit deception involved in the covert recording, but also trick a target to a greater or lesser degree by creating an opportunity to confess that would not otherwise arise. Arguments here may be centred upon an avoidance of Code C of PACE, the Code that governs the detention and questioning of suspects and requires them to be notified of their due process rights, including the right to immediate free legal advice[50] and their right not to have to answer questioning under caution.[51] However, these arguments, although linked to PACE, have a deeper and more fundamental rationale. The basis for the premise that evidence should be suppressed is that the presumption of innocence has been violated through wrongfully obtained admissions and that it would therefore be unfair to utilise this evidence at trial.

The claim that the privilege against self incrimination has been violated in these circumstances has not generated much sympathy with the Court of

Appeal. In *Christou and Wright*,[52] the court considered, on the facts, that providing opportunity to dispose of stolen goods through a sting operation did not amount to deceptive practice or to an evasion of Code C. In order to combat a high rate of burglary and robbery then prevalent in the area, police posed as purchasers of second hand jewellery and occupied a shop for that specific purpose. Transactions in the shop were recorded by means of cameras and sound recording equipment. The two appellants were charged with burglary or, alternatively, handling stolen goods, as a result of the operation. Lord Taylor accepted that the 'police were clearly engaged in a trick or deceit', though they did not themselves participate in offences, nor did they act as *agents provocateurs*. The Court of Appeal agreed with the analysis of the trial judge that 'the criteria of unfairness are the same whether the trial judge is exercising his discretion at common law or under statute'. Section 78 was therefore to be applied in accordance with the pre-PACE prejudice versus probity evaluation. Lord Taylor stated 'it is not every trick producing evidence against an accused which results in unfairness'.[53] There was a distinction made between the deception involved in obtaining a confession by a positive lie, such as falsely informing a suspect that his fingerprints had been found on incriminating evidence,[54] and the deception in *Christou* where, in the course of running the shop, undercover officers requested receipts thereby obtaining the fingerprints of customers. This latter deceit 'was not unfair'. The rationale for this distinction was, at least in part, that the appellants had assumed the risk of their betrayal by voluntarily applying themselves to the trick.[55] Arguments based on an evasion of Code C of PACE were dismissed on the basis that the appellants were not 'being questioned about an offence by a police officer acting as a police officer for the purposes of obtaining evidence'.[56]

Another form of deception by conduct occurred in *R v Bailey, R v Smith*.[57] In this case the police acted out a charade in which the investigating officers pretended that they did not wish the accused to share a cell and that this arrangement had been imposed on them by the custody officer. In fact, the plan was to put the two accused together in a bugged cell and to allay suspicion by this play acting. Despite a warning from one of the solicitors acting for the defendants, incriminating admissions were made and they were convicted of robbery. Whilst conceding that the question of admissibility was a matter separate from the factual guilt or innocence of the suspects,[58] Simon Brown L.J. adopted the 'assumption of risk' rationale in stating that they did not have 'to be protected from any opportunity to speak incriminatingly to each other if they chose to so'.[59] The statements made were voluntary and thus no breach of the privilege against self-incrimination had occurred.

Even where pressure to make admissions *does* occur, the Court of Appeal has declined to exclude them when they are made to a fellow accused. In *Roberts*,[60] a potential co-accused pleaded with the appellant to admit his part in a robbery and to exculpate the other therefrom. This request was made no less than 34 times. In addition, the appellant was questioned about other offences. The resultant admissions, made in a bugged cell, were relied on to convict Roberts. Whilst the Court of Appeal was satisfied that no deal had been done with police officers, the motivation for the potential co-accused to shift blame onto the appellant and to induce him to confess was self-evident. Further, under PACE, since both men had been charged, no further police interrogation was permissible. One justification for upholding the conviction was that there had been no deceptive police practice, but the bugging of the cells was in itself a deception by conduct, since no notification was given to the detainees that their expectation of privacy was being violated.

The use by the police of friends or of fellow cell mates, who have been wired to obtain admissions, is a situation that has received scrutiny in other common law jurisdictions. In the previous chapter, reference was made to the cases of *Kuhlman v Wilson*[61] and *R v Herbert*.[62] In both the United States and in Canada, the critical test is whether there has been 'passive surveillance' or whether there has been a purposeful elicitation of admissions. Whether a constitutional right not to incriminate oneself is the crux of the matter, or whether a court is evaluating the fairness of trial proceedings, the court will admit evidence obtained through the induction of misplaced confidence so long as no active pressure has been exerted by law enforcement officers to make the suspect confess.[63] Thus the outcome concerning the suppression of evidence may well be the same, although the route to achieve that outcome is a different one. The Australian cases of *R v Swaffield and Pavic v R*[64] appear to apply a cruder test. In Swaffield's case, evidence obtained through conversations with an undercover officer was deemed to violate his right of silence. However, in Pavic's case, a friend acting at the behest of the police obtained admissions as a result of numerous and direct questions. The majority of the High Court decided that the evidence had not been wrongly admitted. The fact that Swaffield engaged in a conversation (albeit unknown to him) with a law enforcement officer seems to have made the difference. Yet, there must be very little distinction, qualitatively speaking, between conversing with a police officer posing as a civilian and conversing with a civilian acting on behalf of the police. Any judicial endorsement of this distinction encourages police officers to use acquaintances, colleagues and perhaps even relatives of a suspect to obtain admissions through a falsely based trust in the confidant.

Electronic Search, Entrapment and Abuse of Process

The use of undercover officers and civilians in police detection is closely linked to the issue of whether wired individuals have entrapped a suspect into offending. Whilst entrapment is still not a substantive defence, section 78 allows for the possibility that evidence obtained in this way may be excluded. The cases subsequent to *Sang* have accepted that this is so.[65] However, there has rarely been an instance of the courts applying the discretion in favour of an accused (Sharpe, 1994) In *R v Smurthwaite*,[66] a case involving the wiring of an undercover officer posing as a potential contract killer, Lord Taylor set out the criteria to be addressed when exercising a discretion to exclude evidence in such circumstances. The matters to be considered include the degree of incitement offered to the suspect and the nature of the entrapment, the degree of activity or passivity of the undercover agent and whether there is 'an unassailable record of what occurred'.[67] The fact that evidence obtained from an electronic search is deemed to be the most reliable form of evidence militates against exclusion of the evidence.[68] In some cases, the courts have overlooked the fact that the circumstances surrounding and forming a background to the recorded conversations may themselves have a crucial part to play in assessing the reliability of that evidence. In *R v Latif, R v Shazad*,[69] the House of Lords was asked to determine whether covertly recorded conversations taking place between the appellants in a bugged hotel room were admissible or should have been excluded under section 78.[70] These recordings were, however, the *culmination* of the negotiations that had allegedly taken place between an informant acting on behalf of the Drugs Enforcement Agency and the appellants. Prior to these recordings, there had been discussions in Pakistan, which, according to the appellants, did not involve a conspiracy to import drugs. The drugs had been imported by a customs officer and the appellants were 'persuaded' to come to England and to take delivery. It was only after this event that the bugging took place. A high level of deception and encouragement occurred, but it did so outside the jurisdiction and was not subjected to the same 'unassailable record' criteria that has been applied in crimes not involving an extra-territorial element. It would seem that when there is a strong policy interest in the suppression of crime, the courts will take an exceptionally wide view of the reliability principle.

The decision in *Latif and Shazad* must now be read subject to the Human Rights Act and to the European Court decision in *Teixero de Castro v Portugal*[71] that the use of entrapment techniques violated Article 6(1) of the Convention. In that case, a buy/bust operation took place at the instigation of police officers. However, the target had no criminal record and, since no preliminary investigation concerning him had been opened, he was presumably not even reasonably suspected of drugs offending.[72] Whilst academics continue to decry the use of predisposition as a justification for entrapment (Choo, 1990 and Sharpe 1996), it would seem that the judiciary condone it. In the House of Lords, Shazad was labelled 'an organiser in the heroin trade',[73] even though this assumption was made on the basis of prosecution assertions as to previous conduct in another jurisdiction. It would seem that the subjectivity involved in a defendant-focused assessment of entrapment may extend to decisions of the European Court and there may be little likelihood, therefore, that either Article 6 or Article 8 will be violated where encouragement is given to a known, or even suspected, offender. The evidence of predisposition need not be a prior conviction. Knowledge of drug terminology, 'proximity to the source of supply, and past experience of the intricacies of such supply'[74] afford justification for police initiated offending.

One argument in favour of excluding evidence that has been obtained through the egregious conduct of law enforcers is that it supports public confidence in the moral integrity of the criminal justice system and prevents debasement of that process. The doctrine of abuse of process has a similar justification. It arises through the inherent power of a court to control its own proceedings. However, it was not until the seminal House of Lords' decision of *Connelly v DPP*[75] that this power was stated to exist in relation to criminal proceedings. The scope of that power was not clearly defined (Choo, 1993:7) so that, although it was acknowledged to exist in respect of prosecutorial delay and manipulation of process, it was not considered to exist in relation to investigative impropriety. It was said that reprehensible conduct in relation to the obtaining of evidence was not a misuse of the court's process.[76] The decision of *R v Horseferry Road Magistrates Court ex parte Bennett*[77] has now put the matter beyond doubt. There *is* an inherent power to stay proceedings because of pre-trial investigative impropriety in order to 'give the accused a fair trial – or because it offends the court's sense of justice and propriety to be asked to try the accused in the circumstances of the particular case'.[78] Lord Griffiths stated in *Bennett* that the judiciary should accept responsibility for overseeing 'executive action' and should 'refuse to countenance behaviour that threatens either basic human rights or the rule of law'.[79]

The judiciary, then, have power to uphold human rights (including the right to privacy) even though the violation of those rights may have occurred prior to the initiation of criminal proceedings. Whether this power should be exercised even when a fair trial is possible is a further matter of debate. Choo (1995:871) is of the view that that the power should be exercised, in line with the protective principle, to protect the moral integrity of the system. In the case of *Latif and Shazad*,[80] Lord Steyn agreed with this approach and accepted that, even though a fair trial was possible, the need to uphold the integrity of the criminal process could require the court to stay proceedings. If it were otherwise, 'the perception will be that the court condones criminal conduct and malpractice by law enforcement agencies'.[81] In deciding when to use this inherent power, the court had to effect a balancing exercise to ensure that there was no failure to protect the public from serious crime and yet to protect public confidence in the system.[82] Yet in undertaking this balancing exercise, the House construed the facts so as to minimise the influence of the informant acting on behalf of the Drugs Enforcement Agency. The appellants were not considered to be 'vulnerable' persons since they were of mature years and were adjudged to possess substantial criminal predisposition. The focus was on the personal characteristics of the targets, rather than on any misconduct by law enforcement agents. This shift in focus allowed Lord Steyn to limit the impact of the deception, persuasion and illegality that took place during the course of the investigation. The customs officer who imported the drugs was not authorised to do so and it was conceded that he had committed an offence under the Customs and Excise Act 1979.[83] Notwithstanding this illegal act and the fact that it constituted the *actus reus* of the offence charged, the House were not inclined to stay the proceedings.

The statements in *Latif* to the effect that the case did not, unlike *ex parte Bennett*, involve any force, nor the breach of any extradition treaty, would have potential to limit the use of stays to investigatory misconduct that does involve physical violence or a breach of international law. This could certainly explain why, in *R v Mullen*,[84] the Court of Appeal allowed a claim of abuse of process when a terrorist suspect was deported from Zimbabwe to England in disregard of existing extradition procedures. Steps were taken to prevent any challenge by the suspect to the deportation by denying him access to legal advice in Zimbabwe. There was therefore a breach of both the national law of Zimbabwe and of international law. Despite the seriousness of the crime for which the appellant was later convicted, the Court of Appeal was forced to conclude that 'but for the unlawful manner of his deportation, he would not have been in this country to be prosecuted' and that there was 'a real prospect' that he would not have been brought to the jurisdiction at all.[85]

Such an approach can be contrasted with that taken by the courts when deceptive and even illegal practices are used to secure electronically recorded evidence. A difficulty arises for an appellant who is convicted after unsuccessfully seeking to have proceedings stayed or evidence excluded. The difficulty has been compounded by the creation of a revised single ground for quashing a conviction (Clarke, 1999). This ground is contained in section 2(1) of the Criminal Appeal Act 1968, as substituted by the Criminal Appeal Act 1995. It provides that an appeal should be allowed only where a conviction is 'unsafe'. Because safety is treated as being synonymous with reliability, there is little chance that a convicted individual can argue that the admission of electronically recorded evidence has made his trial 'unfair'. It is most probable that the need to prevent degradation of the criminal justice system and the circumstances surrounding the acquisition of the evidence, rather than the probity of that evidence, are the matters relied upon as a basis to suppress the evidence or stay the proceedings. It has already been seen that in *Chalkley*[86] the Court of Appeal declined to extend the application of section 78 purely to uphold the integrity principle. It would also seem that a court will not readily exercise its inherent power to stay proceedings where investigatory misconduct has occurred, but a fair trial is yet considered possible. It is even worse for an appellant who, in the face of an adverse admissibility decision of the trial judge, pleads guilty. In this situation, it is certain that the Court of Appeal will uphold the plea. In *Chalkley*, the view was taken that first instance judicial determinations to admit Crown evidence do not make it impossible for an accused to assert his innocence. They merely made it harder for him to do so.[87]

In *R v Rajcoomar*,[88] the appellant pleaded guilty to being concerned in the supply of a controlled drug. The evidence consisted of telephone and oral contact between the appellant and an undercover police officer and of a secretly video recorded transaction in a hotel room booked by that officer. The initial contact had been made whilst the appellant had been in prison on a previous occasion and had been effected through a police informer and a series of undercover officers. Many, but no means all, of these earlier conversations were recorded. The defence alleged entrapment and this gave rise to pre-trial rulings on disclosure of unused material and abuse of process. The abuse claim was linked to late disclosure by the Crown as to the existence and status of their undercover officers and of their taped conversations. It also related to their alleged entrapment of the appellant. The trial judge rejected all defence arguments and the appellant pleaded guilty. The Court of Appeal, relying on *Chalkley*, rejected an application for leave to appeal stating that none of the challenged rulings, whether in respect of abuse of process or of disclosure, rendered an acquittal 'legally impossible'. *Mullen*,[89] was distinguished on the basis that there the accused had 'contested his guilt throughout and been found guilty by the jury'. It would seem that an accused facing trial on the basis of covertly recorded evidence has little chance of acquittal either at trial or on appeal. The evidence is so probative that, despite any wrongful exercise of discretion by a trial judge, the conviction will be safe. If the accused continues to plead not guilty to preserve his position, he will risk losing any sentence discount that he might otherwise have in the hope that the Court of Appeal might consider police conduct sufficiently egregious to allow the appeal.

Intercepted Evidence in England and Wales

There was a particular anomaly with regard to the adduction of evidence obtained through telephone interception. As stated in the previous chapter, section 9 of IOCA prevents evidence obtained through a warrant to intercept a public telecommunications system being adduced in a court of law. Yet where evidence was obtained without use of a warrant, for example because the interceptor claimed reasonable belief in consent to the interception from one party to the conversation, this evidence could be admitted.[90] Evidence has also been held to be admissible when the interception takes place in another jurisdiction,[91] or over a private telephone system[92] and even when a civilian, rather than a law enforcement officer makes the intercept.[93] Such inconsistencies are regrettable, although the House of Lords decision in *Morgans v DPP*[94] has removed at least the first of these anomalies. It has already been explained that in *Choudhary v United Kingdom*,[95] the European Court of Human Rights, in deliberating on the admission in evidence of a 'consensually' obtained interception, considered that the inability of the accused to challenge the validity of belief in consent did not infringe Article 6(3)(d) of the Convention. The other argument raised by Choudhary was that his right to silence had been violated. In considering this argument, the Court took an extremely narrow view of statements obtained in breach of the privilege against self-incrimination. Whilst it was accepted that this right is closely linked to the presumption of innocence, it was said that the privilege was 'primarily concerned with respecting the will of the accused to remain silent'. Adopting the approach taken in *Saunders v UK*,[96] the Court stated that the privilege only applied to testimonial evidence. Further, even in relation to testimonial evidence, the privilege only protects those statements made 'through methods of coercion or oppression in defiance of the will of the accused'. The confinement of the protection to compulsion and the failure to extend the concept to deliberate trickery effectively removes the privilege from those subjected to covert surveillance. It is inconsistent with the approach taken in Canada, where the active elicitation of information by deceit may infringe the right to silence.[97]

Even where the circumstances surrounding the interception are not veiled from challenge behind section 9 of IOCA, because there is no issue concerning consent to interception of the conversation, a court is unlikely to exclude the evidence on the basis that a conversant has a motive in inducing the accused to make admissions. The reliability of the intercepted speech and its strong probative value overrides the fact that the accused would not have said what he did if 'he had known the true position' and even the fact that 'the evidence was obtained through a participating informant'.[98] Where a common purpose or a conspiracy is alleged as the basis of offending, there is not even any need for the accused to be a participant to the intercepted conversation. In *R v Jones, Williams and Barham*,[99] the case against Barham, on a charge of importing cannabis, consisted of circumstantial evidence of association between B and the other participants and of recorded telephone conversations, held between other defendants and third parties, in which reference was made to him. The Court of Appeal held that the conversations were 'contemporary evidence of the progress of the offence charged'. Provided that reasonable evidence of common offending could be established by independent evidence apart from the relevant conversations, it was no objection to admissibility that an accused did not take part in a recorded conversation, nor that he was not even present when it took place.

Whilst this recognised exception to the hearsay rule[100] applies to all oral evidence and not simply to recorded telephone intercepts, there may be an additional privacy issue involved in admitting such evidence when it is obtained through bugging or interception. It is not simply the privacy of the conversants that that is being invaded, but the privacy of third parties who may not, prior to the bugging or interception, be reasonably suspected of offending. It allows law enforcers to obtain evidence by serendipity and to supplement it thereafter by further investigation in order to obtain independent proof. Yet the reliability of third party references (which may frequently be in terms of coded messages) may not be beyond challenge either because of the verbal ambiguity of the references themselves, or because those speaking may have a biased or ill-informed view of the involvement of the subject concerned. As in other areas of covert surveillance, the verbatim electronic record overrides any challenge as to the circumstances of its obtainment.

The Canadian Approach to Exclusion and Abuse

Before the adoption of the Charter of Rights and Freedoms, the common law position in Canada concerning the exclusion of evidence was very close to that espoused by the English judiciary prior to PACE. In *R v Wray*,[101] illegally obtained evidence was stated to be admissible, if otherwise relevant. The Supreme Court adopted the dicta of Lord Goddard in *Kuruma v The Queen*[102] and, in a statement that was to prove to be in direct contradiction to the subsequently enacted Charter provisions, Judson J. said that there was no judicial discretion to exclude relevant evidence even if a judge 'thinks that it will operate unfairly against the accused or, according to his opinion, bring the administration of justice into disrepute'. Paccioco (1996) confirms that, as in England and Wales, evidence would be excluded only if it was gravely prejudicial (in the sense that it could distort fact finding) and was of trifling probative value. The prejudice against probity equation ruled out the suppression of real evidence. Then in 1982 a judicial sea change was made possible by virtue of section 24 of the Charter. The section reads in full

(1) Anyone whose rights or freedoms, as guaranteed by this Charter, have been infringed or denied may apply to a court of competent jurisdiction to obtain such remedy as the court considers appropriate and just in the circumstances.

(2) Where, in proceedings under subsection (1), a court concludes that evidence was obtained in a manner that infringed or denied any rights or freedoms guaranteed by this Charter, the evidence shall be excluded if it is established that, having regard to all the circumstances, the admission of it in the proceedings would bring the administration of justice into disrepute.

It has been pointed out that the wording of section 24 sends out something of a mixed message concerning its theoretical rationale. Subsection 24(1) appears to envisage the use of suppression as a 'remedial' measure, whereas subsection 24(2) is grounded firmly in the protective principle and, irrespective of any wrong suffered by a defendant, looks to preserving the reputation of the process itself (Paccioco, 1996).

It is instructive to compare the dynamics of the Supreme Court's application of the Charter provisions in respect of criminal evidence with those of English judges interpreting section 78 of PACE. English judges were faced with a parallel situation in that they were expressly empowered to exclude evidence that would have an adverse effect on trial proceedings. There were no case law precedents to bind them, no detailed statutory criteria to be met.

Section 78 is unstructured and judicial creativity was therefore unconstrained. As with section 24 of the Charter, the exclusionary power is a half-way house between the 'automatic' exclusionary rule of the United States and the common law rule that all relevant evidence was admissible (Sopinka *et al*, 1992).[103] Yet, whilst the judges in England have retreated back to the situation that existed before the enactment of PACE and have severely curtailed the prospect of exclusion in respect of illegally obtained real evidence,[104] Canadian judges have seized the opportunity to rewrite the law and to take an active role in maintaining the integrity of the criminal justice system. The genesis of this approach is the case of *Collins v The Queen*.[105] Indeed, Fontana (1997:542) considers that this case is 'as important to a consideration of s.24(2) and the test "would bring the administration of justice into disrepute", as *Hunter v Southam Inc*. is to s.8'. Both cases are 'keystone decisions'. Before analysing the criteria that flow from the decision, it should to be noted that *Collins* also resolved any doubts that there may have been concerning the stringency of the exclusionary rule. Literally read the English and French translations of subsection 24(2) differ. The English version reads that the admission of the evidence 'would' bring the administration of justice into disrepute. The French text uses the lower threshold of 'could'. In *Collins*, Lamer J. determined that defendants must be given the benefit of the doubt and that this less onerous test would apply.[106] None the less, the burden of persuasion is on the defendant. This, again according to Lamer J.,[107] requires an accused to persuade the court on the balance of probabilities.

The case of *Collins* involved factually unexceptional offending, a charge of possession of heroin with intent to supply. However, the grasping, by a law enforcement officer, of the throat of the appellant in an apparent attempt to prevent her swallowing drugs, proved to have a legal significance way beyond what might have been envisaged at the time. Because this action was not based upon probable cause, it was unreasonable and it therefore tainted a subsequent seizure of heroin from the accused. That seizure was from the hand, not the mouth of the appellant, as her mouth was, in fact, empty. The Supreme Court allowed the appeal and ordered a new trial. In doing so, the possibility of excluding reliable evidence obtained through an illegal search became a reality. However, suppression will only take place where the exclusion of the evidence would bring the administration of justice into *'further disrepute'* than that already sustained by virtue of police misconduct.[108] This further disrepute could arise *either* because the admission of the evidence would deprive an accused of a fair hearing, *or* 'from judicial condonation of unacceptable conduct by the investigatory and prosecutorial agencies'.[109] Any disrepute that may result from excluding the evidence must also be considered. The balancing exercise does not, therefore, depend entirely, as does section 78 of PACE, on an evaluation of the fairness of the trial. The maintenance of the integrity of the process is an express and sufficient justification to suppress evidence.

Major questions that arise are whether a trial can ever be rendered 'unfair' through the admission of illegally obtained search evidence and in what circumstances 'further disrepute' would attach to the system by admitting evidence obtained in breach of the Charter. The question of unfairness depends more upon the 'nature of the evidence' than upon the manner in which a Charter right has been violated. The use of real evidence will rarely operate unfairly since it 'existed irrespective of the violation of the Charter'.[110] This limitation on unfairness does not apply to conscripted evidence, for instance self-incriminating evidence obtained following a denial of the right to counsel. The linkage between conscription and fairness therefore allows for the possibility that, should an accused himself be compelled to assist in an illegal search, the admission of any resultant real evidence might render the trial unfair.[111] It was stated in *Stillman v The Queen*[112]

> The crucial element which distinguishes non-conscriptive evidence from conscriptive evidence is not whether the evidence may be characterised as 'real' or not. Rather it is whether the accused was compelled to make a statement or provide a bodily substance in violation of the Charter.

L'Hereux-Dube J., dissenting, disagreed with this rationale and preferred to limit unfairness to conscripted testimonial evidence only.[113] Whilst the wider view is to be preferred, its application is unlikely to be a liberal one. Indeed, lack of conscription can be used to justify the admission of evidence, thus turning the argument on its head.[114]

The more likely basis for the exclusion of evidence obtained through an illegal search is that the admission of the evidence would bring the administration of justice into further disrepute. The safety of the conviction is irrelevant; what matters is the gravity of the infringement of constitutional or of human rights that has taken place. In *R v Dyment*,[115] the Supreme Court excluded a blood sample relied upon by the prosecution to prove a charge of driving under the influence of alcohol. The sample had been taken by a doctor from a wound sustained by the accused and handed to the police. La Forest J. considered that the 'violation of the sanctity of a person's body'[116] that occurred was sufficiently serious to require exclusion under subsection 24(2). He stated

> Grounded in man's physical and moral autonomy, privacy is essential to the
> well-being of the individual. For this reason alone, it is worthy of constitutional
> protection, but it also has profound significance for public order. The restraints
> imposed on government to pry into the lives of a citizen go to the essence of a
> democratic state.[117]

This robust rhetoric was not just a transient, if euphoric, response to the new power of exclusion granted to the judiciary. Cases subsequent to *Dyment* have continued to assert that both bodily samples and the tangible evidence of physical searches may be excluded even though the probity of the evidence is beyond doubt.[118] There are, however, some borderline cases where the Charter breach is technical and the evidence incontrovertible. For example, in *Knox v The Queen*,[119] a blood sample was taken from the appellant in hospital as a consequence of which he was convicted of causing bodily harm through driving a vehicle under the influence of alcohol. The Crown did not have to prove consent to the taking of the sample, but it was necessary to establish compliance. The demand for the sample was legally deficient, as there was no assurance given that it would only be taken by a medically qualified practitioner. There was therefore a contravention of sections 7 and 8 of the Charter and the case was remitted for retrial to determine whether the evidence should be excluded. This case must be a very borderline example of its kind and, indeed, the Supreme Court expressed the view that, if an accused actually complied with the demand in the absence of medical assurances and the sample had been taken by a suitably qualified person, the admission of the evidence would not bring the administration of justice into disrepute.

The wrongful invasion of bodily autonomy has been treated as so grave a harm that, even where the crime charged is one that may be viewed as seriously threatening the fabric of society, the evidence may be suppressed. In *Greffe v The Queen*,[120] a strip search for narcotics proved unsuccessful. The subject of the search was informed that he was being arrested for outstanding traffic warrants. He was then taken to a hospital where a rectal examination took place and narcotics were removed. Since the police could not establish that reasonable and probable grounds existed for the search, the Supreme Court, albeit with reluctance, restored the appellant's acquittal. Lamer J. stated that despite the 'manifest culpability of the appellant', the integrity of the justice system and 'the respect owed to our Charter are more important than the conviction of this offender'. In contrast to judicial attitudes toward the exclusion of evidence in England and Wales (Sharpe, 1998a), the public interest in the conviction of serious offenders does not inevitably override objections based on police illegality. This open minded approach has been endorsed in *Burlingham v The Queen*,[121] where Iacobucci J. stated

> We should never lose sight of the fact that even a person accused of the most heinous crimes, and no matter the likelihood that he actually committed these crimes, is entitled to the full protection of the Charter. Short-cutting or short-circuiting those rights affects not only the accused but also the entire reputation of the criminal justice system. It must be emphasised that the goals of preserving the integrity of the criminal justice system as well as promoting the decency of investigatory techniques are of fundamental importance in applying s.24(2).

The circumstances surrounding the Charter violation are, frequently, crucial in determining the seriousness of that violation. In *Collins*,[122] it was said that that the availability of other investigatory techniques would make a Charter violation more serious. It was also stated that, whilst evidence was more likely to be excluded for a trivial breach where an alleged offence was less serious, the seriousness of the offence was a factor in *favour* of exclusion where the fairness of the trial rather than the reputation of the criminal justice system was the determining factor. A critical issue may be whether the breach of the Charter was in good faith or was flagrantly done in wilful defiance of the law. In *Croucher*,[123] a distinction was made between violations affecting trial fairness, where good or bad faith was irrelevant, and violations affecting the reputation of the process where *mala fides* would clearly increase the seriousness of the impugned conduct. An example of such conduct occurs in *Greffe*,[124] where the arrest of the accused for outstanding traffic warrants had been a 'convenient artifice' to keep the appellant in custody and this meant that the breach was 'deliberate, blatant and flagrant'.

On the other hand, where a Charter breach is innocent, in the sense that it has been made under an honest mistake, this may incline a court to admit the evidence. In *Duarte v The Queen*,[125] the use made by undercover officers of bugged premises and unauthorised telephone interceptions did violate section 8 fairly substantially. Nonetheless, the Supreme Court did not suppress the evidence because the officers were found to be acting in good faith 'in accordance with what they had good reason to believe was the law' and as it 'had been for many years before the advent of the Charter'. Similarly in *R v Wong*,[126] the unauthorised bugging of a hotel room was said to stem from 'an entirely reasonable misunderstanding of the law by police officers'. This approach replicates some of the case law in England and Wales where failures to observe the requirements of PACE or of the Codes made thereunder have been described as emanating from a 'misunderstanding' of the law and therefore as not justifying exclusion under section 78.[127] However, the longer the period of time that has passed since the enactment of the relevant due process legislation, the less likely it is that law enforcers can continue to blame failures to obey that legislation on honest mistake. The case of *Duarte* must surely create its own dynamic in favour of excluding evidence, since it now makes clear those circumstances in which authorisation for electronic search is required and sets a precedent for future police activity.

Another factor that may 'mitigate' a breach of the Charter is that exigent circumstances exist and that 'the constitutional violation was motivated by urgency or necessity to prevent the loss or destruction of evidence'.[128] This factor may lead to the admission of evidence even when there is a very serious breach of a Charter right. Thus in *R v Silveira*,[129] the police wrongly and forcibly entered premises to seize drugs prior to the issue of a warrant. The perceived urgency of the need to preserve the evidence was held to be sufficient to defeat any argument based on maintaining the integrity of the system. Crime control values clearly predominated in a judgment that referred to drug trafficking as a 'serious crime' and adopted a probity test in stating that the real evidence found 'was vital to the proof of the case against the appellant'. This judgment is hard to reconcile with cases such as *Stillman* and *Croucher* and it raises issues about the extent to which subjectivity enters into judicial evaluations concerning the exclusion of illegally obtained evidence (Sharpe, 1998a).

In one respect the Canadian approach to exclusion is clearly more generous to a suspect. Derivative evidence, that is evidence obtained through a search made consequent upon an inadmissible confession, is also inadmissible if it would not have been found but for the Charter breach. In *Burlingham*,[130] the police found a gun at the bottom of a river. The only person who knew of its location was the appellant. A distinction was made between evidence that the police would have discovered in any event 'with or without the assistance' of the accused[131] and that which would not have been found but for the statement of the accused. The statement in *Burlingham*, made in violation of the right to counsel and after improper pressure had been placed on the accused, tainted the subsequent search. Iacobbucci J. stated[132]

> The rationale behind the exclusion of evidence lying in close proximity to the Charter breach stems from the fact that, in the case at bar, such evidence, if tendered at trial, detracts from the integrity of the trial and thereby infringes both the fairness principle and the reliability principle. In any event, even if the improperly obtained evidence were reliable, considerations of reliability are no

longer determinative, given that the Charter has made the rights of the individual and the fairness and integrity of the judicial system paramount.

The position in England and Wales is very different. Section 76(4) of PACE provides that the fact that a confession is excluded in pursuance of that section shall not affect the admissibility in evidence 'of any facts discovered as a result of that confession'. The crucial issue is not whether the real evidence has been found through the wrongful coercion or trickery of a suspect, but whether the evidence can stand alone as proof. The question is simply whether the item found and/or the location in which it may be found can, without reference to the confession, provide relevant evidence for the prosecution. Thus if an incriminating item is found on the premises of the accused,[133] or bears the fingerprints or bodily traces of the accused, the item may be put in evidence regardless of the fact that the confession leading to its discovery has been suppressed.

There is still at least one matter that remains unresolved about the interpretation and application of the Charter to the exclusion of criminal evidence. Both subsections 24(1) and 24(2) give a court the power to enforce Charter rights. What is less clear is whether there is exclusivity in respect of the methods by which these rights may be enforced. Sopinka *et al* (1992:391) considers that, if exclusion is only permitted under subsection (2) and cannot provide a 'remedy' under subsection (1), a court may be unduly restricted and may be unable to exclude evidence, even when this may be the most appropriate remedy, because the administration of justice would not be brought into disrepute by its admission. He therefore prefers the view espoused in *Therens*[134] that exclusion is possible under either subsection. Fontana (1997:497) is non committal on this point and states simply that the matter 'remains to be judicially determined'. It may be that the only remedy available under subsection 24(1) is the quashing of any improperly obtained warrants, the return of any wrongfully seized goods and damages.

Section 24 of the Charter is, however, not the only way in which evidence may be suppressed. An exercise of the more drastic power to stay proceedings for an abuse of process will also have this effect. The ethos, engendered by the Charter, in favour of preserving the integrity of the justice system, appears to have spilled over into the judicial use that is made of this inherent power to stay proceedings. Paciocco (1991:325) points out that, at least in respect of entrapment, the Supreme Court has made a complete *volt face* from sanctioning 'the most conservative abuse of process regime among major commonwealth countries' to approving the use of abuse of process as a means of redressing the wrong of entrapment. The power to stay proceedings is classically described in *R v Jewitt*[135] where Dickson C.J. stated that it was time to 'end the uncertainty' about the availability of the remedy. The remedy is to be used

> Where compelling an accused to stand trial would violate those fundamental principles of justice which underlie the community's sense of fair play and decency and to prevent abuse of the court's process through oppressive or vexatious proceedings.[136]

This statement, derived from the English case of *Connelly*,[137] leaves open the possibility that the power to stay may be used in precisely the same circumstances as those justifying the exclusion of evidence. The power is entirely process centred.

For instance, in *Mack v R*[138] the persistent importuning of the accused to acquire drugs on the part of a police officer and an alleged threat made to the accused by that officer, was considered to be conduct that offended against the concept of decency and resulted in proceedings for possession of cocaine being stayed. The decision to exercise the power had 'nothing to do with a determination of whether the particular accused should be excused from the crime'. The question was rather whether the conduct of the police had exceeded acceptable limits.[139] The Supreme Court was concerned to show that

> there are inherent limits on the power of the state to manipulate people and events for the purpose of attaining the specific objective of obtaining convictions.[140]

Similarly, in *R v Xenos*,[141] the conduct of the police in participating in a scheme whereby informants were paid conditionally upon their evidence resulting in conviction, was considered to be 'absolutely unacceptable in a free and democratic society'. Brossard J. said that he would not

> be reticent to order a stay of proceedings if unlawful actions or proceedings were consciously or deliberately used by the Crown and constituted the sole basis of a charge, without which no verdict of guilty could have been considered.

However, in this case evidence independent of the informer prevented the need to stay the proceedings. A retrial with exclusion of the tainted evidence was ordered.

The case raises the question of the relationship between abuse of process and section 24 of the Charter. Investigative illegality or impropriety may be a factor justifying either the suppression of evidence or the stay of proceedings. It is a moot point when one rather than the other remedy is appropriate, particularly when the entire evidence against an accused is tainted by illegality. In *Burlingham*,[142] the court, having found that a 'serious Charter violation' had occurred, was faced with determining the just and appropriate remedy. The decision of the lower court that it was inappropriate to stay the proceedings was not disturbed. Iacobucci J. expressed a view that stays should be 'limited to the clearest of cases' and that this was not such a case.[143] Yet, despite this assertion, the incriminating statements in *Burlingham*, that culminated in the finding of real evidence, were all obtained through a series of constitutional violations. This real evidence was suppressed because its admission would effectively eviscerate the Charter of its protective value.[144] If this were indeed the case, it is difficult to see where the dividing line lies between the two remedies. In both section 24 suppression and in the case of a stay for abuse, the question is whether a reasonable person in the community would be shocked by the usage of the evidence to secure a conviction.

The dividing line was specifically considered in the Australian case of *Ridgeway v R*,[145] where, in a situation that closely paralleled the facts of *Latif and Shazad*, a Malaysian police officer imported a quantity of heroin. The appellant was arrested when an informant delivered the heroin to him in Australia. The issue for the High Court was whether the involvement of the Australian Federal Police in the illegal importation should have led to a stay of proceedings or to the exclusion of evidence of the appellant's guilt. Mason C.J. conceded that it was 'true that there is an artificiality in the distinction between an exclusion of all evidence and a stay of proceedings'. He purported, none the less, to make a 'significant distinction in principle' between staying criminal proceedings on the ground 'that the proceedings themselves constitute an abuse of process' and 'staying further steps in the proceedings on the ground that, due to the effect of the evidentiary rulings made in them, they must fail'.[146] On the facts, it was held that there had been 'grave and calculated police criminality; the creation of an actual element of the charged offence'. The 'objective of the criminal conduct' would be achieved if the evidence were admitted. The solution was to exclude 'on public policy grounds' all the evidence that tended to show illegal importation of the heroin supplied to the appellant. The result of such a ruling would be that the necessary elements of offending could not be proved and further proceedings 'would inevitably fail'.[147]

It would seem, therefore, that if the suppressed evidence leaves no case remaining against an accused, the remedy of a stay might be more appropriate.

It might also be more appropriate where alleged investigative illegality combines with procedural irregularity to prevent a proper assessment being made of the seriousness of the Charter violation. This argument was raised in the case of *R v Campbell*.[148] A reverse sting operation had been undertaken by the RCMP and a large quantity of cannabis was sold to drug organisation executives. The sting had apparently been undertaken after consultation with the Department of Justice. The Supreme Court allowed the appellant's appeal, based on abuse, in part and ordered a retrial with the stipulation that the trial judge should review documentation concerning the advice given by the Department of Justice and consider whether additional disclosure should be made to the appellants. The advice was subject to a disputed claim of legal professional privilege. Disclosure would throw light on the view of government lawyers as to the legality of the RCMP's action and on any claim of 'good faith' on their part. The relationship between disclosure of unused prosecution material and the ability to challenge prosecution evidence is discussed below. Clearly, it is only possible to argue an infringement of due process rights if the information supporting that infringement is made available to the defence.

The Suppression of Evidence in the United States

The United States has been condemned for adopting a so called 'automatic' exclusionary rule in respect of evidence that has been obtained in breach of the Fourth Amendment.[149] In reality, this automatic rule has become hedged about by exceptions and qualifications and it is not, in any sense, absolute. There was a fairly long gestation period during which the rule developed and widened in its application. Initially it applied in Federal trials only. In respect of such trials, *Weeks v United States*,[150] resolved any previous uncertainty in the law in favour of excluding evidence obtained by means of an unreasonable search, at least where the property seized was legitimately owned and was not contraband (Stewart, 1983:1375). In the later decision of *Agnello v United States*,[151] the Supreme Court refused to make a distinction between legitimate property wrongfully seized and the illegitimate possession of cocaine. It mattered not that the person dispossessed was in no position to seek the return of the evidence. Constitutional considerations were from thenceforth to override proprietorial ones (White, 1983). The question of whether this exclusionary rule applied to State trials was eventually settled by the case of *Mapp v Ohio*.[152] The case held that the Fourteenth Amendment due process clause, when read with the Fourth Amendment, required that identical prohibitions concerning the use of the evidence apply in both Federal and State cases.

Stewart (1883:1381) points out that there is no 'residual support in the Constitution itself' for suggesting that exclusion is a mandated remedy for an unreasonable search. It is, after all, logically possible to admit the evidence and, at the same time, punish an officer for his misconduct in obtaining it (Stuntz, 1989:119). The rule has been attacked because of its allegedly unproven efficiency in deterring investigative illegality (Oaks, 1970). It has also been attacked as being too costly in that 'it often leads to inaccurate results by excluding relevant evidence from consideration' (Stuntz, 1989:124). The 'not worth the cost argument' (replicated in England and Wales by an application of the reliability principle in preference to the disciplinary principle or protective principle) is apparent in decisions such as *US v Calandra*.[153] In *Calandra*, evidence obtained through an illegal search was admitted because to remove the evidence concerned 'would achieve a speculative and undoubtedly minimal advance in the deterrence of police misconduct at the expense of substantially impeding the grand jury'. This approach downgrades suppression from a constitutionally mandated right, to just one of the possible remedies that may be used to give effect to the Fourth Amendment. It received endorsement in *Stone v Powell*,[154] where it was said that the exclusionary rule was justified only on the basis that it deterred police illegality. It was 'not a personal constitutional right'. It was further stated that, whilst courts must be concerned to preserve the integrity of the judicial process, 'this concern has a limited force as a justification for the exclusion of highly probative evidence'. The counter argument is that

> Far from being disproportionately costly, the exclusionary remedy is remarkably proportionate to the wrong. When the Government has evidence of crime that it should not have under the fourth amendment, the exclusionary rule puts the Government where the fourth amendment says it should be – without the evidence.[155]

Whatever the merits or demerits of the exclusionary rule, or its strict rationale, the determination of the judiciary in the United States to admit reliable and probative evidence, notwithstanding the absence of a warrant or of probable cause, has led to the creation of 'exceptions' to the rule. These exceptions exist by virtue of creative interpretation of factual situations enabling a court to state that a search was consensual, or that there was no reasonable expectation of privacy, or that the investigation was not a search. The argument in respect of 'consent' searches is that a party may waive his constitutional rights in respect of a search of a person or of premises. The prosecution has to prove the voluntariness of the consent and awareness of the right of choice.[156] However, *Schneckloth v Bustamonte*[157] held that it is not necessary that the police explain the right to refuse to the individual concerned in the same way that they must administer a *Miranda* warning. This view of consent has been described as 'expansive' (Kamisar, 1987:41) and it certainly leaves room for uncertainty concerning the reality of any consent given by an individual in a potentially coercive situation.[158] *Schneckloth v Bustamonte* was affirmed and extended in *US v Matlock*[159] where it was stated that a 'consent search is fundamentally different in nature from the waiver of a trial right'. The prosecution is not limited to proof that consent was given by the defendant, but may show that 'permission to search was obtained from a third party who possessed common authority over or sufficient relationship to the premises or effects sought to be inspected'.

The alternative to disapplying the Fourth Amendment through waiver is to construe the circumstances surrounding the search as giving rise to no reasonable expectation of privacy within *Katz v US*,[160] or to utilise the closely linked analysis that no 'search' has taken place. In *Alderman v US*,[161] Mr. Justice White held that the 'established principle is that suppression of the product of a Fourth Amendment violation can be successfully argued only by those whose rights have been violated'. Thus if the accused himself has no reasonable expectation of privacy, incriminating evidence, even though obtained through an unlawful search, will be admitted. Such searches may be targeted at a third party's property or may be the result of electronic surveillance of other individuals. The crucial point is that it is not the accused's Fourth Amendment rights that have been infringed. This reduction in the scope of privacy protection can be demonstrated in cases such as *US v Quinn*,[162] where the respondent, Quinn, purchased a vessel for the purpose of drug importation, but 'turned over' the vessel to the individual whom he had solicited to assist in the importation. The boat was subsequently searched and marijuana was discovered. The Supreme Court determined that the respondent had no reasonable expectation of privacy in the vessel and therefore he was unable to establish a Fourth Amendment violation. Again, in *US v Padilla*,[163] it was stated that 'expectations of privacy and property interests govern the analysis of the Fourth Amendment search and seizure claims'. Whilst participants in a criminal conspiracy might have such expectations or interests, the existence of a joint enterprise or agreement 'neither adds nor detracts from them'.

The 'open fields' doctrine also prevents an accused from asserting that a reasonable expectation of privacy exists. In *Dow Chemical Company v US*,[164] the Supreme Court affirmed a decision of the Sixth Circuit Court of Appeals to the effect that there was no reasonable expectation of privacy in respect of aerial surveillance. A commercial aerial photographer had taken pictures of a manufacturing facility whilst in legal airspace. The Environmental Protection Agency was not, therefore, prohibited from effecting a search in this way. On the same day, the case of *California v Ciraolo*,[165] also decided that a suspect could not claim a violation of privacy in respect of a targeted aerial surveillance that had taken place over his property. The fact that marijuana plants (the subject of subsequent criminal proceedings) were screened at ground level by a six foot outer fence did not create a reasonable expectation of privacy. The police plane was in publicly navigable airspace and the fact that the observation was carried out by officers trained to recognise marijuana was irrelevant to the issue. There was 'no constitutional difference between police observations conducted whilst in a public place and standing in the open fields'. A literal and narrow interpretation given to the Fourth Amendment protection of 'persons, houses, papers and effects' has re-introduced proprietory concepts into constitutional rights and, arguably, thereby limited them.

An associated method of restricting the application of the Fourth Amendment is to confine the concept of what constitutes a 'search'. This approach has resulted in the Supreme Court holding that installing a beeper inside a car and monitoring the signals thereafter did not give rise to a search.[166] The rationale is linked to a denial of a reasonable expectation of privacy on the part of one who drives an automobile on public highways. The installation of a pen register is not a search for similar reasons. In *Smith v Maryland*,[167] it was stated that there was neither an actual, nor a 'legitimate' expectation of privacy in respect of the numbers dialled by telephone subscribers. Again, in *US v Place*,[168] a 'sniff test' carried out by a trained narcotics detection dog was held not to amount to a search. In all these situations, the limited information obtainable from the investigation, or the superficiality of the intrusion, entitled the court to deny that the accused had a valid expectation that his activities were protected from scrutiny. A further and distinct legitimation for denying the protection of the Fourth Amendment is to limit its application to government agents so that if privacy interests have 'already been frustrated as a result of private conduct' there is no possibility of suppressing the search.[169]

In all three jurisdictions, judges make determinations to achieve desired outcomes. However, neither the pedantic jurisprudence that governs decision making in the United States, nor the unstructured and largely unaccountable discretion operated by judges in England and Wales under section 78 of PACE, adopts the protective principle as the primary basis for suppressing evidence. It is only in Canada that maintaining the integrity of the criminal process is an overt and actual justification for excluding evidence that has been obtained through illegality or gross impropriety. In respect of search evidence, in particular, this different approach produces noticeably different trial outcomes.

Public Interest Immunity/Informant Privilege

There is always a risk that sensitive undercover operations might be severely prejudiced, or that those co-operating with the police by giving information might be endangered, if the nature of police activity or the identity of informants is made known to the defence. Judges manage this risk through the doctrine of public interest immunity. This immunity shields what might otherwise be relevant and probative evidence from the defence. Mention has already been made, in the context of warrant applications, of the difficulty that this creates in challenging probable cause.[170] This difficulty continues throughout the criminal process. The reason is that the immunity allows for a controlled information deficit to exist in respect of the case against the accused. Concern over the safety of those participating in covert operations has increased. The Criminal Procedure and Investigations Act 1996 was passed, in part, in response to the view of the Royal Commission on Criminal Procedure[171] that not all sensitive material was being adequately protected and that more should be done. The proposed solution was 'a new regime' involving a two stage disclosure process between the prosecution and defence. This regime would narrow the range of material that could be sought by the defence and, as an incidental effect, reduce the amount of sensitive material that became susceptible to disclosure (Sharpe, 1999).[172] Examples of 'sensitive' information, as redefined under the CPIA Code,[173] include material relating to intelligence gathering and national security, the identity or activities of informers or undercover officers, the location of surveillance posts, the techniques and methods used in the course of criminal investigation and the material upon which search warrants were obtained. Many of these examples relate, in particular, to information obtained through search and surveillance.

Decision making in respect of public interest immunity has, therefore, to be viewed in the context of law enforcement concerns to protect agents and investigative strategies from revelation. However, this creates a tension with the counter concern, now a right embodied in Article 6(3)(a) of the European Convention, that a defendant be fully informed of 'the nature and cause of the accusation' against him. It also conflicts with the right of the accused, in Article 6(3)(d), to examine and cross-examine witnesses against him. The common law of public interest immunity has been preserved in respect of criminal investigation by subsection 21(2) of CPIA. This immunity justifies an exception to the disclosure scheme set out in CPIA. It therefore enables a prosecutor to withhold information which, in his opinion, 'might undermine the case for the prosecution against the accused'[174] or which 'might be reasonably expected to assist the accused's defence as disclosed by the defence statement'.[175] Any determination as to whether disclosure should be refused, because it is not in the public interest, must be made by a judge on the application of a prosecutor.[176] However, the determination is made on the basis of information recounted to the judge by the Crown. In turn, the Crown is relaying this information on the basis of information given to the prosecution by the police. The question of whether the totality and accuracy of the information is sufficient to justify the application is a matter for each individual judge. Furthermore, there is no automatic right for defence counsel to be present at the hearing of the application. The recent European Court decisions in *Rowe and Davies v United Kingdom*,[177] *Fitt v United Kingdom*,[178] and *Jasper v United Kingdom*,[179] have declared that the use of *ex parte* proceedings in public interest immunity applications is not *per se* a violation of Article 6 of the European Convention. The Court in *Jasper* stated that it was not necessary to appoint 'special counsel' to review the material in such circumstances since assessment by the trial judge of the need for disclosure adequately protected the interests of the accused.[180] The Commission (whose decisions on the merits were confirmed in each of the cases by the full Court) took the view that

> Even though the applicant and his representative were not aware of the category of material sought to be withheld, the trial judge did know it and having also known the risk of damage sought in the public interest to be prevented by withholding the material, he was able to assess how serious was the risk and how serious was the potential damage.[181]

It was stated that a judge must be sure that he has 'sufficient knowledge of the contents of the material' before making a ruling on non-disclosure,[182] but that such knowledge might be based on what a prosecutor tells the judge about the information rather than an actual inspection of the disputed material.[183]

The question that a judge must ask himself in relation to an immunity claim is whether 'the disputed material may prove the defendant's innocence or avoid a miscarriage of justice'. If the material might have this effect, then the 'sensitive' information must be disclosed unless the prosecution choose to abandon the proceedings rather than make disclosure. Where innocence is at stake, according to *R v Keane*,[184] the 'balance comes down resoundingly in favour of disclosing it'. However, evidence obtained through search or surveillance is so inherently reliable that only in circumstances where 'plant' or 'set up' is alleged will the undisclosed background to the obtaining of that evidence be relevant to the facts in issue. Thus in *Keane* itself, the issue was whether counterfeit money and implements that could be used to make such money had been planted in a car which the appellant had been driving. He claimed that a passenger, turned informant, had planted these items on the instruction of an undercover officer. Similarly, in *R v Turner*,[185] the incriminating items (a gun and clothing) had been found by the police as a result of a tip off concerning a robbery that had taken place two days beforehand. The informant had not been named and the accused raised an alibi defence, leading to the inevitable inference that he had been set up. Although the appeal was allowed, Lord Taylor took the opportunity to deliver a warning that judges should be 'astute to see that assertions of a need to know such details, because they are essential to the running of the defence, are justified'.[186] This warning was given in the context of Lord Taylor's view that defences of set up and of duress had 'multiplied'.

It is not easy for a defendant to contest an immunity ruling. This is because he is contesting a vacuum in the case against him; an absence of information. It may be that he has a suspicion that he has been framed or entrapped by an individual, but unless he has 'reasonable cause' to believe this, he may not apply to the court for an order seeking disclosure.[187] Even if the prosecution should concede, by making an application, that there may be undisclosed material relevant to the case, there is no *locus standi* for defence lawyers in relation to an immunity application. It is therefore almost impossible to challenge any decision made. It may be that only if, fortuitously, suppressed material is later discovered and found to be crucial to the outcome of the case, a defendant may be vindicated. This occurred in *Rowe and Davis*[188] where substantial payments were found to have been made to accessories whose evidence formed the mainstay of the prosecution case, but only after the appellants had been convicted.

In Canada and the United States, the criteria for the disclosure of evidence, in the face of a claim of informer privilege, are not far removed from those operated under the common law of England and Wales. In all three jurisdictions, courts must balance the right to present a meaningful defence against the public interest in preserving informant anonymity and encouraging citizens to report crime. In *R v Hunter*,[189] the Canadian Supreme Court acknowledged that these interests were conflicting ones. It was difficult for a citizen to determine if he had been the victim of an unreasonable search if he did not have access to the information that was the basis for issuing the search warrant, and impossible for him to make full answer and defence 'as he cannot attack the validity of the search warrant'. On the other hand, informer privilege is 'of great importance to society in the detection of crime and criminals' and 'should not be lightly set aside'.[190] The enactment of the Canadian Charter caused the courts to reassess their approach to this difficult conflict. In *Hunter* itself, a comparison was made with the Fourth Amendment case law of the United States. Following a review of this case law,[191] it was stated that a trial judge should examine the contested material and attempt to reconcile the matter by deleting all references to the identity of the informant. This edited material should then be made available to the accused. If the Crown was unhappy that, even after editing, an informant's identity might be discovered, a prosecutor might have to elect whether to proceed.[192]

However, if the material is edited more extensively than is necessary, there may be a successful appeal by an accused. In *Farinacci et al v The Queen*,[193] the appellants were charged after an extended police investigation that involved a considerable volume of wiretap evidence. Challenge was made to the validity of the intercept authorisations and, in order to substantiate their challenge, the appellants had sought access to sealed packets in which the relevant material was held. The trial judge had edited that information with the concurrence of Crown counsel. On appeal, it was alleged that the editing had gone too far and that the appellants' ability to make a full answer and defence was prejudiced. The Supreme Court upheld their contention and ordered a retrial. In the course of the judgment, Sopinka J. stated that there was a presumption of disclosure of *all* relevant information that was in the possession of the State and that in order to justify non-disclosure, the Crown must bring itself within an exception to that general rule. Disclosure of the full affidavit 'should be the starting premise'.[194] The Court highlighted factors that were relevant to the editing of material. Consideration of these matters would assist in ensuring that there was compliance with the Charter right to make full answer and defence to a criminal charge. The factors relate to the protection of informants from danger, the protection of ongoing police investigations and investigators, and the protection of innocent persons. Although these factors are described in terms of their objectives rather than in terms of particular categories of information, they overlap considerably with the detailed list of items that comprise sensitive material within the Code made pursuant to CPIA.

It is still possible for an accused to assert that the balance comes down in favour of full disclosure and that no editing should take place. The need to establish innocence is the only basis to seek such disclosure. McLachlin J. said in *Leipert v The Queen*[195] that informer privilege 'is subject to only one exception, known as the "innocence at stake" exception'. Whilst the innocence at stake exception is the only exception recognised by the courts, this may arise in variety of circumstances. In *Scott v The Queen*,[196] three examples were given of situations where the defendant might claim that he needed to know the identity of an informant in order to assert his innocence. The first was where the informer was 'a material witness to the crime'. The second arose where 'the informer has acted as an *agent provocateur*'. An accused would, as a general rule, be expected to provide some evidentiary basis for the defence.[197] The third situation arose in the context of section 8 of the Charter where the accused argued that there had been an unreasonable search. In this last situation, the editing of material should be used to manage the conflict of interests between the accused and the Crown and disclosure of identity should only be ordered 'where it is absolutely essential'. This third situation must now be read subject to the statement made in *Leipert*[198] that the innocence at stake exception effectively confines the right to know the source of information on which a search warrant is based to the circumstance where the defence alleges 'that the goods seized in the execution of the warrant were planted'.

Despite the presumption that there should be disclosure of all relevant information in the hands of the prosecution, it was said in *Leipert* there is no inherent conflict between this Charter right and the common law rule of informer privilege.[199] Indeed, McLachlin J. went further by stating that the privilege 'is of such importance that it cannot be balanced against other interests'. It extends not only to the Crown, but also to the informer which 'raises special concerns in the case of anonymous informants'.[200] The consequence is that the immunity has a broad scope and extends not only to disclosure of the name of the informant, but also to disclosure of any information that might indirectly reveal his identity.[201] Thus, in *Leipert*, the police acted on an anonymous tip from a Crime Stoppers organisation. That tip then led to further investigation and to the issuance of a warrant. The Crown claimed that, since the informer could not be contacted, it was not in a position to determine whether any part of the information contained in the tip off might reveal the identity of the individual concerned. The Supreme Court agreed that, since it was not possible for such a determination to be made, the

Crown was justified in claiming privilege for all the information provided by the informer.

It is hardly surprising, in view of the fact that Canada has looked to the United States for guidance on the balancing of interests involved, that there should be a concordance of approach toward informer immunity. The Fourteenth Amendment due process clause creates a requirement that criminal prosecutions must comply with prevailing notions of fundamental fairness. Thus, in order to allow an accused to present a meaningful defence, the prosecution is under a constitutional duty to disclose material that is relevant, exculpatory and unavailable to the defence from other sources (Mauet, 1995). *Brady v Maryland* [202] stated that the suppression of prosecution evidence that 'is material to either guilt or punishment' violates due process. In the more recent case of *Kyles v Whitely*,[203] this statement was clarified and was said that the question was whether suppression of the evidence had affected the fairness of the trial in the sense that it might result in a verdict not 'worthy of confidence'. This presumptive duty of disclosure may be overridden where the public interest in the protection of informers overrides fair trial arguments. In *Roviaro v US*,[204] the Supreme Court denied that there was any 'fixed rule' with respect to disclosure in these circumstances and stated that the particular circumstances of each case must be considered, including the crime charged, the possible defences and the possible significance of the informer's testimony. In order to tip the balance in favour of disclosure, an accused has to demonstrate the possibility of an unsafe conviction. Crucial factors are likely to be that the government holds significant material and exculpatory information,[205] that the material is otherwise unavailable to the defence and that the informant was an active participant in the crime.[206]

Since there is an 'innocence at stake' exception to the immunity, an attempt to seek disclosure of the identity of an informant, merely to establish that an unreasonable search has taken place, will probably fail. *McCray v Illinois*[207] concerned the arrest of an accused for possession of drugs. The arrest and the subsequent search of the defendant's person had been triggered by a tip received from an informer. The Court held that where the issue is not guilt or innocence, but is whether there is probable cause for an arrest or search, police officers need not disclose the informant's identity. That, at least, is the situation if the trial judge is satisfied that the officers relied in good faith on credible information supplied by a reliable informer. Thus, as in England under CPIA, there is little chance of discovering the content or source of information upon which a search took place unless this information may substantiate a claim that the accused has been framed or set up in some way by another.

The consistency of the law concerning informer privilege demonstrates that concern over the extent of serious and organised crime has allowed for exceptions to be created in respect of the normative disclosure rules in each of the three jurisdictions. These exceptions have been maintained in the face of constitutional rights to privacy and there is no reason, therefore, to imagine that the implementation of the Human Rights Act will have any significant impact on the doctrine of public interest immunity so far as it attaches to informant evidence. Notwithstanding this uniformity of approach, there is a valid objection to the width of the privilege. Mauet points out that 'much of the recent increase in informant use is in the area of paid informants'. Such people are hardly unbiased, since they are paid 'contingent on the seizure of things' (Mauet, 1995:564). McCollum (1975:120) puts the matter even more strongly when he says that 'society suffers because it must give to a group "generally regarded with aversion and nauseous disdain" a safe haven for working their intrigues'. Against this it is suggested[208] that the requirement of showing probable cause helps to diminish the danger of the public dissemination of false information.[209] There are ethical objections to withholding relevant material from a court of trial and to protecting those who may be distorting the truth. However, investigations into serious crime are unlikely to suffer any narrowing of informer immunity. Whilst some informers may be as corrupt and dangerous as those against whom they are informing,[210] their need for protection is not apparently diminished by their own lawlessness.

Notes

1. Article 6(3)(a).
2. Article 6(3)(c). There is a right to state funded assistance for indigent accused 'when the interests of justice so require'.
3. Article 6(3)(d).
4. See chapter 4.
5. [1996] 23 EHRR29.
6. The Fourteenth Amendment applies the due process clause to States and prevents State derogation from Federally mandated safeguards.
7. *R v Leatham* (1861) 8 Cox CC 498 and *Kuruma v R* [1955] AC 197.
8. Above. Some members of the House of Lords in *Sang* [1980] AC 402 considered that *Kuruma* was wrongly interpreted in subsequent case law.
9. *Kuruma* [1955] AC 197 at 204.
10. At 203.
11. [1964] 1 QB 495.

12. [1978] 1 QB 490.
13. *E.g.* the wiring of individuals, consensual telephone interceptions and consensual bugging; see chapter 5.
14. *R v Court* [1962] Crim. L.R. 697; *R v Payne* [1963] 1 WLR 37 and cp. *R v Apicella* (1985) 82 Cr. App. R. 295.
15. See the comments on these cases by Lord Scarman in *Sang* at 455 and Viscount Dilhorne at 436.
16. [1980] AC 402.
17. *Ibid* at 447.
18. *Ibid* at 450. Lord Fraser was considerably influenced by Scottish case law which had, by then, developed a more structured exclusionary approach to illegally obtained evidence.
19. *Ibid* at 450–453.
20. *Ibid* at 455.
21. At 434. Lord Diplock viewed the discretion in its purely historical context as a means of controlling the admission of character evidence.
22. At 440–441. *I.e.*the cases of *Payne, Callis v Gunn* and *Jeffery v Black*.
23. Per Lord Diplock at 436.
24. Or, as in the Canadian Charter, that the administration of justice is not brought into disrepute.
25. See Mirfield (1997) and Sharpe (1998a) for a discussion of the issue.
26. The passage of the 1982 PACE Bill was interrupted by a general election and was reintroduced in October 1983.
27. 'Confession' is defined as including 'any statement wholly or partly adverse to the person who made it, whether made to a person in authority or not and whether made in words or otherwise'; subsect. 82(1).
28. Subsect. 76(2)(a).
29. Subsect. 76(2)(b). For a fuller discussion of this section see Mirfield and Sharpe (above).
30. See RCCP (1981) Cmnd. 8092 at para. 4.118. There was an unsuccessful attempt to introduce an exclusionary rule for evidence obtained as a consequence of an illegal search at the Committee Stage of the 1982 Bill.
31. Hansard vol. 454 cols. 931–932. This clause owed much to the exclusionary principles developed in Australia; see *Bunning v Cross* (1978) 19 ALR 641.
32. Hansard vol. 455 cols. 653–657. Improperly obtained evidence may be in issue where there has been no specific breach of primary or subordinate legislation, *e.g* a deception on the part of investigators.
33. Hansard vol. 455 cols. 654–656.
34. At p. 14.
35. This general discretion is inconsistent with the express wording of subsect. 76(1) which states that a confession may be given in evidence against a person if it is relevant and is not excluded by the court 'in pursuance of this section'.
36. *I.e.* by an officer of insufficient rank such as a superintendent.
37. *Viz.* that there are no grounds to support a belief that the bugging is likely to be of substantial value in the detection of serious crime.
38. In which case, there should be prior judicial authorisation.
39. [1996] 3 ALL ER 289; discussed in chapter 5.
40. *Ibid* at 297. Lord Taylor in the C.A. also cited these dicta.
41. *Ibid.*

42. See above.
43. See *R v Fulling* (1987) 85 Cr. App. R. 136.
44. Lord Herschell in *Bank of England v Vagliano* [1891] AC 107 at 144 and see Lord Taylor in *Smurthwaite* [1994] 1 ALL ER 896 at 902.
45. *Khan* (above) at 301.
46. [1998] 2 ALL ER 155.
47. This was a pre Police Act case; see chapter 5.
48. At 178.
49. At 180. See also Choo and Nash (1999)
50. Sect. 58 grants this right subject only to limited powers to delay its exercise in the case of serious arrestable offences.
51. Code C10. But note that, under sect. 34 of CRIMPO, adverse inferences may be drawn from silence.
52. [1992] 4 ALL ER 559.
53. *Ibid* at 564.
54. See *R v Mason* [1987] 3 ALL ER 481.
55. Cp. *US v White* (1971) 401 US 745 for a rationale against suppression which is based on assumption of risk.
56. *Christou* (above) at 566.
57. (1993) 97 Cr. App. R. 368.
58. *Ibid* at 368.
59. *Ibid* at 374 and cp. *Kuhlman v Wilson* (1986) 477 US 436.
60. [1997] 1 Cr. App. R. 217.
61. See above.
62. (1990) 57 CCC (3d) 1.
63. *E.g. Jelen and Katz* (1990) 90 Cr. App. R.456.
64. (1998) 151 ALR 98. These two cases were heard together by the High Court.
65. *E.g. Gill and Ranuana* [1989] Crim. L.R. 358; *Edwards* [1991] Crim. L.R. 45 and *Smurthwaite* [1994] 1 ALL ER 898.
66. Above.
67. At 903.
68. In *Smurthwaite*, counsel made much of the fact that the first meeting with the undercover officer was not recorded. There was corroborative evidence, however. See also *R v Callaghan* (1999) 97/8628/X4 and *R v Bryce* [1992] 4 ALL ER 567.
69. [1996] 1 ALL ER 353.
70. This was in addition to an argument based on abuse of process (discussed below) and an argument that an essential element of the substantive offence had been committed by a customs officer and not by the appellants.
71. (1998) 44/1997/828/1034.
72. In contrast to the earlier case of *Ludi v Switzerland* (1992) 15 EHRR 434 where the German police had opened a preliminary investigation and an investigating judge had been aware of the undercover role of a police officer.
73. [1996] 1 ALL ER 353 at 359.
74. *R v Callaghan* (1999) 97/8628X4 and see *R v Edwards* (above).
75. [1964] AC 1254.
76. *R v Heston-Francis* [1984] 1 QB 278 at 290.
77. [1994] 1 AC 42.

78. *Ibid* Lord Lowry at 74.
79. *Ibid* at 62.
80. [1996] 1 ALL ER 353; discussed above.
81. At page 360 and see *R v Campbell* (1999) 1 SCR 565.
82. At 360.
83. *Ibid.*
84. [1999] 2 Cr. App. R. 143.
85. *Ibid* at 157. Mullen might have been deported to Eire instead.
86. [1998] 2 ALL ER 155
87. At 166–167 and see Choo and Nash (1999)
88. [1999] Crim.L.R.728 No. 980299/Y5 C.A. 18th February 1999.
89. [1999] 2 Cr. App. R. 143.
90. See *R v Preston* [1994] AC 130; *R v Rasool* [1997] 1 WLR 1092 and *Morgans v DPP* [1999] 2 Cr. App. R. 99.
91. See *R v Aujla* [1998] 2 Cr. App. R.16.
92. See *R v Effick* [1994] 3 ALL ER 458.
93. See *R v Sargeant* C.A. 8th January 1999.
94. 17th February 2000 Internet Judgments and see chapter 5.
95. (1999) App. No. 40084/98 and see chapter 5.
96. [1996] 23 EHRR 313 and see chapter 4.
97. *E.g. R v Herbert* (1990) 57 CCC (3d) 1 and *Broyles v The Queen* (1991) 68 CCC (3d) 308.
98. *R v Hallsworth* C.A. 3rd April 1998 and cp. *R v Roberts* [1997] 1 Cr. App. R. 217.
99. [1997] 2 Cr. App. R. 119 and see also *R v Gray* [1995] 2 Cr. App. R. 100.
100. See *R v Blake and Tye* (1844) 6 QB 126; *Tripodi v R* (1961) 104 CLR1 and *Ahern v R* (1988) 165 CLR 87.
101. (1970) 11 DLR (3d) 673.
102. [1955] AC 197; discussed above.
103. And see Dickson C.J. in *R v Simmons* (1988) 45 CCC (3d) 296.
104. See the discussion above.
105. (1987) 38 DLR (4th) 508.
106. *Ibid* at 528.
107. *Ibid* at 523.
108. *Ibid.*
109. *Ibid.*
110. *Collins* at 526.
111. See *R v Genest* (1989) 1 SCR 59 and *R v Black* (1989) 2 SCR 138.
112. (1997) 141 DLR (4th) 193 at 224 and see *R v Mellenthin* (1992) 76 CCC (3d) 481.
113. At 257–259. Cp. Lord Diplock in *Sang* [1980] AC 403. See also *Thompson Newspapers Ltd v Canada (Director of Investigation & Research Restrictive Trade Practices Commission)* (1990) 54 CCC (3d) 417.
114. See *R v Wise* (1992) 1 SCR 527.
115. (1988) 55 DLR (4th) 503 and see chapter 4.
116. At 513. La Forest J. relied on the judgment of Lamer J. in *Pohoretsky v The Queen* (1987) 33 CCC (3d) 389 where a doctor took a blood sample from a delirious patient at the request of a police officer.
117. At 513.

118. *E.g. Stillman v The Queen* (1997) 141 DLR (4th) 193.
119. (1996) 139 DLR (4th) 1 and cp. *R v Borden* (1991) 119 DLR (4th) 74 and *R v Colarusso* (1997) 1 SCR 20.
120. (1990) 55 CC (3d) 161.
121. (1996) 97 CCC (3d) 385 at 408.
122. (1987) 38 DLR (4th) 508 at 527.
123. (1996) 112 CCC (3d) 428 at 447–448.
124. (1990) 55 CCC (3d) 161 and see above.
125. (1990) 65 DLR (4th) 240 at 262 and see chapter 5.
126. (1990) 3 SCR 36.
127. See *R v Hughes* [1988] Crim. L.R. 519 where erroneous information about the availability of a defence solicitor was given as a result of a 'misunderstanding' rather than as a deliberate breach of PACE and *R v Hoyte* [1994] Crim. L.R. 215 where police conducted an identification procedure in good faith despite it being in breach of PACE.
128. *R v Therens* (1985) 1 SCR 613.
129. (1995) 2 SCR 297.
130. (1995) 97 CCC (3d) 385.
131. See *R v Black* (1989) 2 SCR 138.
132. At 405.
133. See *R v Warickshall* (1783) 1 Leach 263; 168 ER 234 and *Lam Chi-ming v The Queen* [1991] 2 ALL ER 212.
134. (1985) 2 SCR 297.
135. (1985) 2 SCR 128.
136. At 136–137. The words come from dicta in the earlier case of *R v Young* (1984) 40 CR (3d) 289.
137. [1964] AC 1254 and see above.
138. (1988) 67 CR (3d) 1.
139. *Ibid* per Lamer J. at 40.
140. *Ibid* at 31.
141. (1991) 70 CCC (3d) 36.
142. (1995) 97 CCC (3d) 385 and above.
143. *Ibid* at 400.
144. *Ibid* at 406.
145. (1995) 129 ALR 41.
146. *Ibid* at 56.
147. *Ibid* at 58. The actual decision in *Ridgeway* has now been 'overcome' by the Crimes Amendment (Controlled Operations) Act 1996 (Cth.) which precludes the rejection of evidence on the ground of 'unlawful' conduct in the course of a 'controlled operation'; and see *Nicholas v The Queen* (1998) 72 ALJR 456 (HC).
148. (1999) 1 SCR 565.
149. See the Royal Commission on Criminal Procedure (1981) Cmnd. 8092 paras. 4.123 to 4.128.
150. (1914) 232 US 383.
151. (1925) 269 US 20.
152. (1961) 367 US 643 and see chapter 3.
153. (1974) 414 US 338.
154. (1976) 428 US 465.

155. Loewy (1983:1265).
156. *Johnson v US* (1948) 333 US 10.
157. (1973) 412 US 218.
158. Cp. the PACE Codes A and B concerning the obtaining of informed consent, discussed in chapter 2.
159. (1974) 415 US 164.
160. (1967) 398 US 347.
161. (1969) 394 US 165.
162. (1986) 475 US 791 and see *Rakas v Illinois* (1978) 439 US 128.
163. (1993) 508 US 77. Cp. *R v Jones, Williams and Barham* [1997] 2 Cr. App. R. 119.
164. (1986) 467 US 227 and see chapter 2.
165. (1986) 476 US 207. This decision was subsequently applied in *Florida v Riley* (1989) 488 US 445, where a helicopter flew at only 400 feet and made naked eye observations through openings in a green house roof. See also Yeager D.B. (1993:249).
166. *United States v Knotts* (1983) 460 US 276 and see chapter 5.
167. (1979) 442 US 735 and see chapter 5.
168. (1983) 462 US 696.
169. *US v Jacobsen* (1984) 466 US 109.
170. See chapter 3.
171. Cm. 2263 (1993) at pp. 91–91.
172. Fears about sensitive information have spilled over into used and therefore disclosed material. In *R v CPS and anor. ex parte J and anor.* The Times July 8th 1999, the Divisional Court held that audio and video surveillance tapes, exhibited to support the statement of an undercover officer, should be viewed in controlled conditions. This was to prevent copying and distribution of the tape, which, in turn, might have led to identification of the officer concerned.
173. Para. 6.12 and see chapter 3.
174. CPIA subsect. 3(1)(b).
175. CPIA subsect. 7(2)(a).
176. CPIA subsects. 3(6); 7(5); and 8(5).
177. Application No. 28901/95 (Judgment 16th February 2000).
178. Application No. 29777/96 (Judgment 16th February 2000).
179. Application No. 27052/95 (Judgment 16th February 2000).
180. *Jasper* (above) at paras. 55–58.
181. *Jasper* (above) at para. 79 of the Commission judgment.
182. *Fitt v United Kingdom* (above) at para. 84 of the Commission judgment.
183. *Ibid* at para. 82.
184. *R v Keane* [1994] 2 ALL ER478 at 484. Cp *Kyles v Whitely* (1995) 514 US 131 and below. See also chapter 3.
185. [1995] 2 Cr. App. R. 94.
186. *Ibid* at 98.
187. CPIA subsect. 8(2).
188. See above.
189. (1987) 34 CCC (3d) 14.
190. Per Cory J. at 17–18.
191. *E.g. Roviaro v US* (1957) 353 US 53; *McCray v Illinois* (1967) 386 US 300 and see below.

192. *R v Hunter* (above) at pp. 26–27.
193. (1994) 88 CCC (3d) 1.
194. *Ibid* at p. 55.
195. (1997) 143 DLR (4th) 38 at 47.
196. (1990) 61 CCC (3d) 300 at 315.
197. Cp. CPIA 1996 sect. 8.
198. Above at 50.
199. *Ibid* at 49.
200. *Ibid* at 45.
201. *Ibid* at 46.
202. (1963) 373 US 83.
203. (1995) 514 US 131.
204. (1957) 353 US 53.
205. *US v Sanchez* (1993) 988 F2d 1382 (5th Cir.); *US v Bender* (1993) 5 F3d 267 (7th Cir.).
206. *US v Sanchez* (above); *US v Bender* (above) and *Rugendorf v US* (1964) 370 US 528. Cp. *R v Keane* [1994] 2 ALL ER 478 and *R v Turner* [1995] 2 Cr. App. R. 94.
207. (1967) 386 US 300.
208. McCollum (1975:122).
209. If a requirement of probable cause is indeed instrumental in safeguarding suspects from false accusation, there should be such a requirement in relation to *all* searches.
210. Informant Working Group (1998).

7   From Evidence to Information

In the foregoing chapters, I have attempted to sketch the development of search and surveillance powers from the earliest right to apprehend a 'hand-having thief'[1] to the development of sophisticated electronic surveillance activities in the twentieth century. While the objective of many of these criminal investigations has been to obtain real evidence for use in proceedings against an accused, increasingly the purpose of an investigation is the gathering of information to be held on a database. Such databases store knowledge that might conceivably be of use in future law enforcement. The gathering of the information is therefore not necessarily directed to solving a crime that has already taken place. It is, of course, possible that, as a fortuitous incidence of storing information, past crimes may be solved. The power to use DNA analysis to assist in closed investigations is one obvious example of how scientific advances can lead to the reopening of long abandoned cases.[2] However, the main purpose of storing material that concerns suspects or convicted individuals is to build up a knowledge database through which law enforcers can trawl, whether in support of an offender profile or simply in support of a 'hunch'. In respect of criminal investigation, knowledge is most definitely power. There are inevitably privacy issues involved in the storage of personal data, even when the subject of that data is a convicted criminal rather than an innocent citizen. In this chapter, there is a discussion of existing law enforcement powers, both national and transnational, to store information without the consent of an individual. I end the chapter by questioning whether wide limitations on the presumptive right of access to personal data[3] raise questions as to whether there should be a reconsideration of privacy rights and, in particular, the converse right 'not to be known about'.

DNA Databases and Information Storage

In April 1995, the first national database was launched in England and Wales. By the end of 1997, there were 229,301 suspect samples on the database and 26,984 crime scene samples. The database had effected some 18,846 matches.[4]

The initial impetus to set up the database came from the police service, but their proposals 'for a clearer legislative approach to the taking and retention of samples for the purpose of monitoring and consulting DNA data bases' were examined by the Royal Commission on Criminal Procedure.[5] This 'clearer' approach was to give the police the power to retain relevant data concerning those who were convicted of offences 'so that in any subsequent investigation where the identity of the offender is unknown but DNA evidence comes to light, the evidence can be checked against the samples in a database'.[6] The power to take this sample would not necessarily be 'relevant to the particular offence concerned'. In other words, the police were seeking a power to take samples not for the immediate purpose of ongoing criminal investigation relating to the accused, but for future use. The Commission stated that this police resource should be available since DNA profiling 'is now so powerful a diagnostic technique and so helpful in establishing guilt or innocence'.[7] It was considered by the Commission that a distinction should be made between those convicted and those acquitted of offending. Only in respect of the former should details of DNA analysis be retained for the purposes of cross matching. In respect of those acquitted, analysis should be retained only in order to provide statistical information (*e.g.* in relation to random occurrence ratios amongst the general population).[8]

PACE subsection 63A(1) provides that

> Fingerprints or samples or the information derived from samples taken under any power conferred by this Part of this Act from a person who has been arrested on suspicion of being involved in a recordable offence may be checked against other fingerprints or samples or the information derived from other samples contained in records held by or on behalf of the police or held in connection with or as a result of an investigation of an offence.

Further, under subsection 63A(4)(b), a person who has previously been convicted of a recordable offence, but has not had a sample (or a suitable or sufficient sample) taken from him, may be required to attend a police station to have a sample taken. Seven days notice is to be given of this requirement.[9] Failure to attend will result in arrest without warrant.[10] PACE originally provided the time limit under which such a request could be made was one month from the date of conviction. However, both the categories of persons from whom samples may be taken and also the time limit within which the requirement can be made have been extended. Steventon (1995:414) wrote somewhat prophetically that 'as technology advances and the cost of DNA profiling decreases, the likelihood of creating a very large database increases'.

The evolving statute law in England and Wales demonstrates that there is an unstoppable dynamic toward extending rather than narrowing the categories of those who are within the database provisions.

The Criminal Evidence (Amendment) Act 1997 section 2 provides that even persons convicted before 10th April 1995 may now be required to provide a non-intimate sample. The offence for which they are convicted must be one of those listed in Schedule 1 of the 1997 Act. In addition, at the 'relevant time' the offender must be serving a sentence of imprisonment, be detained as a young offender during Her Majesty's pleasure, or be detained under a hospital order pursuant to the Mental Health Act 1983. The 'relevant time' is stated in section 5 to be 'the time when it is sought to take the sample'. The sample is taken at the place of detention. Although the database was supposed to contain genetic fingerprinting taken only from those who were found guilty, the requirement that a person be 'convicted' is extended, by section 2, to cover insanity verdicts and verdicts of unfitness to plead. The list of offences contained in Schedule 1 includes murder, manslaughter, firearms offences, wounding with intent and aggravated burglary, but also causing grievous bodily harm under section 20 of the Offences Against the Person Act 1861, occasioning bodily harm under the same Act[11] and burglary. Whilst the category of offences is not so wide as the concept of a recordable offence, which includes all imprisonable and some non-imprisonable offences,[12] it is a wide enough concept to embrace those who have committed middle range offences. The Schedule also includes all sexual offences under the Sexual Offences Act 1956 (except certain prostitution offences), indecency with children and the possession of indecent material relating to children. The inclusion of virtually all sexual offences within the database provisions is consistent with a current public *animus* toward sexual offenders that has led to distinctions being made in respect of sentencing[13] and in respect of trial procedures.[14] Such persons are deemed to be serious and dangerous offenders by virtue of the type of crime committed with little subtlety in distinction between violent rapists and those committing indecent assaults. All those who might possibly pose a threat to society on release are within the Criminal Evidence (Amendment) Act.

The recommended distinction between samples taken from those convicted and samples taken from those acquitted is currently maintained in PACE. Section 64 provides that a suspect who is acquitted of an offence, or not proceeded against for an offence, is entitled to the destruction of fingerprints or samples taken from him in 'connection with such an investigation'. Not surprisingly, samples or fingerprints taken from a non-suspect (*e.g.* the occupier of premises that have been burgled where prints are necessary for elimination purposes) are also required to be destroyed 'as soon as they have fulfilled the purpose for which they were taken'. However, subsection 64(3A) provides that samples may be retained where another person involved in the investigation has been convicted, but the information derived therefrom may not be used as evidence against an unconvicted person, nor 'for the purpose of any investigation of an offence'. This complex provision is explained by Steventon (1995:416) as covering the practical problem caused by different samples (for instance one taken from the rape victim and one taken from the alleged rapist) being processed together for the purpose of DNA profiling. In such a situation, it might not be possible to destroy one sample without destroying the other. A new subsection 64(3B)[15] provides that where samples are required to be destroyed, the information derived from them need not be destroyed, but may not be used in evidence in subsequent criminal investigation or proceedings. The provision paves the way for the creation of a DNA database by authorising the collection of information for statistical purposes. This creates a 'half-way house' between the destruction of sample evidence and the retention of sample evidence specifically in order to cross- match it in the case of future offending. A convicted person has no right to request the destruction of his fingerprints or of a sample taken from him. He must be informed when it is taken that it may be used to effect a 'speculative search'.[16] A 'speculative search' is defined in section 65 of PACE as 'a check against other fingerprints or samples'. This cross-checking is made against fingerprints, samples, or the information derived therefrom 'contained in the records held by or on behalf of the police or held in connection with or as a result of an investigation into an offence'.[17]

There are obvious concerns that privacy is substantially invaded by the retention of information derived from the samples of those who have not been convicted even when the retention is not for investigative purposes. The Forensic Science Service acts as an agency of national police forces and of Customs and Excise. Information is not, therefore, held by a neutral 'independent body'.[18] Further, there are problems about the anonymity of personal data that is held for statistical purposes due to the need to prevent a duplication of entries.[19] Whilst it may be argued that certain types of privacy rights may be lost on conviction, this should not apply to those who are subsequently cleared of offending and cannot apply to those who are not even suspected of offending. Concerns over the potential for misuse of such data seem to have been outweighed by the efficacy of the information in respect of crime enforcement. Schumacher (1999) points out that DNA profiles 'can be stored in numeric code, thereby requiring minimal technology'. Thus, at a practical level, databases are easy to maintain. He also points out that

> without the use of random DNA profiles to check it against, a sample of DNA recovered from a crime scene would only be valuable if there were a suspect in custody who provided a sample matching the unknown sample.

The utility of these databases in criminal investigations has led to proposals being made for a further widening of the potential for random profiling. The Home Office[20] is concerned that the use of mass DNA screening, combined with the use of offender profiling, may lead to possible suspects being approached a number of times in the course of investigations into serious crime. The fear is that, although an initial request to volunteer a sample may be complied with, 'people will refuse to give further samples if they continue to be approached on different occasions for different offences'. The suggestion is to amend PACE so that samples and the DNA profiles derived from samples, can be retained 'for use in future investigations' with the written consent of the volunteer. This mooted rewriting of section 64 of PACE would remove the distinction, considered by the Royal Commission on Criminal Procedure to be a crucial one, between the retention of samples obtained from convicted offenders and those obtained from innocent citizens. It is difficult to see how this can be 'mutually beneficial' both to the police and to the volunteer, as stated in the Home Office Consultation Document. There is a recognition that the right to withdraw consent 'at any time' would be a necessary safeguard,[21] but should a volunteer later withdraw consent, it is likely that the police would be justified in treating such a withdrawal as a suspect action if it takes place whilst they are investigating a later crime.

It is also proposed by the Home Office that there should be express statutory authority to check DNA samples and fingerprints against information derived outside the jurisdiction. Thus DNA profiling would become a recognised tool in international crime control. At the other end of the spectrum, there is likely to be a widening of police powers to access fingerprint data at street level. The Home Office[22] has recommended that new technology, allowing for the electronic imaging of a hand, should be expressly legitimated within PACE. This new technology 'will enable officers on patrol who suspect the involvement of an individual in an offence to verify that person's identity on the spot'. This allows for the virtually instantaneous identification of suspects and for a cross-check to be made with records held on a Police National Computer to discover (amongst other things) whether there is a history of 'violence or contagious disease'. This suggestion leads inexorably to the further recommendation that lower ranking officers should be able to authorise the compulsory taking of fingerprints where there are reasonable grounds for suspecting a person's involvement in a criminal offence. Whilst the cross-check will only prove fruitful where there are already prints on record, the potential extension of this power to the relatively uncontrolled environment 'on the street' could pave the way for abuse. Reasonable suspicion may be a contentious matter and there would seem to be no proposal for a requirement that a person has been arrested prior to the taking of prints. Thus any level of suspected offending, however minor, would justify this invasion of privacy. The Home Office Document continues its support for expediency over privacy by recommending that there should be power to take fingerprints by compulsion from those young offenders who receive an official 'warning'.[23] Thus, even though the young offender has not been technically convicted of an offence, the details of his warning for a recordable offence, held in National Police Computer records, could be evidenced by 'supporting fingerprints'.

In England and Wales, the law has not yet gone so far as to require all of its citizens to submit DNA samples for medical research, or other purposes.[24] However, it is certainly a role model for other jurisdictions looking to expand the potential scope of a criminal database. The American National Commission on the Future of DNA Evidence has considered whether to adopt the 'relevant parts' of the English system in the United States.[25] The Commission considered that the concept of extending the database to arrestees was desirable in principle and that only practical constraints, such as backlogs in the collection of data from already convicted individuals and lack of funding, were reasons to delay the implementation of this change. In Canada, the DNA Identification Act 1998 provides for the creation of a national databank containing DNA profiles from convicted offenders and from unsolved crime scenes. The bank is expected to be operational by June 2000. There is a provision within the statute for the removal of information concerning a person who is subsequently acquitted on appeal and also, in respect of those who receive a discharge for the offence, for the removal of information within a specified number of years if no reconviction takes place. In Europe, there has been a perceptible shift in attitude. In 1992, the Committee of Ministers accepted that DNA had a use in 'the fight against crime', but recommended that an analysis and the information so derived should not be kept after the final decision in the case, or after it was no longer necessary in relation to the purposes for which it had been used. The only exceptions were where the individual concerned had been 'convicted of serious offences against life, integrity and security of person' or where the security of the State was involved. Even in these exceptional circumstances, it was thought that 'strict storage periods should be defined by domestic law'.[26] Yet in 1997, the Council of Ministers issued a Resolution inviting member States to consider establishing national DNA databases with a view to the mutual exchange of the results of DNA analysis. It is up to each State to determine the offences and conditions that justify storage of the information.[27]

It can be objected that the 'ever-widening scope of the target groups from whom law enforcement collects DNA' may arguably lead to a general rather than a limited purpose for forensic databases.[28] The potential for misuse is worrying, not least because DNA samples may reveal genetic conditions and, perhaps, even genetic markers for aggression, substance abuse, mental illness and criminal tendency.[29] This genetic information is relevant not only to the individual whose sample is being taken, but also to those who are related to that individual. The fear is that even strict controls on the dissemination of this information may not, ultimately, prevent the data being used for purposes unconnected with the investigation of crime.

National Surveillance Databases

Her Majesty's Inspectorate of Constabulary considers that 'good quality intelligence is the life blood of the modern police service' and that the challenge posed by 'professional' criminals 'cannot be underestimated'.[30] One of the most potent tools in the armoury of police intelligence is the National Criminal Intelligence Service. This organisation was established under the Police Act 1997. Subsection 2(2) of that Act states that the function of NCIS shall be

    (a)   to gather, store and analyse information in order to provide criminal intelligence,

    (b)   to provide criminal intelligence to police forces in great Britain, the Royal Ulster Constabulary, the National Crime Squad and other law enforcement agencies, and

    (c)   to act in support of such police forces, the Royal Ulster Constabulary, the National Crime Squad and other law enforcement agencies carrying out their criminal intelligence activities.

The use of surveillance strategies and of 'sophisticated surveillance equipment' are recognised means to acquire criminal intelligence.[31] The storage of personal data resulting from such operations raises just as many privacy issues as the storage of DNA samples. The position is now regulated by the voluntary NCIS Codes and by the Code of Practice laid under the Police Act 1997.

Under the Police Act Code, officers have power to retain material that 'might be relevant', not only to the current investigation, but also 'to any other investigation or to pending or future civil or criminal proceedings'.[32] Indeed, the Code goes so far as to state that officers should take steps to inform the Commissioner of their belief that the material might have future relevance in order to prevent its destruction.[33] Destruction of material is justified on the negative basis that it is 'wholly unrelated to a criminal investigation or to any person who is subject to the investigation and that there is no reason to believe that it will be relevant to future civil or criminal proceedings'.[34] Mere belief in possible future relevance therefore prevents the fruits of a bugging activity from being destroyed, even when the surveillance has not produced usable material in respect of the target. The Code specifically allows the use of information obtained through properly authorised intrusive surveillance 'in other investigations', although it is stated that such use by bodies or individuals other than law enforcement agencies or the courts should be permitted 'only in the most exceptional circumstances'.[35] Surveillance that is outside the Police Act[36] and governed by the NCIS Codes is subject to the same principle of preservation for contingent future use.[37]

In respect of telephone interception, information obtained under IOCA 1985 is governed by that statute. The Secretary of State issuing the warrant is responsible for making arrangements to restrict disclosure of the interception(s) and ensuring that the material is destroyed as soon as 'its retention is no longer necessary' for the purposes for which the warrant was issued.[38] There is, of course, no external judicial scrutiny of these arrangements and, since the material will not be used in court, its destruction will be especially difficult to monitor, as there is no evidence that it even exists. Consensual interceptions and interceptions of calls made from private systems or by means of wireless telegraphy are governed by the NCIS Code on Interception of Communications and by the Code on the Recording and Dissemination of Intelligence Material. Preservation of such intercepted material is again permitted on the basis that it 'could be relevant in pending or future criminal or civil proceedings'. The wording is positive rather then negative. Paragraph 7.3 of the Interceptions Code mandates that, once an investigation has been cancelled or concluded, the material shall be destroyed if there is no belief that it will be required in any pending or future investigation. However, the same paragraph contains a sting in the tail. Destruction is not required, even if there is no belief in possible future use, if its retention is required on grounds of 'significant public interest' under paragraph 5.3 of the NCIS Code on Recording and Dissemination of Intelligence Material.[39] Significant public interest includes 'the maintenance of security and integrity of law enforcement agencies and other public authorities'. This somewhat imprecise definition allows for a potentially wide basis of retention, such retention being only subject to systemically internal control.

The subject access provisions of the Data Protection Act 1998, giving the right to know what is recorded about one, do not apply to intelligence material,[40] since there are exceptions in respect of national security and the detection of crime, but the Code on Recording and Dissemination states in paragraph 1.7

> Notwithstanding that the requirement for openness may be set aside in appropriate circumstances, the law enforcement agencies must have a legitimate basis for processing data and observe the data protection principles regarding data quality and security in their handling of intelligence material.

In particular, this Code requires law enforcers to evaluate the reliability and worth of the information before it is recorded, to ensure that it is retained 'only for so long as it remains relevant' and to permit access to databases only 'in connection with official business'.

However, there is, inevitably, no external scrutiny of the compilation or distribution of such material and, as in the case of interceptions under IOCA, no way of knowing whether information is held at all, since it may not have been relied upon in any criminal proceedings. There is a potentially wide definition of 'intelligence material' in paragraph 1.8.1 where it is stated to include 'personal information of value to national security, the prevention or detection of crime or disorder, the maintenance of community safety or collection of any tax or duty'. The databases may therefore contain information, not only in relation to past offending, but also data that might be used should there be a suspicion of future offending and data on those who might cause public disorder through political activities.[41] Disclosure of this material is subject to authorisation, the level of authorisation required largely depending on whether dissemination is effected within or outside of the United Kingdom. Material may be transferred between United Kingdom police forces and Customs and Excise on the authority of an 'individual officer'.[42] An individual officer may also disseminate material to the Security and Intelligence Services and prosecuting agencies. There is a requirement in paragraph 3.5 that where 'confidential material'[43] is involved, 'any proposed dissemination must take account of any restrictions on its use or requirement for special handling imposed by the officer who authorised the collection'. Again, compliance with this condition may only be monitored internally. Dissemination to bodies or parties other than the above may be authorised by an officer of the rank of inspector.[44]

The authorisation of an inspector is also required when intelligence material is disseminated out of the United Kingdom but within the European Economic Area.[45] Transfer of such data to Europe is likely to occur with far greater regularity with the implementation of the Europol Convention.[46] There is provision within the Code for the dissemination of information to countries that are not within the European Area for the 'purpose of the prevention or detection of international crime and terrorism'.[47] No definition of these terms appears within the Code and it could therefore be argued that any offending involving criminal activity in more than one jurisdiction is 'international crime'. Trans jurisdictional deceptions and frauds and any importation of prohibited substances could fall within this provision. Dissemination to a country outside the European Economic Area is prohibited by the Data Protection Act 1998 unless either the recipient 'ensures an adequate level of protection for the rights and freedoms of data subjects', or 'a substantial public interest would be served by the transfer'.[48] If the recipient country is deemed not to possess 'an adequate level of protection', an assessment must be made of any 'risks to the subject arising from the transfer of the intelligence'.[49] An additional control is imposed by the requirement in paragraph 4.6 of the Code that authorisation for such transfer must be given by an officer of the rank of superintendent. The final safeguard contained within this Code concerns the destruction of material. Intelligence data will be subject to 'regular review and weeding'.[50] The intention of the law enforcement agencies is clearly to act in accordance with the terms of the Data Protection Act and to comply with the Human Rights Act 1998 to the extent that privacy rights are affected through the creation of national databases. The major problem is that, since the Codes are not statutory and since they are subject to internal monitoring, adherence to them must, to a large extent, be taken as a matter of good faith. The sensitivity of the material that may be involved is another factor that is likely to preclude openness and accountability in respect of recording practices. The right to know what is known about one and by whom is trumped by competing governmental interests in law and order. These competing interests become even more significant when they are linked with those of other States and when the European Union takes a commanding role in the control of personal data.

European Databases and Information Exchange

The Schengen Agreement was originally signed by five of the Member States of the European Community in June 1985.[51] The objective of the agreement was to abolish internal border controls and to create an area of co-operation between those States endorsing the agreement. The Schengen Implementation Convention was finally signed in June 1990. Several other States joined in these arrangements thereafter.[52] The abolition of cross-border controls, that is an essential part of the Convention, is counterbalanced by increased powers in respect of police co-operation and the exchange of information between forces. The Convention provides for the establishment of a 'joint information system'. As yet, the United Kingdom is not a signatory to this Convention. However, the Maastricht and Amsterdam Treaties which the United Kingdom *has* signed, have the effect of incorporating Schengen into the European Union's institutional framework.[53] This is an almost inevitable consequence of the movement towards closer homogeneity within the membership of the European Union and the establishment, by the Maastricht Treaty, of the 'Third Pillar' of the Union, covering justice and home affairs. The 'Third Pillar' has now been formalised in the institution of the Council of Ministers of Justice and Home Affairs. The Council's terms of reference include crime and, in particular, drug offending and serious organised crime. The impact on human rights, and on the accountability of governments, of this closer co-operation has been debated elsewhere (Colvin and Noorlander, 1998). It is beyond the scope of this text to provide a general assessment of the constitutional limitations of E.U. systems, or the compatibility of those systems with concepts of parliamentary democracy and human rights. The important issue, in the context of surveillance and evidence gathering, is that Schengen provides a European wide framework within which police authorities shall 'in compliance with national legislation and within the limits of their responsibilities, assist each other for the purposes of preventing or detecting criminal offences'.[54]

One aspect of this is to permit surveillance by foreign police officers provided there is authorisation from the country in which the observation is to take place. Article 40 provides

> Police officers of one of the Contracting Parties, who within the framework of a criminal investigation, are keeping under observation in their country, a person who is presumed to have taken part in a criminal offence to which extradition may apply, shall be authorized to continue their observation in the territory of another Contracting Party where the latter has authorized cross-border

observation in response to a request for assistance which has previously been submitted. Conditions may be attached to the authorization.

Schengen goes even beyond this in that under Article 40(2), prior authorisation may be dispensed with provided that authorisation has been obtained within five hours after a national border has been crossed. The offences in respect of which this cross-border activity may take place include offences against the person (such as murder, rape, kidnapping and hostage taking), offences against property (such as arson and counterfeiting) and drugs and terrorist activities. The powers of the police officers who cross their national boundary are limited in that they may not enter private premises, nor arrest any person being observed.[55] All operations shall be subject to a report to the authorities of the Contracting Party in whose territory they took place.[56] However, the term 'observation' is not explained in the Convention. It is not included in the definitions in Article 1. This absence of precision in terminology pervades Schengen and, in respect of Article 40, raises questions as to whether electronic (as well as visual) surveillance is within the scope of the permitted activity. It is also unclear whether the 'observation' must be land based or whether aerial or satellite observation is within the terms of the Article. The extent to which observation can include infiltration is debatable, but it is probable that even under Article 73, which provides for 'monitored deliveries' involving illicit drugs, passive observation is all that is authorised (Joubert and Bevers, 1996:189).

Article 44 provides that the Contracting Parties shall set up 'telephone, radio, and telex lines and other direct links to facilitate police and customs co-operation, in particular for the transmission of information in good time for the purposes of observation and cross-border pursuit'. These provisions are intended to supplement the European Convention on Mutual Assistance in Criminal Matters[57] which provides for assistance between Contracting Parties in respect of the obtaining of evidence through letters rogatory, the service of judicial process and the making available of judicial records. Co-operation is further promoted by Title Four of the Schengen Agreement which provides that the Contracting Parties shall set up and maintain the Schengen Information System. This shall comprise a national section for each country and a technical support function. Article 92 states that the System shall enable the authorities to have access to (*inter alia*)

> reports on persons and objects for the purposes of border checks and controls and other police and customs checks carried out within the country in accordance with national law.

The technical support function is located in Strasbourg. It comprises a data file which ensures that the data files of the national sections are kept identical by the on-line transmission of information. The technical support data file shall contain reports on persons and objects where these concern all the Contracting Parties.[58] The Information System has a capability of eight million personal records and seven million records on objects. It is used to exchange information on asylum applications, identification papers, aliens listed as undesirable by one of the Contracting Parties, persons expelled or extradited and persons wanted for criminal prosecution (Bennyon *et al*, 1993). Information relating to persons shall include no more detail than their name, aliases, permanent physical features, the date and place of birth, their sex and nationality, whether the person is armed or violent, the reason for the report and the action taken.[59]

Article 99 provides that data relating to persons or vehicles shall be included, in compliance with the national law of the reporting Contractual Party where a 'discreet surveillance' report or a 'specific check' has taken place. Such reports and checks may be made for the purposes of prosecuting criminal offences and for the prevention of threats to public safety where either

(a) there are real indications to suggest that the person concerned intends to commit or is committing numerous and extremely serious criminal offences, or

(b) an overall evaluation of the person concerned, in particular on the basis of offences committed hitherto, gives reason to suppose that he will also commit extremely serious offences in the future.

A report may also be made where there is reason to suppose that this information is necessary to prevent a serious threat to State security.[60] There is no specific definition of these key concepts. The terms 'numerous' and 'serious' and 'security' must apparently be left to the subjective interpretation of Member States.

It is arguable that the purposes for which data may be gathered are as ill defined as the purpose of the information system itself, which is to 'maintain public order and security, including State security'.[61] It has been pointed out that this could include everything from terrorism through various forms of social unrest to political demonstrations deemed to be a threat to public order (Mathiesen, 1999:5). Further the scope of the data is not as narrow as might at first appear. The reported information may also include the identity of persons accompanying the person who is the target of the surveillance or the occupants of the vehicle concerned.[62] Where the request for data is a 'specific check' rather than covert surveillance, then, in accordance with the national law of the State, persons, vehicles and objects may be searched.[63] Article 100(1) provides that 'data relating to objects sought for the purpose of seizure or of evidence in criminal proceedings shall be included in the Schengen Information System'. Identifying details of associates of the target, or even casual acquaintances may therefore be entered on the database along with the outcome of any search, whether or not this results in a subsequent criminal prosecution.

There are restrictions contained within the Agreement as to those having access to data on the System.[64] Use of that data may only be for the purposes set out in Schengen.[65] However, as Mathiesen (1999:7) states, SIS 'is only one of the systems for information exchange in Schengen'. The other system, known as SIRENE, is a network for police and security co-operation between the Schengen countries. The possibilities of information exchange under SIRENE are virtually limitless because the national SIRENE offices handle non-standardised information and are not limited by the constraints of Title Four of the Agreement. The manual that exists in relation to SIRENE is confidential and therefore not available for scrutiny. However, enough has been 'leaked' for it to be public knowledge that both oral (telephone) and written communication may take place between offices and that photographs, fingerprints and written texts are transmitted electronically.[66] It is bizarre, to say the least, that this potentially huge networked database should not be adverted to in the Schengen Agreement itself and it could be thought sinister that this secret information system is not governed by the common data protection regulations that apply to the more accessible Schengen provisions.[67]

On 1st October 1998, the Europol Convention came into force. Europol became operational in July 1999. This organisation emanated from the Maastricht Treaty. It was decided that the former TREVI[68] European Drugs Intelligence Unit was to be transferred into the European Drugs Unit/Europol. Despite this transformation, Europol is not yet an integrated police unit as is the FBI. The Convention does not, as yet, provide for operational or executive police powers. It only provides for information sharing and technical and expert support along the lines of the Interpol model. Thus, there is another European wide criminal information system. The content of the Convention was drawn up in secret by members of a Working Group comprised of police officers and ministry officials. There was no consultation within the European Parliament, despite a requirement in the Maastricht Treaty that this should take place.[69] The resultant Convention establishes a computerised system for the collection of information. National units (NCIS in the case of the United

Kingdom) will supply Europol with 'information and intelligence'. The objective to be served from this gathering of data is the prevention and combating of

> terrorism, unlawful drug trafficking and other serious forms of international crime where there are factual indications that an organized criminal structure is involved and two or more Member States are affected by the forms of crime in question in such a way as to require a common approach by the Member States owing to the scale, significance and consequences of the offences concerned.[70]

The scope of activity is to be incrementally increased to encompass 'other forms of crime listed in the Annex to this Convention'. The ultimate objective is to collect data not only in relation to drug trafficking, illegal immigration, vehicular crime and crimes likely to be committed in the course of terrorist activities, but also in relation to murder or grievous bodily harm, kidnapping and false imprisonment, organised robbery and illicit trafficking in arms and endangered species. There are some curiously vague forms of offending specified in the Annex such as 'racism and xenophobia', 'racketeering and extortion' and 'corruption'. There is also a list of property offences which might arguably encompass less than serious crime such as 'swindling and fraud' and 'counterfeiting and product piracy'. Europol may also deal with related money laundering activities and 'related criminal offences'.[71]

Under Article 8, the central information system houses data on those suspected of both past and future offending. In the case of past offending, the level of suspicion need not be consistent. In each case it is based on 'the national law of the Member State'. With the expansion of the European Community, this raises an issue about the extent to which the data will necessarily relate to those against whom probable cause exists and the extent to which the privacy of citizens who have not given any reasonable cause for intrusion will be violated. At least in the case of future offending, there must be 'serious grounds under national law' for believing that the individual will commit offences within the remit of Europol. The data itself may include the names, date of birth, nationality and sex of an individual and 'other characteristics likely to assist in identification'. However, Article 8 also provides for the storage of data on criminal offences and alleged crimes, the means which were or may be used to commit the crimes, suspected membership of a criminal organisation and past criminal convictions. Any further 'additional information' may be held by Europol, or by national units, so long as this is in accordance with 'national law'.[72]

The information may not only be stored, it may also be analysed. Article 10 authorises the setting up of temporary work files. These files may contain extensive information[73] about persons who are not actually registered in the system. These other persons include potential witnesses, victims, associates of the suspect and informants. The breadth of this provision means that even unsuspected citizens may now be the subject of personal data that is held on an international criminal database. The provisions as to dissemination of data are equally broad. The information may be forwarded to Europol by E.U. States and Europol may gain access to data under 'other Conventions'.[74] Conversely, Europol may 'communicate personal data' to third States and third bodies.[75] The most significant danger in respect of these provisions is that information may be received from countries that have no adherence to human rights legislation or to the concepts of due process of law. The quality of the data supplied might be adversely affected to the extent that it is factually unreliable (Justice, 1998:103). The Council Act of November 1998, adopting rules applicable to Europol analysis files, reiterates the provisions in the Europol Convention concerning responsibility for data. Prior to incorporation in an analysis work file, the data is the responsibility of the member State supplying the data. Thereafter it is the responsibility of Europol.[76]

Europol, Schengen and Interpol have been described as three 'mutually interlocking' and 'overlapping' policing initiatives (Mathiesen, 1999:24). There is, however, another and even wider based information system that is currently being put in place. The system is founded in collaboration between the European Union and the Federal Bureau of Investigation. The purpose of the system is to 'combat serious crime and to protect national security' and the method of achieving this is through the interception of telephone calls, electronic mail and faxed communications. In November 1995, A Memorandum of Understanding on the Legal Interception of Telecommunications[77] was signed by the E.U. member States at a meeting of the Council of Justice and Home Affairs Ministers. Despite being dismissed by the then Home Secretary as 'not a significant document' and therefore not meeting the criteria for Parliamentary scrutiny,[78] it can be argued that this Memorandum is the most significant movement yet made in the direction of global surveillance. This new system is not, officially, part of the system governing military intelligence (the ECHELON System).[79] However, since ECHELON is an existing world-wide operation that intercepts electronic communications via satellites, the technology facilitating satellite interception will be substantially compatible with that required under the E.U./FBI system. An integration may easily take place both in respect of equipment and in respect of personnel. The risks of merging intelligence activity and criminal investigation have already been adverted to in respect of land based surveillance activities.[80] The dangers of unwarranted privacy intrusions are even greater when the surveillance is in respect of global communication and when there is uncertainty as to which national law governs the interception.[81] There is an obvious potential for infringements of human rights to occur when no clear distinction exists in the objective of the surveillance between suspected criminality and political dissidence.[82] The need to suppress serious, organised and international offending may be the excuse for a huge erosion of the rights of all citizens, both law abiding and others, 'not to be known about'.

Data Protection Principles and the Right to Access Data

The Data Protection Act 1998 (hereinafter DPA) is the successor to the Data Protection Act 1984 and was enacted in order to comply with the 1995 Directive of the European Community.[83] The Directive does not, strictly, apply to the European Union's Third Pillar, but the 1998 Act applies 'data protection principles' to 'any data' processed in the United Kingdom.[84] The meaning of processing is much wider than that given in the previous definition in the 1984 Act. Subsection 1(1) of the DPA defines it as

> obtaining, recording or holding the information or data or carrying out any operation or set of operations on the information or data, including –
> (a) organisation, adaptation or alteration of the information or data,
> (b) retrieval, consultation or use of the information or data,
> (c) disclosure of the information or data by transmission, dissemination or otherwise making available, or
> (d) alignment, combination, blocking, erasure or destruction of the information or data.

This provides a concept of processing that effectively includes anything that can be done with data. It certainly covers the storage of information relating to criminal investigation and targeted surveillance. It also includes non targeted surveillance such as the use of CCTV in public places.

Article 6 of the 1995 European Directive requires member States to make provisions concerning the processing of data to ensure that it is both lawful and fair and that it is collected for legitimate purposes. Data should be accurate and should be kept up to date. These principles are incorporated into the DPA. Schedule 1 states (*inter alia*) –

1.   Personal data shall be processed fairly and lawfully and, in particular, shall not be processed unless –
     (a)   at least one of the conditions in Schedule 2 is met, and
     (b)   in the case of sensitive personal data, at least one of the conditions in Schedule 3 is also met.
2.   Personal data shall be obtained only for one or more specified and lawful purposes, and shall not be further processed in any manner incompatible with that purpose or those purposes.
3.   Personal data shall be adequate, relevant and not excessive in relation to the purpose or purposes for which they are processed.
4.   Personal data shall be accurate and, where necessary, kept up to date.
5.   Personal data processed for any purpose or purposes shall not be kept longer than is necessary for that purpose or those purposes.

The relevant conditions listed in Schedule 2 include that data processing is necessary in pursuance of a legal obligation, is necessary in the exercise of government functions, or is necessary for the administration of justice. The relevant conditions listed in Schedule 3 are that processing is necessary for the purpose of, or in connection with, any legal proceedings (including prospective legal proceedings), or is necessary for the administration of justice, or the execution of government functions.[85] It is most probable, therefore, that data, even sensitive personal data, may be processed for the purposes of criminal investigation and even for intelligence gathering.[86] Sensitive personal data is defined in section 2 of the DPA as data consisting of information as to racial and ethnic origins, political opinions, religious beliefs, membership of trade unions, physical and mental health, sexual orientation and practices and details of any alleged or committed offences.

Under the DPA, there is a presumptive of 'right access to personal data'. Section 7 provides that an individual is entitled 'to be informed by any data controller whether personal data of which that individual is the data subject are being processed by or on behalf of that data controller'.[87] A data controller is defined in subsection 1(1) as a person who, either alone or jointly, or in common with other persons, determines the purposes for which such data are processed and the manner of the processing. This definition is, again, wider than under the 1984 Act and the result is that there may be more than one data controller in respect of each piece of information.[88] The right to be told 'in an intelligible form' of the information constituting any personal data of which the individual is the subject and also of any information available to the data controller as to the source of that data[89] is, of course, fundamental to privacy rights (Justice 1998:94). Without access to this information, it is impossible to check the accuracy of databases or to seek a remedy for any wrongful invasion of privacy. However, this presumptive right is subject to 'exemptions'. The most significant exemptions from the point of view of search and surveillance issues are contained in sections 28 and 29 of the Act.

Section 28 deals with exemptions 'required for the purpose of safeguarding national security' and section 29 with data processed for

(a)   the prevention or detection of crime,
(b)   the apprehension or prosecution of offenders, or
(c)   the assessment or collection of any tax or duty or other imposition of a similar nature.

Both sections exclude the right of subject access granted under section 7,[90] but in relation to crime and taxation, the exemption only bites where subject access 'would be likely to prejudice' police operations.[91] However, it is hard to imagine any situation arising in the context of criminal investigation and prosecution where the police could not successfully argue that disclosure would be likely to prejudice their activities. The subject is not in a strong position to challenge any assertion of 'prejudice' because the subject does not know, at that point, if information is held, or if it is, what the content of that information might be.[92] As with contested claims of public interest immunity, the difficulty of arguing that there is a wrongful withholding of unknown information is almost insurmountable.

Even in the unusual circumstance that access to data would be granted to an individual in respect of a criminal database, the subject of the application may have to face other hurdles. If the data has become part of the Europol information system, access may be refused under Article 19 of the Europol Convention on the basis that a refusal is necessary 'to enable Europol to fulfil its duties properly' or to 'protect security and public order in the Member States or to prevent crime'. Refusal may also be made where this is necessary to 'protect the rights and freedoms of third parties'. Thus, even if under domestic law, no point of prejudice is taken, there may be a refusal of access at a higher level and that refusal may be on extremely wide grounds. Article 109 of the Schengen Agreement provides that if the information has been transferred to the Schengen Information System, rights of access are governed by national law. The National Supervisory Authority for each Contracting Party is responsible for controlling the right of subject access to SIS. However, even if the national law permits subject access, it 'shall be refused on the basis that it may undermine the performance of the legal task specified in the report or in order to protect the rights and freedoms of others'. It shall, in any event, be refused during the period of reporting for the purpose of discreet surveillance.

The DPA exemptions in respect of national security are so wide ranging that little is left by way of statutory protection in respect of such data.[93] The exemptions in respect of crime and taxation are less comprehensive. Apart from the subject access provisions, other exemptions are the first data protection principle (except to the extent that it incorporates the second and third Schedules) and the disclosure provisions. The exemption concerning the first data protection principle has a rather uncertain scope. Since lawfulness and unfairness are irrelevant to the processing of material concerning criminal activity, it is arguable that illegally obtained information may be processed despite any court ruling that the resultant evidence was inadmissible or despite any statutory provision requiring that it should be destroyed.[94] In any event, it may well be impossible to establish that processing is occurring since subject access is most likely to be denied. The exemption concerning disclosure raises a wider issue. This is the extent to which legitimate rights to privacy may be infringed by the dissemination of data. Such legitimate rights might be violated either because data is inaccurate and prejudicial to the subject, or because it is sent to a party who has no justifiable interest in seeing the information.

It has already been noted that there is a close co-operation between European law enforcement agencies resulting in the creation of European (if not global) databases containing information concerning suspected offenders and others considered to threaten public order and security. The eighth data protection principle provides that

> Personal data shall not be transferred to a country or territory outside the European Economic Area unless that country or territory ensures an adequate level of protection for the rights and freedoms of data subjects in relation to the processing of personal data.

This principle results from Article 25 of the 1995 European Directive. That Article envisages that the European Commission will make rulings on the adequacy of protection afforded by third countries and provides that member States 'shall take measures necessary to prevent the transfer of data' to a third country whose protection procedures are found wanting.[95] Schedule 4 of the DPA states that the eighth principle does not apply where the transfer 'is necessary for reasons of substantial public interest'. Circumstances when a transfer is so justified may be specified by the Secretary of State. As outlined above, the Europol Convention permits the sending to and receiving of information from a third country.[96] When information is received from or sent to third countries or bodies, Articles 10(4) and 18(1) provide that Europol must be satisfied that an adequate level of data protection is ensured. The rules to be observed by Europol in transmitting data are to be drawn up by the European Council. Unfortunately, the key concept of 'an adequate level of data protection' is left undefined and the fear is that practical exigencies may drive law enforcers to ignore the rules in order to achieve mutual assistance and more effective crime control.

The Schengen agreement also incorporates data disclosure protections. Article 101 provides that access to SIS and the right to search SIS data shall be reserved exclusively for the authorities responsible for border checks, police and customs checks and visa control. 'Users may only search data which are necessary for the performance of their tasks.'[97] Under Article 113, data is preserved for a maximum period of ten years, although data relating to identity documents will be retained for a maximum of five years, and data kept for the purpose of locating persons, only for the time required to achieve that purpose. Data may only be used for the 'purposes laid down for each type of report' authorised by SIS.[98] However, since under both the Europol Convention and the Schengen Agreement, subject rights of access may be even more limited than under the DPA, it may be impossible to ensure that data is reliable, or that it has not been distributed to countries or bodies for unauthorised purposes.

At a national level, as stated above, the second data protection principle provides that

> Personal data shall be obtained only for one or more specified and lawful purposes, and shall not be further processed in any manner incompatible with that purpose or those purposes.

The purposes will be those specified by the data controller to the data subject or set out in a notification given to the Commissioner.[99] The 'purposes' for which the police are authorised to obtain and process data are extremely wide ranging and therefore include the non targeted gathering of criminal intelligence. Section 29(3) of the DPA states that personal data that are to be processed for the prevention or detection of crime or the apprehension or prosecution of offenders are exempt from the non disclosure provisions so far as any restriction on disclosure would be likely to 'prejudice' those purposes. Therefore, even beyond the wide remit of purposes for which the police may themselves gather data, there is express statutory power allowing information gathered from agencies or individuals not involved in law enforcement to be used by the police in order to prevent or detect crime. The police may therefore garner intelligence from commercial bodies such as telephone companies and utility companies, or from public bodies such as local health authorities. The only restrictions on the acquisition of this information are the restrictions contained in PACE concerning special procedure and excluded material.[100] Law enforcement agencies have great flexibility of action. However, the subject of data relating to criminal investigation or criminal intelligence has only a nominal right to know if there is any entry on a database concerning him and, if there is, whether this information is accurate.

Towards a Reconsideration of Privacy

It has been stated that 'of all the human rights in the international catalogue, privacy is perhaps the most difficult to define and circumscribe'.[101] The various facets of this right include privacy in respect of personal property and space, privacy in respect of personal physical autonomy, privacy in respect of communications and privacy in respect of information. The law has evolved gradually to extend protection to these different aspects of privacy. In this text, I have attempted to outline such evolution. The earliest judicial recognition arose in the context of the protections afforded to domestic occupiers in respect of warrantless searches. Protections were then later extended not only to tangible searches, but to searches effected by surveillance and by the interception of communications. In some jurisdictions, bodily intrusion is also regarded as a search that may violate privacy. The most embryonic of protections in respect to the right of privacy exist in the area of information acquisition, retention and dissemination. As discussed above, there should be a right not to have inaccurate or damaging personal information held or distributed by any organisation. There should be a right to insist that only those organisations with a legally recognised interest have access to personal data.

It could be argued that, in the context of criminal investigation, the privacy rights surrounding information storage and dissemination will become the most fundamental of all. This is, at least partly, because databases are always the ultimate product of investigation and intelligence gathering by law enforcement officers. Databases represent the acme of information garnering, analysis and compilation. Databases allow public agencies to acquire a more complete picture of an individual, as opposed to the limited knowledge of a particular fact or facts about him. Such knowledge enhances the power of law

enforcers and is a potent tool in their crime control armoury. Pol⁄
longer purely reactive, solving crimes that have occurred through re⁄
and *ad hoc* investigation. The modern police force looks to gather iⅡⅴ⁓
to pre-empt crime as well as to solve it. There is also a wider dimension. That
is the control of public order and of individuals as social beings. The more
that is known about a person's lifestyle, habits, race and criminal convictions,
the easier it is for States to control the activities of those citizens who might
threaten the stability of government or simply the established norms of society.
Such control has become increasingly feasible as data recording processes
become cheaper and more efficient. As Miller (1969:1103) points out, in
accordance with Parkinson's Law, 'as capacity for information-handling
increases there is a tendency to engage in more extensive manipulation and
analysis of recorded data'.

There is great difficulty for an individual in showing that the line has
been crossed beyond which knowledge is deemed to be invasive and an
illegitimate infringement of privacy. The major problem is that the citizen is
unlikely to be able to challenge the legitimacy of information storage or
dissemination, or indeed that such information has ever been acquired. It has
been seen above that rights of subject access in respect of databases concerning
crime or national security are nebulous in the extreme. If an individual cannot
find out what is known about himself, it is impossible to claim that
inappropriate, prejudicial or misleading information is being held. It is also
impossible to claim that it is being shown to those who have no right to see it.
Yet, it has recently been stated that police forces, 'even in countries with
strong privacy laws, still maintain extensive files on citizens for political
purposes' and that in many Eastern Bloc countries, there are still controversies
over the passing of files 'to the secret police'.[102] On a structural level, lack of
subject access concerns *all* citizens for 'when the individual is deprived of
control over the information spigot, he in some measure becomes subservient
to those people and institutions that are able to gain access to it' (Miller,
1969:1108).

The problem with reliance upon subject access as a control mechanism to
enforce privacy rights is compounded by the fact that much of the information
that is being held on such databases has been covertly obtained. The subject
is not even aware, therefore, that data has come into existence. In the days
when investigation was limited to the physical search of persons and of property
there would be less likelihood of a search taking place without the knowledge
of the target. Of course, premises and vehicles may be searched in the absence
of the occupier, but even when this occurs, the main objective of police activity

in this context is evidence gathering and the fruits of the search (if any) will be put before the court. The court then determines whether to admit the evidence and to validate the search that has occurred. The question is the legality of the search activity, not whether it has taken place. In the days of a technology driven, information based society, the goal posts have moved. Law enforcers are now seeking to gather data that might be useful in situations yet to occur. Subjects are included on the basis of offender profiles rather then on the basis of individualised suspicion for a particular crime under investigation. The police and other agencies may have as their primary objective the gathering of intelligence without the knowledge of the targets of surveillance, because knowledge of such activity might induce the targets to modify their behaviour or speech or to remain silent and to refrain from certain actions altogether.

The tension between the use of secret police surveillance, intelligence gathering and the individual's rights of freedom of opinion, association and expression have been acknowledged (albeit infrequently) in the case law of the United States and Canada.[103] Articles 9, 10 and 11 of the European Convention guarantee these three linked rights. In the United States, the First Amendment and, in Canada, section 2 of the Charter of Rights contain similar guarantees. Judicial consideration of these provisions has, traditionally, been confined to the right to speak, assemble or to publish in public or to the public. I would contend that there is a need to re-evaluate the significance and scope of these freedoms that protect our thoughts, words and actions. There is a pressing argument that the freedom 'not to be known about' should be an important aspect of these guaranteed rights. Words spoken to friends or to close associates and words and actions taking place in the private domain should surely be *more* protected than those intended for public consumption. Whilst the connection once made between the Fourth and Fifth Amendments has now been largely discredited,[104] it might be appropriate for a new association of freedoms to be made as a way of protecting these fundamental constitutional and human rights. Despite the assertion by Akhil Reed Amar (1997:66) that the mental privacy of murderers and rapists is not within the core of the First Amendment, there is a case for arguing that the ever growing encroachments upon the mental privacy of potential criminal suspects ultimately impinge on the privacy of us all. By linking the right of mental and physical privacy to freedom of thought, speech and deed, we cease to define human rights in one dimensional terms and begin to take account of the effect of those freedoms on all members of society. A society nurturing the right to mental and physical privacy is likely to be more spontaneous and uninhibited than a society in which persons fear to communicate freely with friends, relatives and associates, or one in which there is a belief that activities are monitored by law enforcers or State officials. A society fearful of being pried upon, a society in which personal data may be collected for uncontrolled speculative use, is not a free society. Miller (1969:1179) states

> The climate or atmosphere of suspicion engendered by an accumulation of invasions of privacy is of far greater concern than the direct harm caused by the incidents themselves.

Perhaps the cost to society as a whole of systemic information gathering and information storage, even in respect of criminal investigation, will eventually prove greater than the benefit that it confers in terms of crime control.

Hufstedler (1979), emphasising that there is no simple solution to the 'crime problem' because it is 'a complex pandemic phenomenon', points out that the empirical effectiveness of governmental information gathering is still unknown. We only learn about insidious intrusions when they produce a 'result' for government agencies. It is impossible, therefore, to attempt a cost benefit analysis in purely utilitarian terms. However, according to Hufstedler (1979:1520), it is possible to

> recognize that we must have zones of individual privacy which cannot be penetrated by the government, because no societal interest can be as compelling as the need of the individual citizen for preservation of autonomy of personality.

The humanitarian values of friendship, trust and respect may, ultimately, be irretrievably damaged if the perceived 'public interest' in suppressing criminal or subversive activity is relied upon to confer on law enforcers increased powers of information gathering and information storage. Since, increasingly, data may be assembled free from judicial control and without any enforceable restrictions concerning probable cause, necessity and proportionality, the movement from the gathering of evidence to the gathering of information should be a major libertarian concern.

Notes

1. See chapter 1 and Pollock and Maitland (1968).
2. Of the many instances occurring in England and Wales in the last few years, one of the most dramatic relates to the murder of Cynthia Bolshaw in 1983. A DNA sample taken

from the blood of the alleged killer matched some semen stains found on the victim's nightgown. The gown had lain undisturbed in the murder file since the initial investigation; The Times 11th November 1999.

3.　Data Protection Act 1998 sects. 7, 8, 9, 27, 28, Schedules 2 and 3 and below.

4.　Home Office Annual Report 1998–1999 chapter 8 para. 8.5. Despite police reservations about resources, the Prime Minister stated in November 1999 that he wished to extend the practice of DNA testing as a matter of routine to *all* imprisonable offences. In the United States, all 50 States have passed legislation to create State DNA databases, but the range of individuals included therein varies from State to State. Most States require a sample from persons convicted of sexual and violent offences. Other States have extended the sample requirement to persons convicted of any felony. The Federal proposal (March 1999) is for the collection of DNA from all arrestees.

5.　Cm. 2263 at p. 15 para. 34.

6.　*Ibid.*

7.　At p. 16 para. 35.

8.　At p. 16 paras. 36–37.

9.　PACE subsect. 63A(6).

10.　PACE subsect. 63A(7).

11.　Both these offences carry a maximum prison sentence of 5 years.

12.　An example of a non-imprisonable recordable offence is having in one's possession a bladed article in a public place.

13.　See the Criminal Justice Act 19991 sect. 1(2)(b) allowing for the abrogation of the proportionality principle in respect of violent and sexual offences and the Sex Offenders Act 1997 requiring *all* convicted sex offenders to register with the police for a stated period. The length of the period varies with the seriousness of the offence, but the minimum period is 5 years.

14.　The Youth Justice and Criminal Evidence Act 1999 now prohibits the cross-examination in person by the alleged offender of the victim of a sexual offence (sect. 34). Further, there are substantial curbs on the kinds of questions that may be asked in the cross-examination of the complainant of a sexual offence (sect. 41).

15.　Added by the Criminal Justice and Public Order Act 1994 subsect. 57(3).

16.　PACE subsects. 61(7A); 62(7A) and 62(8B).

17.　Subsect. 63A(1) of PACE.

18.　RCCJ (1993) Cm. 2263 at p. 16 para. 36.

19.　*Ibid.*

20.　Proposals for Revising Legislative Measures on Fingerprints Footprints and DNA Samples (1999) at pp. 11–12.

21.　*Ibid* at p. 11.

22.　*Ibid* at pp. 4–5.

23.　*Ibid* at pp. 7–8 and see the Crime and Disorder Act 1998.

24.　This has occurred in Iceland where the 270,000 inhabitants have a remarkably uniform genetic inheritance.

25.　National Commission Proceedings of 1st March 1999 and 5th May 1999 on the Future of DNA Evidence.

26.　Recommendation No. R(92)1 of the Committee of Ministers to Member States on the Use of Analysis of DNA within the Framework of Criminal Justice (1992).

27.　Council Resolution of 9th June 1997 on the exchange of DNA analysis results.

28. Response by Steinhard B., Associate Director, American Civil Liberties Union, to the National Commission above.
29. *Ibid.*
30. HMIC (1997) at p. 1.
31. *Ibid* at para. 2.16.
32. Police Act Code para. 2.34.
33. *Ibid.*
34. *Ibid* para.2.35.
35. *Ibid* para.2.36.
36. *E.g.* consensual or non intrusive surveillance.
37. NCIS Code of Practice on Surveillance para. 5.1. Cp. para. 4.1 of the Code on Undercover Operations and para. 5.1 of the Code on the Use of Informants.
38. NCIS Interception of Communications Code para. 7.1 and sect. 6 of IOCA.
39. This Code does *not* apply to disclosure between agencies on a statutory basis (*e.g.* under the Customs and Excise (Management) Act 1979, the Immigration Act 1971 or the Vat Act 1974) nor to the disclosure of evidential material to foreign law enforcement agencies through mutual legal assistance; see paras. 1.5 and 4.2–4.4).
40. See below.
41. Cp. the Schengen Information System and the Europol Convention, discussed below.
42. NCIS Code para. 3.
43. As defined throughout the 'package' of NCIS Codes *i.e.* matters subject to legal privilege and material that would be excluded material under PACE.
44. Or equivalent rank in Customs and Excise or NCIS, para. 3.8.
45. The EEA comprises the 15 'Member States' of the European Union, Iceland, Liechtenstein and Norway.
46. See below.
47. See below.
48. DPA 8th principle, see below and para. 4.3 of the Code.
49. Para. 4.4 of the Code.
50. Para. 5.2; although, 'significant public interest' justifies retention, see para. 5.3 above.
51. Germany, France and the Benelux States were the original signatories.
52. Spain, Portugal, Italy, Austria, Greece, Denmark and Sweden are signatories. Norway and Iceland (though not E.U. Members) participate in the Schengen area.
53. The Amsterdam Treaty has established a protocol incorporating the existing Schengen Agreement into Union law.
54. Title Three Chapter 1 Article 39.
55. Article 40(3).
56. Cross border pursuit is permitted by Article 41 on similar terms.
57. 20th April 1959.
58. Article 92.
59. Article 94.
60. Article 99(3).
61. Article 93.
62. Article 99 (4)(d).
63. Article 99(1) and 99(5).
64. Article 101. Access may be given to police, customs officers and immigration officers.
65. Article 102 (*viz.* for the purposes set out in Articles 95–100).

66. Mathiesen (1999:8).
67. See below and the discussion of the Data Protection Act.
68. TREVI was established in 1976 and was the title given to an initiative to promote co-operation in combating international violence (terrorism). Its focus later extended to drugs crime and to other serious organised crime.
69. Under Article K6 and see the criticism by Bunyan (1996).
70. Article 2 of the Europol Convention.
71. Article 2(3).
72. Article 8(4).
73. The personal data that may be stored on those registered in the system under Article 10(1) is set out in the Council Act (1998) Doc. No. 499 Y0130(02). The list is more than two pages long and includes employment (past and present), education, economic and financial standing (including assets and tax position) and behavioural data (including places frequented).
74. Articles 10(4) and 10(5).
75. Article 18. Third parties might be Interpol, the SIS and the FBI, or another non E.U. country.
76. Article 3 of the Council Act Doc. No. 499 YO130 (02) and see Europol Convention Article 15(1). Responsibility for the verification of data supplied by a non E.U. State rests entirely within Europol.
77. ENFOPOL 112,10037/95. Brussels 25th November 1995.
78. Michael Howard replying to a letter from the Select Committee on European Committees (Correspondence with Ministers 9th Session 1995–96 HoL 74 p. 26).
79. This system was designed and is co-ordinated in the USA by the National Security Agency and involves intelligence agencies in the US, New Zealand, the United Kingdom (GCHQ), Canada and Australia.
80. See chapter 5.
81. This might be the law of the requesting interceptor or the law of the place where the communication is intercepted (the visited State). Italy hosts the 'Iridium' ground station and thus will be a major intercepting jurisdiction for satellite communications.
82. See the position of the United Kingdom in respect of surveillance by MI5, discussed in chapter 5.
83. Directive on the protection of personal data (95/46/EC). It entered into effect on 25th October 1998.
84. DPA 1998 sect. 5.
85. The Secretary of State may make additional requirements for (or exclude the operation of) the justifications based on the administration of justice or the execution of government functions.
86. Justice (1998) points out that it remains unclear whether Schedules 2 and 3 provide the necessary legal basis for law enforcement purposes. This is expected to be clarified by order. Note that (apart from Schedules 2 and 3) the first data protection principle does not apply to law enforcement; see below.
87. DPA subsect. 7(1)(a).
88. *E.g.* NCIS, Customs and Excise and regional police forces.
89. DPA subsect. 7(1)(c).
90. DPA subsects. 28(1) and 29(1).
91. Subsect. 29(1).

92. Justice (1998:94) cites the example of football fans (wrongly targeted as hooligans) whose personal data were disseminated throughout Europe. Even the Data Protection Commissioner is not empowered to go behind the face of the information furnished by the data controller.
93. Exemptions are given from all the data protection principles, the rights of data subjects, notification provisions, enforcement provisions and the offence of unlawfully obtaining data.
94. IOCA subsect. 6(5) and the Police Act 1997 subsect. 103(3) – destruction may be ordered where the Commissioner quashes an authorisation.
95. The DPA 1998 Schedule 1 Part 2 para. 13 sets out the criteria that will determine whether an adequate level of protection exists.
96. Europol Article 10(4) and 18 (and above). Thus information disseminated to an EEA State may be sent on to a third State.
97. Article 101(3) Schengen Agreement.
98. Article 102.
99. DPA Schedule 1 Part 2 para. 5.
100. Should the body concerned object to providing the information; see chapters 3 and 4.
101. Michael J.(1994) *Privacy and Human Rights* UNESCO p.1.
102. Electronic Privacy Information Center and Privacy International (1999) *Privacy and Human Rights 1999 An International Survey of Privacy Laws and Developments* Privacy International [http://www.privacy.international.org/].
103. *Warden v Hayden* (1967) 387 US 294 per Douglas J.; *US v White* (1971) 401 US 745 per Mr. Justice Haarlen (dissenting) and *R v Duarte* (1990) 65 DLR (4th) 240 per La Forest J.
104. See O'Brien (1979) and Akhil Reed Amar (1997).

Select Bibliography

Akhil Reed Amar (1994) 'The Fourth Amendment First Principles' 107 *Harvard Law Review* 757

Akhil Reed Amar (1997) *The Constitution and Criminal Procedure* Yale University Press

Allen C.J.W. (1990) 'Discretion and Security: Excluding Evidence under Section 78(1) of The Police and Criminal Evidence Act' *Cambridge Law Journal* 80

Amsterdam A. (1974) 'Perspectives On The Fourth Amendment' 58 *Minnesota Law Review* 349

Ashworth A. (1998) 'Should The Police Be Allowed To Use Deceptive Practices?' 114 *Law Quarterly Review* 108

Ashworth A. (1998a) *The Criminal Process: An Evaluative Study* Clarendon Press

Audit Commission Report (1993) *Helping With Enquiries: Tackling Crime Effectively* HMSO

Bennyon J., *et al* (1993) *Police Co-operation in Europe: An Investigation* Centre for the Study of Public Order, University of Leicester

Blackstone's Criminal Practice (1999) ed. Murphy P. *et al* (9th ed.) Blackstone Press

Bottomley K. *et al* (1991) *The Impact Of PACE, Policing In A Northern Force*, Centre for Criminal Justice, The University of Hull

Bottoms A. and McClean J. (1976) *Defendants in the Criminal Process* Routledge

Bunyan T. (1996) *The Europol Convention* Statewatch, London

Burnside R. (1987) 'The Electronic Communications Privacy Act of 1986: The Challenge Of Applying Ambiguous Statutory Language To Intricate Telecommunications Technologies' 13 *Rutgers Computer & Technology Law Journal* 451

Butler A. 'The Bill of Rights Debate: Why the New Zealand Bill of Rights Act 1990 is a Bad Model for Britain' (1997) 17 *Oxford Journal Legal Studies* 323.

Cameron I. (1986) 'Telephone Tapping And The Interception Of Communications Act 1985' 37 *Northern Ireland Law Quarterly* 126

Clancy T.K. (1995) ' Extending The Good Faith Exception To The Fourth Amendments Exclusionary Rule To Warrantless Searches That Serve As A Basis For The Search Warrant' 32 *Houston Law Review* 697

Clarke A (1999) 'Safety or Supervision? The Unified Ground of Appeal and its Consequences in the Law of Abuse of Process and Exclusion of Evidence' *Criminal Law Review* 108

Choo A. (1990) 'A Defence of Entrapment' 53 *Modern Law Review* 453

Choo A. (1993) *Abuse Of Process And Judicial Stays Of Criminal Proceedings* Clarendon Press

Choo A. (1995) 'Halting Criminal Prosecutions: The Abuse of Process Doctrine Revisited' *Criminal Law Review* 864

Choo A. and Nash S. (1999) 'What's the Matter with Section 78?' *Criminal Law Review* 929

Colvin M. and Noorlander P. (1998) 'Human Rights and Accountability after the Treaty of Amsterdam' *European Human Rights Law Review* 191

Cross and Tapper (1999) *On Evidence* Butterworths

Duke S. (1986) 'Making Leon Worse' 95 *Yale Law Journal* 1405

Feldman D. (1986) *The Law Relating to Entry Search and Seizure* Butterworths

Fontana J. (1997) *The Law of Search and Seizure in Canada* Butterworths Canada Ltd.

Goldsmith M. (1987) 'Eavesdropping Reform: The Legality of Roving Surveillance' 3 *Univ. Illinois Law Review* 401

Goldsmith M. and Balmforth K. (1991) 'The Electronic Surveillance Of Privileged Communications: A Conflict in Doctrines' 64 *Southern California Law Review* 903

Goldstein A. (1987) 'The Search Warrant, The Magistrate, And Judicial Review' 62(6) *New York University Law Review* 1173

Graham C. and Walker C. (1989) 'The Continued Assault on the Vaults – Bank Accounts and Criminal Investigations' *Criminal Law Review* 185

Hedderman C. and Moxon D. (1992) *Magistrates' Court or Crown Court? Mode Of Trial Decisions And Sentencing* Home Office Research Study no.125 HMSO London.

Heydon J.D. (1973) 'Illegally Obtained Evidence' *Criminal Law Review* 603.

HMIC (1997) *Policing With Intelligence: HMIC Thematic Inspection Report On Good Practice* Home Office, London

Home Office (1998–1999) Annual Report, Home Office, London

Home Office (1999) Interception of Communications in the United Kingdom: A Consultation Paper Cm. 4368 HMSO

Home Office (1999) The Annual Report on the Interception of Communications Act 1985 Cm. 4364 HMSO

Home Office Statistical Bulletin 2/99 Operation of Certain Police Powers under PACE

Home Office Publication under Section 95 of the Criminal Justice Act 1991 (1999)

Home Office (1999) Proposals for Revising Legislative Measures on Fingerprints, Footprints and DNA Samples

Hufstedler S. (1979) 'Invisible Searches For Intangible Things: Regulation Of Governmental Information Gathering' 127 *University of Pennsylvania Law Review* 1483

Informant Working Group (1998) *Informing the Community* Metropolitan Police and PCA

Joubert C. and Bevers H. (1996) *Schengen Investigated* Kluwer Law International

Justice Report (1998) *Under Surveillance* Justice, London

Kamisar Y. (1987) 'Comparative Reprehensibility and the Fourth Amendment Exclusionary Rule' 86 *Michigan Law Review* 1

LaDue J. (1990) 'Electronic Surveillance and Conversations in Plain View' 65 *Notre Dame Law Review* 490

Law Reform Commission of Canada (1983) *Report on Writs of Assistance and Telecommunications* No. 19.

Lidstone K. and Palmer C. (1996) *The Investigation of Crime: A Guide to Police Powers* Butterworths

Local Government Information Unit (1999) *A Watching Brief: A Code of Practice for CCTV* LGIU

Loewy A.H. (1983) 'The Fourth Amendment As A Device For Protecting The Innocent' 81 *Michigan Law Review* 1229

Maguire M. and Norris C. (1993) *The Conduct and Supervision of Criminal Investigations* Research Study no. 5 to the Royal Commission On Criminal Justice HMSO.

Mathieson T. (1999) *On Globalisation of Control: Towards an Integrated Surveillance System in Europe* Statewatch, London

Mauet T.A. (1995) 'Informant Disclosure and Production: A Second Look at Paid Informants' 37 *Arizona Law Review* 563

McConville M., Sanders A. and Leng R. (1991) *The Case for the Prosecution* Clarendon Press

McCullum T. (1975) 'Sketching The Parameters Of The Informer Privileges' 13 *The American Criminal Law Review* 117

Miller A. (1969) 'Personal Privacy In The Computer Age: The Challenge Of A New Technology In An Information-Oriented Society' 67 *Michigan Law Review* 1091

Mirfield P. (1997) *Silence, Confessions and Improperly Obtained Evidence* Clarendon Press

Newbold A. (1990) 'The Crime Fraud Exception to Legal Professional Privilege' 53 *Modern Law Review* 472

Oaks D. (1970) 'Studying the Exclusionary Rule in Search and Seizure' *University Chicago Law Review* 665

O'Brien D.M. (1979) *Privacy, Law And Public Policy* Praegar.

Orfield M.W. (1987) 'The Exclusionary Rule and Deterrence: An Empirical Study of Chicago Narcotics Officers' 54 *University Chicago Law Review* 1018

Paccioco D.M. (1991) 'The Stay of Proceedings as a Remedy in Criminal Cases: Abusing the Abuse of Process Concept' 15 *Journal of Criminal Law* 315

Paccioco D.M. (1996) 'Improperly Obtained Evidence' in *Recent Issues and Developments in Criminal Law* Canadian Bar Association, Ontario

Passmore C. (1999) 'The future of legal professional privilege' 3(2) *International Journal of Evidence and Proof* 71

Pollock F. and Maitland F.W. (1968) *The History of English Law* Cambridge University Press

Polyviou P.G. (1982) *Search and Seizure Constitutional and Common Law* Duckworth

Power R. (1989) 'Technology and the Fourth Amendment: A Proposed Formulation for Visual Searches' 80(1) *The Journal of Criminal Law and Criminology* 1

Redmayne M. (1995) 'Doubts and Burdens: DNA Evidence, Probability and the Courts' *Criminal Law Review* 464

Report of the Royal Commission on Criminal Procedure (1981) Cmnd. 8092, HMSO London

Report of the Committee of Privy Councillors Appointed to Inquire into the Interception of Communications (1957) Cmnd. 283, HMSO London

Rogers M. (1987) 'Bodily Intrusion in Search of Evidence: A Study in Fourth Amendment Decision Making' 62 *Indiana Law Journal* 1181

Scarman (Sir Lesley) *The Brixton Disorders: 10-12ᵗʰ April 1981* Cmnd. 8427, HMSO London

Schumacher R.W. (1999) 'Expanding New York's Database: The Future Of Law Enforcement' 26 *Fordham Urban Journal* 1635

Sharpe S. (1994) 'Covert Police Operations and the Discretionary Exclusion of Evidence' *Criminal Law Review* 793

Sharpe S. (1996) 'Covert Policing; A Comparative View' 25(2) *Anglo- American L.R.* 163

Sharpe S. (1997) 'The European Convention: A Suspects' Charter?' *Criminal Law Review* 848

Sharpe S. (1998) 'The Privilege Against Self-Incrimination: Do We Need A Preservation Order?' 27(4) *Anglo-American Law Review* 494

Sharpe S. (1998a) *Judicial Discretion and Criminal Investigation* Sweet and Maxwell

Sharpe S. (1999) 'Disclosure, Immunity and Fair Trials' 63(1) *Journal of Criminal Law* 67

Sharpe S. (1999a) 'Search warrants: process protection or process validation?' 3(2) *The International Journal of Evidence and Proof* 101

Smith D. and Gray J. (1983) *Police and People in London, The Police in Action* Policy Studies Institute Gower

Spiotto J.E. (1975) 'Search and Seizure: An Empirical Study Of The Exclusionary Rule And Its Alternatives' 2 *Journal of Legal Studies* 243

Spiotto J., Lederman S.N. and Bryant A. (1992) *The Law Of Evidence In Canada* Butterworths, Toronto

Statewatch bulletin (1999) volume 9 Statewatch, London

Steventon B. (1995) 'Creating a DNA database' *The Journal of Criminal Law* 411

Stewart P. (1983) 'The Road to Mapp v Ohio and Beyond. The Origins, Development and Future of the Exclusionary Rule in Search-and-Seizure Cases' 83 *Columbia Law Review* 1365

Stuntz W.J. (1989) 'The American Exclusionary Rule and Defendants' Changing Rights' *Criminal Law Review* 117

Sundstrom S. (1998) 'You've Got Mail! (and the Government Knows It): Applying the Fourth Amendment to Workplace E-Mail Monitoring' 73 *New York Univ. Law Review* 2064

Van Duizand R., Sutton L. and Carter C. (1984) *The Search Warrant Process: Preconceptions, Perceptions and Practices* National Center for State Courts

Vennard J. (1985) 'The Outcome of Contested Trials' in Moxon D. (ed.) *Managing Criminal Justice* HMSO London

Warren S. and Brandeis L. (1890) 'The Right To Privacy' iv (5) *Harvard Law Review* 193

Watts D. (1979) *Law of Electronic Surveillance* Carswell, Canada

White J.B. (1983) 'Forgotten Points In The "Exclusionary Rule" Debate' *Michigan Law Review* 1273

Yeager D.B. (1993) ' Search, Seizure And The Positive Law: Expectations Of Privacy Outside The Fourth Amendment' 84(2) *The Journal* of *Criminal Law and Criminology, N.W. Univ. School of Law* 249

Zuckerman A. (1990) ' The Weakness of the PACE Special Procedure for Protecting Confidential Material' *Criminal Law Review* 472

Zuckerman A. (1987) 'Illegally Obtained Evidence – Discretion as a Guardian of Legitimacy' *Current Legal Problems* 55

Index